| MADE IN **AMERICA** |

MADE IN **AMERICA**

IMMIGRANT STUDENTS IN
OUR PUBLIC SCHOOLS

Laurie Olsen

THE NEW PRESS
New York

For purposes of confidentiality and protection, the names of the city and school and individuals which are the subject of this book have been changed; in some cases, the author has created composite characters.

Library of Congress Cataloging Card Number 97-35821

ISBN 1-56584-471-8

Published in the United States by The New Press, New York
Distributed by W. W. Norton & Company, Inc., New York

The New Press was established in 1990 as a not-for-profit alternative to the large, commercial publishing houses currently dominating the book publishing industry. The New Press operates in the public interest rather than for private gain, and is committed to publishing, in innovative ways, works of educational, cultural, and community value that might not normally be commercially viable. The New Press's editorial offices are located at the City University of New York.

BOOK DESIGN BY ANN ANTOSHAK

PRINTED IN THE UNITED STATES OF AMERICA

9 8 7 6 5 4 3 2 1

This book is dedicated to my first, best, and most enduring teachers, my parents, Tillie and Jack Olsen. My understanding of the world stems from the gifts they have given me: a commitment to justice and human life, an appreciation of the way people struggle daily against injustice, a sense of the importance of telling that story, a belief that the social and political world we live in is created by people and can therefore be changed by people, a passion for engaging in trying to understand and change this world of ours, and the courage to put forth my own voice.

CONTENTS

SOMETIMES IT is possible to discover a particular story that is fascinating and illuminating and at the same time larger than itself, a mini-world in which major social, political, and cultural dramas provide insight into our entire national life. Laurie Olsen has done just that in this book. She tells the story of the way in which immigrant students learn to become "Americans" at a school she calls Madison High. This is a passionate and personal tale transformed by sensitive anthropological insight and progressive educational theory into a study of how immigrant youth are socialized into accepting the construction of race and inclusion, and the particular nature of economics and democracy in the United States. It is also about how schools, rather than simply reproducing the culture of the society, can become places of contest where some teachers and educators choose to oppose racism, support diversity, and provide youth with a sense that participatory democracy can overcome problems of class and oppression.

I found much of the book painful and familiar. Recently I had a talk with one of my college students, a young African American woman who had grown up in Europe and attended international schools. She was, in a way, a migrant who had found herself in an immigrant situation. She said she had not experienced racism in her early life and had grown up with diversity and equality among people with power. Her first US experience was at college and there she learned what race meant in America. She was treated as "a Black student," an expert on race relations in the United States, a trophy friend—anything but herself, a young woman trying to learn chemistry and develop personal relationships in a good college. She was also treated as someone who had not earned her place at the school even though her parents were paying full tuition. She began, for the first time, to think of "white people and us" and began to wonder whether she could ever live in the United States without sinking into rage and resentment. She is a gentle person; for the first six months she was shell-shocked. She had not been a partisan in racial politics before and not been looked upon as a minority in the past, but as an American among Europeans. It was hard for her to have to come to America and learn that she wasn't considered a full equal of white Americans. Roberta found herself forced to be a student of color. It was neither her intent nor her will. The overwhelming momentum of race caused her to redefine herself and become militant and sad.

Militancy and sadness is the fate of many immigrants, even more so for young people who do not come from the kind of privileged background that Roberta did. And most immigrant children do not have the backing, resources, and opportunities to escape that Roberta does.

The students Laurie Olsen describes do not have the same opportunities and are shell-shocked by their American experiences. They remind me of one of my Cambodian students who told me that she came from the killing fields of the Khmer Rouge to Minneapolis, only to find herself considered a cause of the disintegration of the city and treated as if she were less than human. I'll never forget what she said in class one day: "I went from seeing children killed in my homeland to being spit on in the streets of America. I don't know where I belong on earth."

Laurie Olsen listens and looks, and writes about the shocks of becoming American. She has a keen eye and writes well and with a quiet passion that shows through the measured and well-documented text. She focuses on school and shows both how the worst in us can be re-informed through education and how militant and committed teachers can, in their opposition and solidarity with their students, insinuate hope into their lives. This is a very important book, mixing theory with drama, personal portrait with pedagogical speculation, and passion with scholarship. It provides an exceptional example of the marriage of theory and practice in the service of children.

ACKNOWLEDGMENTS

IT HAS been a long intense journey from the day I began graduate studies a decade ago, to the completion of my dissertation, and then the rewriting of that academic treatise into this book.

From the first moment I contemplated this journey to the placement of last punctuation mark on this manuscript, Lily Wong Fillmore has been my mentor. It was Lily's passion for social justice and insistence on using the tools of academia as a springboard for building a movement for language rights that first made me consider graduate studies. Lily continues to be a model for me in addition to countless others who seek to be a force in creating a more just world. I am indebted to Jean Lave, who first introduced me to the world of social theory and then served as my guide and beacon, and offered me the deepest learning in my graduate school career with her unrelenting push for deeper and deeper thinking and her consistent belief that I had a place in theoretical discourse. Ron Takaki added immeasurably to my historical understandings.

My husband Michael Margulis and my sons Jesse and Josh are my lifelines. They kept me balanced when all else threatened to topple me in the struggle to work full time, get my doctorate, and write this book. They absorbed the burdens and stresses this journey has put on our family life, and always let me know that if there was meaning and heart for me in doing this book, I should "go for it." Rebekah Edwards, Lynn Keslar, and Kathie Olsen provided essential encouragement, perfectly timed cups of tea and conversation, and loving support throughout this decade of work on the project.

I have been blessed with an extended family and friends who offered not only general support for me as I did the research and wrote the book, but also very concrete involvement in grappling with the task of turning an academic dissertation into a book for a general readership. My remarkable mother Tillie Olsen and sister Julie Edwards were with me through this long journey, working through draft after draft and persistently holding to the belief that I had important things to say, and that I had to and could find ways to say it in direct, passionate, and nonacademic ways. Beth Bernstein has performed in the multiple roles of friend, colleague, and reader of multiple drafts as I struggled to get the story "right." Her loving and intelligent imprint is on most pages of this book. Zaida McCall Perez consistently offered to help me understand what I was seeing and always encouraging me to continue. Her intellectual contribution was coupled with continuing passion about the importance of telling this story. I thank Hedy Chang, Lew Butler, Carol Dowell, and Joyce Germaine Watts for the friendship that extended far beyond the realm of our work together at California Tomorrow. Your support kept me going. Thanks to my editor, Ellen Reeves, André Schiffrin, Grace Farrell, and the whole crew at The New Press for their faith in this project and the investment to make this into a book.

Finally, I want to make explicit my gratitude to the people who are the heart of this story. First and foremost, I am grateful to the students whose smiles warmed me and whose stories both touched and taught me. To the teachers, administrators, and others at Madison High, I extend my admiration for the sincerity and effort brought to their daily struggle to work together in the crossfire of demographic change.

ALMOST ONE hundred years have passed since the last great wave of immigration, and we are engaged in a new Americanization project in our public schools. In many ways, the spirit and dimensions of this new Americanization effort resonate with what has gone on in bygone eras. But this is a distinctly contemporary version. There are three parts to this process: (1) the marginalizing and separating of immigrant students academically; (2) requiring immigrant students to become English-speaking (despite huge barriers) and to drop one's native language in order to participate in the academic and social life of the high school; and (3) pressuring one to find and take his or her place in the racial hierarchy of the United States. In the process of "Americanizing" newcomers, all of us engage in a massive struggle over the values of this nation, the meaning of diversity, the content of our race and language relations, and our visions of fairness, democracy, and inclusion.

This book tells the stories of immigrant students as they learn "America" in school. It also tells the stories of the teachers who teach them, the educators who have shaped their educational program, and their English-speaking, U.S.-born schoolmates. Our story follows the students of one community—both immigrant and U.S.-born—as they during their daily encounters shape a new society. Their schooling is in the hands of adults who are themselves buffeted by the political and societal crises engulfing our nation as we struggle with what our response will be to our growing diversity. This book explores what it is like to go to school and to teach in school during a time of increasingly complex cultural relations and political dissension, and amidst the pressures of a large urban, fiscally strapped public school system. Ultimately, this is the story of the latest chapter in a profound and mighty struggle within our United States.

How are we as a society going to respond to our diversity in this last decade of the twentieth century? Will we embrace a diversity of cultures and languages, forging a strong, inclusive, and united community? Or will we end up enforcing a more narrow and exclusive vision out of fear that diversity will weaken our cohesion? Are we in danger of turning into a Bosnia? Is this a new opportunity, a transition to a far more accepting and truly democratic society rich in its diversity? Is this to be an era of new levels of exclusion and conformity, or of new levels of inclusion and diversity? Such matters are never determined by decree, but are decided by individuals in communities throughout this nation who make choices about how they will interact with one another.

To document how this occurs, I spent two and a half years at a school I'll call Madison High—an urban high school in California—during the first half of the 1990s. I spoke with and listened carefully to students and teachers, watched them go about their business in classes and school life in general, went to meetings and read the local media and school-site press. A few teachers, several classrooms of students, and I designed special projects to engage students and teachers in examining their school and reflecting on matters of language, race, culture, and the mighty changes in their community. And in the process, I got a glimpse of some deeply troubling aspects of our society.

The community that this school serves has become increasingly multicultural as a major immigration wave has brought people from all parts of the world to reside there. Amidst these rapid changes, the city officially prides itself on its growing diversity. The school district has boasted innovations in the school program to accommodate the shifting student population. And yet, in the life of the campus something is wrong. The veneer of unity and the promises of diversity are only on the surface. Students are separated—immigrant from U.S. born, racial group from racial group—both socially and academically, where students who can't speak English are shut out of opportunities to learn and make contact with their American schoolmates. Students are sorted by skin color and class into programs that prepare them for very different futures. And teachers and administrators struggle with each other over how to respond to the increasing diversity. There is tremendous resistance to changes that would address the language barriers facing the immigrant students and to programs that might deliver on the promises of educational equity. Rumblings of resentment and anger have emerged because resources in this financially strapped school district are going to "foreigners." Meanwhile, a growing movement among advocates for immigrant inclusion, bilingual education, and educational opportunity in the district has resulted in some innovations, but they remain limited and contained at the margins of school life.

Most of the educators at Madison believe in integration, fairness, and equal opportunity. They mostly say they enjoy and appreciate living in a diverse community. But the way they perceive the world is that students are all equally positioned and free to participate in school and that matters of achievement are the result of the individual choices students make. What they collude in not seeing is the active process of exclusion and sorting that goes on in the school's program and practice, a sorting that consigns students by skin color, class, and English fluency into positions of very unequal access to resources, opportunities, and education.

The reality is that few immigrants get the preparation they need academically or the language development required for academic success. The reality is that they are largely precluded from access to the curriculum that their English-fluent and U.S.-born schoolmates receive. And as they begin to develop some fluency in English, they learn that it is not the only requirement for being accepted in their new land. They begin to see that to become American is to take one's place on the "racial map" of our nation. The task of learning English is accompanied by another major task—becoming racialized into our highly structured social order, where one's position is determined by skin color.[1] For immigrants, this means figuring out the peculiar meanings of racial categories in the United States, and doing so in the midst of intense negotiation among American teens about those racial places. In making the transition to life here, newcomers face tremendous pressures to adopt racial identities that limit them. For most immigrants, Americanization means leaving behind their fuller national, cultural, and language identities, and abandoning hope that others will see and accept them in their full humanness.

How does this happen? How is it possible that a school that speaks with pride of its diversity, full of educators who believe they are involved in opening options to students, could still produce such patterns? It is not a conscious or intentional process on the parts of most of the people involved in shaping and implementing such a system. Yet, the outcomes are clear. Why does the existence of a richly multicultural school not result in wider choices, more appreciation and support for multiple human identities? This is the paradox that the story of Madison High begins to explain for us all. And it provides mirrors for us that reflect what our society is about in these last years of the twentieth century.

In the story of Madison High is all the pain and shame of racism and exclusion that have run deep in this nation for centuries. We see the perpetuation of an unequal society whose response to differences is fearful demands for conformity. But it is also a story that provides us glimpses of new possibilities and the portraits of the slow but determined process of change. Madison reveals the conflict between very different perspectives and understandings of what it means to be a diverse society. The interactions between the profoundly differing visions of response to diversity illuminate for us how our schools are shaping a new generation of young people. Fundamentally, they force us to ask, what kind of society do we want to be? Do we really want to perpetuate a system of racial separation and racism, of monoculturalism and conformity? Do we want to continue to insist that people abandon their mother tongues and cut themselves off from their native traditions as a condition of belonging? Or do we wish to create a new and more inclusive, more richly diverse, fairer and more democratic, and more fully human way of being?

Every day we open the newspapers or tune in to talk shows, and we hear the latest manifestation of this struggle. In the past few years, these struggles have followed hot on the heels of one another: angry debates over Western civilization requirements on college campuses and the adoption of social studies textbooks for K–12 public schools, fights over bilingual-education policy, new initiatives to declare English the official language of this nation, proposals to exclude undocumented immigrant children from schools, new policies to deny legal immigrants public services, policy battles over maintaining or destroying affirmative action. These are the manifestations of our era's struggle in what has been an ongoing battle throughout the history of these United States over our diversity, over language and cultural relations, over racial exclusion, over who will be drawn within the circle and who will be drawn outside. These battles are always more intense at times of large-scale immigration, economic recession, and changes in the labor market. This is undeniably such a time.

In our nation's history, we have crafted some proud chapters in that long struggle. It was a major leap forward for those with democratic visions when almost two centuries ago the property classification for enrollment in schools was dropped, thereby creating a "common" public schooling system for the children of rich and poor alike. It was also a major leap forward (though it took more than a hundred years of bitter fights) when the Supreme Court finally decided the *Brown v. Board of Education* case (1954), ending legal segregation in the schools of this land. There have been proud chapters but also shameful chapters in our history, when fear, racism, xenophobia, and greed have won out. These include moments such as the forced enrollment of Native American children in boarding schools designed to sever their ties from their families and tribes, to eradicate their tribal tongues, and to "civilize" and "Americanize" them so they would never return to their communities. There is a rich and important history to study, to know, and to learn from, but the key question facing us today is, what kind of chapter will *we* write?

THE CURRENT IMMIGRATION WAVE AS A CONTEXT FOR SCHOOLS

After a lapse of half a century, the United States has again become a nation of immigration. During the 1980s, the United States experienced the largest flow of immigrants since the turn of the last century.[2] Fully one-third of the population growth in the nation this last decade was due to immigration. In the past decade, an unprecedented immigration wave has brought millions of people from every continent on the earth to join an already culturally and linguistically diverse U.S.-born population. According to the U.S. Census, by 1990 there were nearly twenty million foreign-born residents in the United States, the most in the nation's history. But unlike the turn of the last century, the magnitude and composition of this new immigration is different and is resulting in a profound alteration of the composition of the United States.

Although the image of boatloads of Eastern Europeans sailing past the Statue of Liberty and arriving at Ellis Island in New York City symbolizes immigration of the turn of the century, it is now quite a different picture. The images in the press and in the public imagination in the 1990s are of people streaming across the Rio Grande River and trekking northward to California and Texas. Immigration is affecting all states in the nation, but three-fourths of those who immigrated in the past decade went to only six states, primarily in the Southwestern and Western United States. This immigration is resulting in profound numerical and proportional changes, from what has been the dominance of a white and English-speaking majority, to a population of increasing diversity in race, culture, and language.

Because of the youthfulness of and high fertility rates among immigrant groups, these changes are being felt most dramatically in the schools, where student enrollment in California alone is projected to grow from the current four million students to approximately seven million by the year 2005. A major component of this growth is immigration, which results in an increasing racial and linguistic diversity of the population. There has been no single ethnic or cultural group constituting a majority in the public school enrollment for several years. By the time of the next census, half of the children in California are projected to be Asian or Hispanic.

In California, these changes are so evident (especially since the publication of 1990 U.S. Census data) that few public policy documents, and few political statements, pass without some reference to the emerging diversity. The change is not easy, however. Underlying much of the public discourse of this era, and threading through many facets of everyday life and practice, is a subtext of fear, anxiety, and turmoil over immigration and demographic changes. Politicians and cultural managers pose new polarities: unity versus diversity, excellence and competitiveness versus equity, the needs of "us" versus the drain of serving "them." Residential separation is increasing as well. Hate crimes (especially anti-immigrant hate crimes) are on the rise. Civil rights activists from "minority" communities are increasingly mounting a political voice for inclusion and access for their peoples amidst increasing attacks on their communities.

The whirling metamorphoses that engulfs California as this major immigration wave continues to change the cultural, racial, and linguistic composition of the state are only projected to intensify. Whether we choose to respond in inclusive ways because of our vision of democracy or clamp down out of fear or greed, and prevent the newcomers from taking their place in this society, is yet to be determined, however. The answer is in our hands.

WHY STUDY A HIGH SCHOOL AS A WAY TO UNDERSTAND THE NATION?

Madison High School is a typical comprehensive high school in an urban area of California. Its basic structure, textbooks, classroom organization, and social activities are similar to what one might find walking into the vast majority of comprehensive high schools in this country, for it has been shaped by a long national history establishing the institution "high school." Madison High could in its structure and basic content be anywhere. And yet, Madison is also undeniably an urban California school in the 1990s, undergoing tremendous change in student population because of the thrusts of the most powerful immigration wave to ever impact on the state. In the past decade, Madison has shifted from having primarily white working-class students to having a student enrollment that has no single majority ethnic or racial group, speaks sixteen different home languages, and is almost one-fourth immigrants. It is a truly multicultural high school campus that celebrates its diversity, yet raises for us the challenge: How is it that despite the rich multiculturalism of the people, despite the creation of some programs and spaces that support a multiculture, the end product is still separation, conformity, and exclusion?

With a student population representing every continent on this earth and speaking more than a dozen different languages, Madison is still undergoing tumultuous demographic changes. Although throughout this nation there are many schools that do not share Madison's degree of diversity, the story of Madison High is nonetheless a story about us all. We are in the thick of heavy choices and decisions about the direction our nation will take. A series of debates rage across the academy, in public conversation and in the media about the meaning and impact of immigration on society, and about the purpose of schools in mediating diversity and reproducing a unifying cultural model. The story of one school is also fundamentally a reflection of those wider struggles about immigration and its impact on our society, the struggle with responses to cultural and linguistic and ethnic diversity, and the ways in which this nation turns to schools to mediate crises over diversity.

These decisions are not occurring only on the level of the big political or academic debates. The renegotiation of power in race, culture, and language relations unfolds in the concrete daily workings of a school—in how people, in the process of going about work and school, live and respond to diversity. Schools are important to understand in terms of the role they play in shaping societal relations, as well as important places to witness more general patterns of how people in our era handle the confrontation with cultures other than their own.

High schools may be a particularly apt place to see how all this plays out. As the institution in charge of helping young adults bridge into adult life, many of the assumptions of our society about who belongs where in adulthood can be revealed.

In this country, race, language, and culture are categories with a long history of meaning and centuries of relegating people to differential experiences steeped in racist, linguistic, and nationalist relations of inequity. We are stratified according to the language spoken, the color of our skin, as well as the income of our family. People live these relationships and create these relationships, and they do so wherever they encounter each other. Because schools are one of the few public arenas in which established residents and immigrant newcomers engage in regular, sustained interactions, the school site is an essential point in that negotiation.

Madison High demonstrates how people engaged in high school cocreate language and cultural and race relations during times of change in the composition of their communities, during times when conflicting views and interests with regard to those relations are present. Schools have legitimized those relationships and contributed toward providing different experiences and access to different groups of people, thereby sorting them for their places in existing power relations in the society.

Yet, schools in this nation also have a history of democratic impulse. There is a long, proud tradition of viewing schools as a vehicle for opening up access, for leveling the playing field, for giving "everyone" a chance. And the public schools of our nation have held forth a proud rhetoric and vision of access for all. The extent to which schools deliver on that promise, however, has always been determined by the outcomes of the struggle within schools and within society over visions of what we mean by democratic inclusion and access for all, and the tenacity of those who seek to slot people into places according to skin color, class, or gender with different levels of access, different resources, and different futures. And so the battles within schools are over what degree they will be instruments of access for those who are from communities that have not been given that access before, or whether they will be institutions that reproduce the existing power relationships.[3]

Teachers and students live together in this process. Amidst rapid changes, it is not only teenagers being socialized to a new world, but also the adults in their lives who are also encountering forces that are fundamentally changing and challenging. Teachers' worlds are being remade by the encounters with students with whom they do not share a culture, language, or national background. The specifics of their work have changed, their efficacy and ability to have an impact have been altered, their basic assumptions shaken about teaching and learning, and they too face a racially and linguistically altered community. What does all this look like?

SEEKING THE ANSWERS: ON THE METHODS OF THIS RESEARCH

Seeking the answers, I began the work on this book in 1992 as part of my mid-life pursuit of a doctoral degree; its seeds had been planted in the five years prior as I worked as a policy researcher who documented the impact and challenges facing schools as a result of the massive immigration wave in California. As director of California Tomorrow, a nonprofit organization focused on building a fair and strong multicultural state, I was engaged in going from school to school, from community to community throughout the state, listening to teachers and students speak of the complexities of teaching and learning and attending and working in schools in the midst of swift demographic changes. I became committed to recording their stories to inform policy and practice about effective school programs in a diverse society. But I was also increasingly convinced there was a deeper story to be told, with implications far beyond what is "effective" school practice.

I could see, from my vantage point as director of a statewide organization focused on the political whirlwinds of racial and language relations, that we as a society were in the midst of a major struggle regarding the direction we would go as a multicultural society. I wanted to speak to that political and rhetorical debate, but knew that I needed to understand what was going on in a deeper, more grounded and concrete way. I saw that teachers and students alike were being shaken and shaped deeply by the interactions and confrontations with people of cultures, national experiences, and languages other than their own. Decades before, I had chosen anthropology as my academic focus, and worked as an assistant to Dr. Margaret Mead. The tumultuous sixties intervened, and I left anthropology for teaching and the field of public education. Now, my previous passion for anthropology was reawoken and joined with the storyteller, the educator, and the advocate in me.

This book then is a product of multiple tasks and multiple approaches. I wrote it as a storyteller, advocate, educator, anthropologist, and theorist. These were not always comfortable partners as the urgent passion of the advocate met the creative impulses of the storyteller, who together had to confront and make peace with the discipline of the social scientist.

THE THEORETICAL FOUNDATION

I entered this research with the perspective that schools are contested territory in struggle with whether they will serve a democratizing purpose of inclusion, creating access and a level playing field in our society, or will be institutions that simply reproduce current class, racial, and language relations. My personal beliefs and a reading of history led me to view the outcomes of that struggle with the purposes of schooling as open to renegotiation in each era. I immersed myself in political and social theory on the reproduction and transformation of current social, political, racial and economic relations. It is a split literature — one body focusing on class and economic relations, another on racial relations. I owe a substantial debt to both bodies of thought, though I was increasingly troubled by the lack of theory that could speak to the complex relationship between class and race. I started this research knowing that to understand the complexities of immigration and Americanization demanded that I try to combine racial and economic theories of reproduction and resistance. I sought to apply, speak to, and contribute toward a more interrelational social theory.

Reproduction theory originally sought to explain how exploitative social class arrangements were perpetuated from generation to generation. This social theory argued that schools reproduced the social relations of production under capitalism (Bourdieu and Passeron 1977; Apple 1979 and 1982; Bowles 1977). Schools, reproduction theorists argued, are critical in this process because class relations and the capitalist division of labor requires a school system that reproduces a system of inequality by selectively transmitting skills according to which class people are in, sorting people by granting credentials from the school into appropriate social positions, and serving to shape an individual's attitudes and identity to fit their class positions. These theorists did not provide the close-up micro portraits of how this occurs, however. But their work has informed and shaped those who have gone on to do that descriptive examination.

Others have produced ethnographies of high schools out of a similar desire to understand the way in which reproduction and resistance occur in daily life. However, this body of ethnography, primarily spawned by neo-Marxist critical theorists associated with the University of Birmingham's Centre for Contemporary Cultural Studies, was specifically focused on the role of oppressed groups in reproduction and resistance to class relations.[4] However, in that body of work, the structure of schools, the curricular content, the behaviors and beliefs of teachers, and the policies are viewed as fixed instruments of reproduction against which students react. The only potential for change is in the cultural production of the students themselves. There is little probing about the role of adult resistance in the system, or of the power of political movements to create change in social relations. The schools exist as reflections and instruments of reproduction, not as potential players in resistance.

I constructed my research, therefore, to examine explicitly the role of adults and adult resistance to reproduction. Furthermore, although these theorists restricted themselves to probing relations between schools and social class systems, I was interested in extending the notion of "reproduction" to other systems of power and hierarchy in our society and particularly those implicated by immigration—namely, the related issues of language, culture, race, and national identity.

I sought then to see how these relations are contested and become changed, and the conditions that make resistance to them more or less tenable. To do this required placing my research in a historical context and examining the contemporary political context of what was occurring in Bayview, California, schools. Put simply, I wanted to see how our era of history, in the context of contemporary politics and political movements, made new solutions possible or closed off potentials for resistance. To do so, I needed to couch the study in some historical analysis of previous eras of Americanization, immigration, and school change. And I needed to frame my study of one school in one community in the larger state- and nationwide political struggles over bilingual education—and trace the connections between the overtly political struggle and the daily efforts of teachers and students to shape their relations.

I did quite a bit of research on the history of public schools in this nation and the role of schools in the Americanization of immigrants and in racial exclusion. In an earlier manuscript, the historical occupies several chapters. That material appears in this final manuscript only as historical reference, but it was essential to my analysis and understanding. The exploration of the contemporary political movements as a context for the forms of resistance and reproduction in daily life at Madison High was also edited down substantially from a prior version; however, it survives in Chapter Ten of this book, enabling the reader to pull back from the microdetail of life at Madison High in order to view the broader national struggle over bilingual education. The broad implications of micro-studies of resistance and reproduction are only visible, I think, where such a political and historical context is provided.

THE ETHNOGRAPHIC METHODOLOGY

Although the theoretical interests prompted me to include the historical and contemporary political context, the basic focus was to provide an up-close view of resistance and reproduction in the schools of today. To do this required an ethnographic approach. In many ways, this research used standard ethnographic methods. For two years I simply spent time at Madison High—in classrooms, on the Quad, observing life, and talking to people. I constructed social maps of the school and engaged students and teachers in developing their own social, and cultural, racial, linguistic maps of the school. I was able to work closely with students in four social studies classes on a three-week unit, in which they constructed social maps of the school, analyzed those maps, and discussed issues raised by their analysis. Overall, I interviewed fifteen faculty members and administrators at Madison High and seven at the Newcomer School, and conducted in-depth interviews with forty-seven students. In addition, I selected ten female students and five teachers to focus on in more depth over the two years of the project.

Conceptually, the primary points of departure for this research were the racial, linguistic, and cultural diversity and demographic changes within the school (and by extension, community). The decision to focus primarily upon female students was a matter of convenience, depth of access, and theoretical interest. Most of the literature on reproduction has attempted to understand class reproduction in terms of those whose places were being constructed at the lower end of a hierarchical, stratified hegemonic system. Most of that literature has then focused on working-class students. Most have also opted to focus on males. Because this inquiry is concerned with gender relations as well as language and race relations in the process of immigrants becoming part of an "American" culture, I elected to focus primarily on females. Gender turned out to be central to the inquiry, in its relationship to how students learn and construct race, language, and culture. I explicitly elected to focus on female students from differing cultural and social groupings in the school in order to illuminate relationships between gender and cultural reproduction. It was not a theoretical or research choice that narrowed the focus to female teachers, however. It simply turned out that the teachers who were the most relevant players with regards to working with immigrant students were female as well.

I ended up with comprehensive biographies of the following students: an Afghan immigrant, a Brazilian immigrant, a Latina (Mexican American) born in the United States, a Fijian immigrant, an East Indian immigrant, a Vietnamese immigrant, a white student born in the local Bayview community, an African American student born in the United States, a Chinese immigrant, and a Mexican immigrant. The teachers included four white teachers, who are relatively new to teaching, and a Latina administrator.

The ten students were also the central starting place for me to study their social circles (which included males and females). I focused my observations and hang-out time around the girls, shadowing them throughout their day, sitting in classes with them, and spending time with them and their friends at school. The central issues we explored were:

- How did they understand "America"? What does it mean to be "American"?

- What borders and boundaries did they create or detect in social relations? What language did they use to articulate and create those borders and boundaries?

- How were the crossings, the borderlands and terrain in between languages, cultures, and national identities experienced, shared, contested?

- How did they experience and view their encounters with each other across languages, cultures, and national identies?

- What was it like for those students and teachers who felt themselves involved in forging new terrains of language, culture, racial, and national identity?

- Why were they in school, and how did they experience school? What relationship did school have to the rest of their lives?

In order to study the contexts and influences in teachers' lives relating to the diversity and demographic changes at school, I met with teachers both at school, in homes, and in cafes and restaurants in their own communities. One teacher spoke into a tape for me as she commuted on her two-hour drive in the morning

and evening to and from school. I spent time with the group of four young teachers simply talking, including some formal whole-day sessions exploring particular
themes or questions that were emerging in my research. And I observed these
teachers at work and spent time with them in many informal discussions as we
tried to make sense of their work. They were in many ways my colleagues and
friends in attempting to unravel and understand issues of diversity in their school.

Finally, the research involved examining processes and mechanisms of
decision making; language policy; student grouping; curriculum content; and
the placement of students and enrollment in specific gate-keeping courses.

THE THREE JOURNALS:
THE STORYTELLER, THE ANTHROPOLOGIST, THE ADVOCATE

I kept three formal journals throughout this research—each representing three
very different lenses and concerns I brought to the task of conducting the
research. One was my "story" journal, another was the formal "field journal,"
and the third was a personal journal. All proved important to informing the
final analysis, though not all ended up represented in the book. Some
researchers and writers would argue against such fragmentation, but I felt it
was necessary for me to have forums to express each of my presences during
the research—and to keep them somewhat separate.

Stories appear and become created in very different ways from interviews,
formal research methodologies, or intellectual analysis. They arise in the
moment of sensing something symbolic or humanly interesting. They do not
just exist to illustrate points, but are a value in and of themselves. There are,
amidst the rich cultural interactions of Madison High, many, many stories to be
told. It was an important part of this research to let myself document those stories—and to do so as a storyteller. I kept a separate journal throughout my years
at the school in which the seeds and pieces of stories were recorded. Some of
these appear in chopped-up versions as quotes or narrative pieces. I allowed
myself the creative joy of writing many of these into a kind of anthology of
vignettes. Some of them appear as edited and shortened vignettes in the introduction to the chapters of this book. Others simply did not fit the basic structure of this book but continued to provide the human meaning and context
and scaffolding around which the analysis was built. The stories are bursting to
be told, wonderful metaphors and illustrations of what this era in history is
about but they perhaps need to wait for another format, other storytellers.
Nonetheless, it was an important part of doing this research to allow myself to
write and tell them in journal form as stories.

The field journal was a standard anthropological field journal used to record observations, maintain interview notes, and keep records of the progress of the research. A personal journal was used to record my reactions, expectations, hunches, disappointments, and experiences in doing the work. This was used also as a tool (in Alan Peshkin's words) to "commit to keeping track of my subjectivity"—to keep track of what sentiments and values were being evoked, of the "hot spots and the cool moments."[5] As a political advocate, it is important to have some place to record my reactions to the politics of Bayview and of California, to note what made me angry and what made me afraid. I had to locate it somewhere, to give it a place of its own. As a white woman with an articulated and deeply felt ideology on matters of diversity and racial and language relations, I was and am positioned in the very struggles I attempted to record. My personal journal became the place I recorded the places of discomfort, those confusions and questions, insecurities and stubbornnesses that are inevitable. I returned often to previous entries to try to see the patterns, and to understand the relationships among those moments. I enlisted friends and colleagues at several points to help me grapple with the content of that journal in terms of its implications for my blindnesses, the voice I would choose in the writing, and ways in which my positioned reactions could be both a strong basis for analysis and a barrier to seeing.

Attempting to study the macro-processes of cultural and social reproduction through the micro-level interactions within a specific high school necessarily raised issues of boundaries. I walked into this community in the middle of the "story," and had to leave it before I could see an "ending." The rapid rise of an anti-immigrant backlash was becoming evident at exactly the time I needed to complete the research. What effect would that have? How will the community respond? Should I "wait" before concluding the research? But the challenge of trying to study issues such as reproduction and resistance is that these are long-term processes, continually contested, with periods of resistance and periods of exclusion. What is an "ending"? And so, I simply ended the research, and it was "time" to write. But I was not ready or able to leave the scene. Having seen the dimensions of the struggle at Madison High and witnessing what appeared to be the conditions of an intensification of backlash against immigrants, the discipline of the social scientist rubbed the political advocate the wrong way. How could I leave? How could I simply retreat to write a book and be done with Madison High at such a pivotal time?

I entered with the purpose of studying the cultural dynamics of the school as a whole, but I ended up with only a slice of Madison High. Although this was partially related to limitations on my time and the complexity of school life, it was more fundamentally a result of the lens, the heart, the history of this ethnographer.

On my first day at Madison High, I sat in the front office and observed for a while, and then spent hours wandering around the campus. I wanted to get a "feel" for the school, but also was unsure how to begin. Three appointments for interviews with administrators were scheduled for later in the day, and I felt at loose ends. I did not know how to be part of the school. I did not know if I was *supposed* to be part of the school. I felt self-conscious with my notebook, and put it away. My field notes describe the few students clustered in the library and a bit of graffiti on the wall near the cafeteria. At around 11:00 A.M., I walked back to the front office and could tell something was up. People were racing around. Closed doors could not mask the sobbing. Police were everywhere. At one point, the principal brushed past me and called to his secretary to alert all teachers to come to the library at lunch. And there, to a faculty who had begun to hear the rumors, he told about a boy in the school who had brandished a gun in a meeting with a counselor, pushed past the counselor and began to run; how the principal (and later police with him) pursued him and were unable to stop him from committing suicide. It was a suicide over a broken heart. The principal and the other administrators would spend the rest of the day with the ex-girlfriend and the boy's parents, and dealing with the newspapers. I canceled my interviews with the administrators, who looked as if they had forgotten who I was and what the appointments were for. On my ride home on the freeways, I felt very small and unimportant. Why would anyone in the midst of the intensity of an inner-city school take the time to talk to me and answer my questions? Why would anyone feel that talking about issues of diversity were at all important?

I walked into the world at Madison High with my own concerns, interests, and lenses—and I held to these. But the sense of questioning whether it was legitimate as a primary lens for telling the story of Madison High continued throughout the two years. This was partially, I think, a factor of any researcher trying to frame the limits and define the parameters of the "question." But it was also a dynamic between myself and the life of this particular school. The majority of the people at Madison High are not sure there is a story to be told, or to be shared, about its diversity and responses to it. The kind of face-to-face confrontation between me as researcher concerned about diversity and a school in the midst of contention about whether or not diversity is even an issue for focus served both to keep me questioning and a little off guard ("Is this a legitimate question?") and also to place me on one side of a polarizing issue in the community. Finding my sea legs as a researcher was difficult in this context. I felt reticent, unsure how to push my way into the life of the school, and unsure when not to. I was unclear as to when I could raise my questions and get responses and when my questions might become part of the overall struggle in the life of the school over the responses to diversity.

This reticence is partly my personality, but it was cocreated at Madison. I tried to pay attention to when I felt most shy, when I felt most "outside," when I felt I had a right to be there.

I wondered to what extent I was picking up on the feelings that many immigrant newcomer teenagers also felt at Madison. It was for them also not an easy school to feel part of. But I also wondered to what extent I was giving their uneasiness and outsiderness more credence because it matched my own. Madison does not welcome people; it does not seek links to the outside. What occurs is most often unarticulated and unspoken. Little is made formal or explicit about how the school functions. There is a comfortable equilibrium in the relations of the many long-term members of the faculty and administration. Newcomers and outsiders are expected to find their own way and put in their time before being embraced as part of the school. Despite presentations to the whole faculty, despite being there for two years, I was never sure whether most of the faculty had any clue as to why I was there.

My issues and my presence were *not* invisible, however, to the immigrant students and the few teachers of English-as-a-second-language and sheltered-content instruction at the school. These teachers shared my interest in issues of diversity and longed for opportunities to have such an interest validated and to have ways to explore it themselves. They too felt marginalized and often invisible. The students were delighted that anyone was interested in their lives. They found me friendly and welcoming, and at times even helpful. I found my welcome and my place there in the margins of the school where newcomer students live and where the young teachers of the low-status classes for newcomers also live, and so that is where I did my research. I am well aware that my research is only a small piece of Madison, a portion of the story, one way of viewing the life of that school. This is not the story that might have emerged had I open access to other parts of the school. This haunts me. I feel in the course of doing this research that I have reproduced the very patterns I have sought to describe, the way in which the adults in this movement for bilingual education and civil rights end up seeking and creating shelters for themselves and their students because of the inability to push past being marginalized, and also to create for themselves a safe and comfortable zone within which they can do their work. However, this awareness also informed my analysis tremendously.

As the findings of this research began to emerge, and as I became increasingly aware of the above dynamics, another aspect of my subjectivity became important. I was not satisfied being only in the researcher role at the school. As codirector of California Tomorrow, as an activist and person in a position of some leadership in the immigrant education movement, my work aside from this piece of research was full of a sense of urgency about the need for institutions to address fully the diversity of their communities. How could I continue to try to be a fly on the wall, a neutral documentor of the struggle over immigrant education issues at Madison High, when in other schools, in other districts across the country I was an active advocate, trainer, and speaker on issues of immigrant education? The teachers at the Bayview Newcomer School and the English-as-a-second-language and sheltered-content teachers viewed me not only as researcher but also as someone with expertise to draw on and leadership to help them. In working with them, I began to feel confused about my role in shaping the school and my role in documenting the world that existed at the school. As the people at Madison engaged in struggles over issues of access, bilingual education, and immigrant education in the district, I sometimes tried to sit back and record what was happening, knowing how much could be learned from watching the encounter. But I also could not help myself at times, and either was drawn in by others or simply jumped in. Mostly, the social scientist won out. But as the research ended, the advocate demanded her time.

Since the completion of this research, I have worked in partnership with dozens of school districts—Bayview among them—an opportunity to begin to apply the understanding I derived from those years of research. It is a challenge to see if this kind of research analysis can in fact help the struggle. It gave those of us working in Bayview some new ideas about what might strengthen our efforts to build a multicultural alternative within the schools. But I still sometimes wonder if it is just my own cyclical dance—the theorist, the social scientist, and storyteller having been given their day, now the advocate demands to be heard. If it is not all on behalf of change and social action, what is the purpose? And so these days, I am working with the determined group of advocates in Bayview to try to tip the scales a little more in the direction of creating a multicultural alternative and more democratic and inclusive schools—engaged together in the daily and hourly task of trying to keep visible and keep voiced the vision and urgency of a more inclusive way of doing schooling, and the arduous and creative task of figuring out how to make that vision a reality. And while we work, I have begun to record the many new stories in the shaping.

MADISON HIGH AND OUR ROLE IN MAKING HISTORY

As the world's children enroll in our schools, students struggle to find creative solutions in response to the enormous pressures of a society slotting them into cultural, racial, and class roles. Teachers grapple with how to teach students with whom they share neither a community nor national background, culture, or language. And teachers, like the ones you will read about at Madison High, are divided over whether and how to respond. Most school sites include some teachers and administrators who greet the new diversity with a welcoming sense of adventure and a commitment to find ways to make schooling appropriate for that diversity. There are some who make it a central focus of their teaching to figure out what the curriculum, instructional approaches, and programs need to be to ensure full educational opportunity for the newcomers. But most schools also encompass many teachers who are frustrated and unsure about what to do. They realize that something is not working right, but they have no time or energy, commitment or support to figure out what to do differently. There are also, in most schools, people who are frankly hostile to doing anything considered "extra" for "those" children.

At Madison, as at many schools, dialogue among these factions is problematic. To admit to not knowing what to do is uncomfortable for most teachers. To raise concerns about the lack of access or the problems in teaching is difficult. To name inequality is believed to be impolite at best, divisive in most contexts. Calling attention to the differences in student needs, the differences in opportunities accorded to students of various language or racial groups, or differences in achievement is potentially explosive. And those who might be effective advocates for more inclusive and fair programs and practices are often silenced or neutralized.

Madison High is not only a single high school being buttressed by these forces of immigration, and is not alone in determining the response to the new diversity. This localized struggle has been shaped by and deeply imprinted by a centuries-long history of such struggles that have created enduring patterns in the relationships between immigration, racial exclusion and our public schooling system in the United States. The high school as an institution has been shaped over two centuries by the crucible of immigration. Large-scale immigration has historically been a factor in forcing our nation to reconsider how it views and molds our high schools to ease the pressures of massive social change and conflict. During such upheaval, tensions over how we as a nation define ourselves and over the nature of our "culture" largely revolve around concerns about what is taught in schools, who should be included in schools, how and where they should be included, and whose values the public schools should reflect. Throughout the history of these United States, public schools have inextricably been involved in the battles over racial inclusion and exclusion, the assimilation of white ethnic immigrants, and the efforts to maintain or to contest a unicultural "American" model for the nation.

Almost two hundred years ago in New England, the immigration of Irish Catholics to the United States was instrumental in pushing what had been a schooling system for propertied white males to drop the property classification and develop into a "common school" model for "all" students (read "white")— a policy prompted in large part by a desire to bring poor Catholic immigrants into the fold of Protestantism. The rhetoric and ideology of the common schools persists to this day in how public schools are perceived by our nation.

Almost one hundred years later, large-scale immigration to the urban centers of the Eastern seaboard resulted in a massive challenge to what had emerged as the American school model. High schools began to be "tracked" into a differentiated curriculum, with special programs that contained and marginalized the efforts of the time to democratize the schools and support a multicultural model. That high school template, the large comprehensive high school with vocational and college preparatory tracks, exists relatively unchanged to this day.

Madison High School in a town I'll call Bayview, California, has a structure rooted in that history. It is a history that strongly embraces the ideology and rhetoric of a "common school" for "all," but has consistently tended toward racial exclusion. It is a history of enthusiasm for "Americanizing" white ethnic immigrants, while sorting children of lower classes, foreign cultures and tongues, and darker skins into contained and marginalized programs with fewer resources and less access.

Here we are now, in the 1990s, once again struggling over which course it will be—fuller access and more inclusion or deeper inequality and more separation and exclusion. Which direction are we going to choose? Will it be toward increased control by a power elite or toward a more open and democratic society? As we become less "white," less "Western," and more worldly and diverse, who will end up where as we arrange ourselves as a society? Can we expect that the conflict and struggle between those who want to hold onto control or maintain the dominance of one group, one culture, one language, and those who want to build a fairer, more inclusive, more embracing society, will again become intense enough actually to change our public schools and public life? What new ideological and political resistance to current power relations can be seen emerging, and where will they lead?

These are lofty questions, with implications far beyond a single high school in a single community. But the story of one high school offers a microcosmic lens with which to examine our answers to these questions and the ways we are constructing the America of the twenty-first century.

Madison High is a story of people encountering each other across cultures, of racial sorting and the Americanization of immigrants, of the losses and exchanges of language and culture. All of this occurs within a context of another modern-day reality of public education. Madison is a school trying to function quite valiantly in an inner-city school district with decreasing resources and increasing needs. A major fiscal crisis, referred to locally as the "budget nightmare," is the backdrop for worsening relations between teachers and the central district office. Strikes and bitterness about overall working conditions cloud all discussions and attempts to call attention to the needs of a new student population. This has had an eroding effect on the ability of teachers to continue to teach, to consider making changes to accomodate the needs of newcomers, and to confront and deal with each other about the role of the school in foreclosing or opening educational opportunity. The exhaustion and sense of scarce and declining resources are part and parcel of the story of why and how one school struggles over its response to immigrants.

It is not an easy road this community faces. The people you are about to meet do their best within their circumstances to construct a new society. They are caught in a moment in history with the mighty challenge, burdens, and awesome responsibility of crafting a response to an unprecedented diversity, and thus helping define our nation's direction and the contemporary version of *e pluribus unum*.

CHAPTER ONE

At the
Crossroads

THE MADISON High School calculus class celebrated having finished their advanced placement exams with an all-day field trip to a reservoir outside of the city. The trip had been donated by local corporations to math teacher Jim Higgins as part of his teacher of the year award. Spirits were high as the bus pulled out of the city and on to the winding country roads. In the middle of the bus, Chinese students clustered around two people who stood in the aisle playing a game. Intense concentration as two people engaged in a fast-paced hand-slapping interaction, followed by bursts of laughter as one of the duo would get confused and be outpaced, and then another student would take her place. Shouts of encouragement, teasing—all in Chinese—accompanied the action. I was sitting next to Patty, one of the few white students on the bus, and asked what the name of the game was called.

"I'm not sure. It's some Chinese game—they play it all the time. I've never been able to figure it out. You have to ask them what it's called. I asked one of the kids once, but couldn't really understand what she was saying."

When we arrived at the reservoir, the students piled off the bus, happy and doing somersaults and cartwheels—obviously feeling released and celebratory. Their teacher, Jim Higgins, watched with pride and affection.

"They really deserve to just let go for a day. These kids worked so hard this year."

These are the college-bound students of the school, the high achievers in the top academic track. Mostly the Chinese students stayed together, speaking Mandarin and playing Chinese hand games. Other students cavorted on the play structures while awaiting their guided tour of the reservoir. Jim spoke to me about the group.

"It's a great group of kids. We have kids who are immigrants, and kids who still don't speak English very well. We have kids from Vietnam, India, Afghanistan, and China. I've taught in this school for years, and it's been amazing to see the changes. It's really a different school now."

On the play structure, Patty had been laughing so hard that she fell off the swing. Two students reached out to help her up, a Chinese student and an Indian. A third person snapped a photo, which found its way into the school yearbook—memorializing the moment. Higgins commented, "Like the United Nations, isn't it?"

■ ■ ■

The story of Madison High School is the story of a community of people at a crossroads—a community altered profoundly by immigration and struggling over the meaning of the new diversity.

Sliced by major freeways and arteries, the city lies halfway between two major cities in northern California. An interstate freeway connecting the south to the north divides the city of Bayview into halves, creating a western and eastern section. Another highway, a major artery for the region, runs east and west across the city. Most people from outside the community know Bayview only by virtue of passing through on the freeways or exiting for a shopping trip to the major retail malls that line the freeways. Traffic on all freeways slows going through Bayview, but high concrete sound walls along the routes obscure the view of the city.

Exiting from the freeways, the mix of old and new is immediately apparent. From a small town two decades ago, Bayview has become a middle-sized city under the pressures of urban sprawl from the major cities to the north and south. Miles of neat, small family homes in 1960s and 1970s suburban architectural style line block after block. These houses, with pick-up trucks, tricycles, small boats, and camper shells in their driveways, are intermittently interspersed with older Victorian houses from another era in Bayview history.

Bayview is a crossroads in more than transportation. In only twenty years, the community has changed from a small white homogeneous working-class community to a richly diverse city, as massive human migration has brought immigrants literally from every continent to settle in Bayview. Bayview has become a community in which cultures, races, language groups, and national groups from around the globe intersect in the attempt to create a community they can all call home.

A THIRTY-YEAR RETROSPECTIVE ON THE CITY OF BAYVIEW

In 1960, Bayview was a small but growing town of 72,700 people, 98.5 percent of them white. It was primarily a working-class town. Jobs centered in the canneries, flower nurseries and farm-related industries of the area. According to the 1960 census, about 5 percent of the city's residents were foreign born, of which 94 percent were white European immigrants.[6]

These census figures only tell part of the story. A large cannery employed thousands of seasonal workers, primarily of Mexican descent. During the Bracero program of the late 1940s and 1950s, many Mexican farm workers were attracted to Bayview.[7] Because of the nature of the cannery industry (the Bayview cannery packed mostly tomatoes, peaches, and apricots) most of its workers came to Bayview only for the canning season, which ran roughly from June until early November. Others established homes in Bayview, but migrated back to their hometowns in the Mexican states of Jalisco and Michoacán for the winter. This labor and residence pattern shifted to more permanent residency in Bayview, and eventually contributed over the next decade to the development of a large and relatively stable population of Spanish-speaking residents in Bayview. This was veiled in the 1960 Census figures because Hispanics were not counted as a distinct group. They were combined in the single classification, "white."

During the 1960s, because of a population boom throughout the region, and the increasing push among young families with school-aged children to buy affordable homes in stable communities, the city grew. Economically, the city also began to shift from an agricultural base to a retail base, which served the burgeoning population. Orchards and fields were torn up to create retail centers and housing development. Bayview Mall was opened in 1964, the first major retail center for the area, heralding a new era for the economy.

By the 1970 census, only a whisper of the coming immigration wave was beginning to be felt. The population of the city still looked a lot like it had a decade earlier.

During the 1970s, the total population barely grew and the school-age population shrank by 19 percent, as the white middle-class families started to move out to new suburbs developing on the other side of the hills.[8] The agricultural base of the city began to decline as property became increasingly valuable for housing for the growing region. In 1978, the cannery, once the largest cannery in the world, closed. More people left. The economy became increasingly built around industrial space, auto dealerships, and retail.[9]

And then, slowly at first and then with drama, immigration began to be felt.[10] By 1980, one out of every four people in Bayview spoke a language other than English as their primary language. The 18.4 percent growth in Bayview in the 1980s was almost exclusively among Asians and Hispanics, many of them immigrants. This fundamentally changed the racial and linguistic composition of the city to an increasingly multiracial, multilingual, and international city. By 1990, the census described the city as only over half white, with significant Hispanic, Asian and African American communities.[11]

In just a twenty-year span in California, where Bayview sits, the public school enrollment shifted from a population that was 75 percent white, to 40 percent white. Today, one-fourth of the students (well over a million) are limited English speaking themselves or come from homes in which English is not the primary language. Over one-fifth were born in another country. In some school districts, as many as 85 percent of the students are limited or non-English speaking. Well over a hundred different languages are now spoken by the school children of California.[12] One out of four students in California is a language minority, that is, coming from a home where English is either not spoken or where English is not the dominant language. Those who do not speak English or are not yet fluent in English are labeled and counted as "limited English proficient," or LEP. More than one million are limited English proficient, and this is expected to double to two million in the next thirteen years. One in five is an immigrant, with a life shaped by another nation and culture. This population has been projected to grow at a rate of 5 to 7 percent annually for the next decade. Officially labeled in terms of their English-speaking proficiency, the cultural, linguistic, and national diversity among this group is astounding.

All of these changes, of course, had great impact on the schools of the Bayview Unified School District. Reflecting the immigration center which the city of Bayview had become, the proportion of public school children with a primary language other than English enrolled in Bayview schools mushroomed throughout the 1980s. In 1984, one out of every eight students in the Bayview schools was limited English proficient. Ten years later, this doubled to one out of every four. During the 1980s, the district had to deal repeatedly with shifting enrollment areas of its schools to accommodate growth and shrinkage of the school-aged population as immigrant newcomers settled in various parts of the city.

In the late 1980s, trying to accommodate the shifts in population, the district closed all junior high schools and shifted the eighth grade into high school. Two years later, the district was faced with the need to close one of the high schools. In the struggle over which of the four comprehensive high schools would close, the mostly Latino-enrolled Washington High lost out. Many of these students were folded into the student body at Madison High, resulting in a sudden increase in the Latino enrollment of that school.

In the 1990s, the growth in the number of students who do not speak English is far outstripping the growth of the general student population. Overall, the number of LEP students in Bayview increased by 87 percent in a ten-year period. Two out of five now are "language minority students," that is, they speak languages other than English at home. More than one in four do not speak English at all. By spring 1993, more than fifty-three languages were spoken by the student body in the Bayview schools.

Although the student population has changed dramatically, the teaching population has not. With close to 20,000 students, the Bayview Unified School District is richly diverse, but the 1,403 teachers and certificated staff differ in racial and linguistic composition from the students they teach, and reflect an older version of the Bayview community. In this mismatch is a seed of major confrontation that occurs over the understanding and response to issues of language, culture, and student behavior.

Thus. The stage is set in which old Bayview (represented by the teaching population) meets new Bayview (represented by the increasingly diverse student population). And in this encounter, they wage a battle over school programs, formal ideology, the role of schools, and the meaning of the new diversity. And in the shadow and on the terrain of the school, immigrant students from every continent interact with their schoolmates who were born on this nation's soil.

THE CHANGING FACES OF MADISON HIGH SCHOOL

In the middle of this changing and diverse city sits Madison High School, one of three comprehensive high schools in the city. It was built in the 1960s, in the flush of the baby boom, with a capacity for 1,800 students. The campus is luxuriously spread out over nine square city blocks. A series of single-story buildings are connected by walkways, with courtyards and lawns in between. A central quad provides a large public space for noontime activities.

A review of life at Madison High School two and three decades ago reflects the demographic changes so evident in census figures for the city of Bayview. The yearbook, *The Golden Bears*, offers a glimpse of this history. Issues published in the 1960s reveal a lively mix of student activities and a heavy emphasis on sports: Fine Arts Club, Future Secretaries Club, Health Club, MESS and MERA (an organization of ushers for cultural events), Science Club, Song Girls, Quill and Scroll Society, the Scholarship Federation, German Club, Spanish Club, Creative Writing, Chess Club, and others. Twelve pages were devoted to football, ten pages devoted to basketball, and the yearbook boasts photos galore of wrestling, baseball, track, tennis, and other sports. Madison appears to be the stereotypical early sixties comprehensive high school. The faces reveal an all-white student population. One black face appears, and she is a student body officer.

By 1965, some slight changes are beginning to be evident. The school is still clearly a robust, comprehensive high school and the activities remain about the same. But the Spanish Club now lists one student with a Spanish surname among its members, and an occasional Asian and African American face can be found. The junior class song is "Ying Yang, Ching Chang, Chow Mein, Chop Suey, Ying Yang, Ching Chang, China Waping." The Song Girls are dressed in Chinese kimonos.

The 1969 issue of *The Golden Bears* attests to both demographic and social change. The Spanish Club has now been renamed the Spanish American Club, and boasts eighteen student members, all with Spanish surnames. The Afro-American society has been established with ten students. The description under its yearbook picture reads:

> The Afro American Society is new to Madison this year, proving that understanding the problems of others is an integral part of any school.

The students voted as "Two Most Likely to Succeed" are both Asians. A newly created United Student Forum is formed with the "purpose of . . . providing a special means of communication between students of varied races and backgrounds." The photo of the forum shows a multiracial group of thirteen students: one Asian, three African Americans, two Hispanics, and seven white students. To the list of student clubs is also added a Young Republicans Club and a Young Democrats Club.

During the 1960s, the school felt the growth in the overall city. The baby boom of the sixties resulted in an increase of high school students four times that of the general population. But in the seventies, new changes are evident: a now shrinking population and the shift toward a more diverse student body. In 1971, the Afro-American Society sponsored a Black History Week, with a soul food breakfast, a black fashion show, and a talent show entitled Ebony of Soul. A gospel choir was formed. The Mexican American Club changed its name to the Latin American Club, "now including all races of Latin background to promote understanding among the races," and it now boasted thirty-five members. A one-semester class about "minorities" had to be taken by all students as a requirement for graduation.

Other social changes are documented as well. Planned Parenthood sent counselors and speakers to the school. Synanon and Project Worth (drug addiction treatment programs) installed projects on campus. The students took over an area of the school, which they called People's Plot, and cultivated it. The social studies department began to offer a "guidance" class. A special *Sixty Minutes* edition featured Bayview on national television as a drug capital, where new drugs were tried before moving inward to the rest of the nation.

By 1975, an Asian student was the Spirit Queen runner up, and sports and student government were visibly becoming racially integrated. The Black Student Union (formerly the Afro-American Club) focused on "understanding our people and the progress of Blacks," and sought to raise scholarship money for their members. A Filipino Student Union was formed with the goal of getting a Filipino studies course adopted and a Philippine teacher hired at Madison. The Latin American Club was described as "proud of their heritage and continuing to fight for equal rights not only in school, but in society. They strongly believed in the things they were working for and will continue fighting until their goals are achieved." White students clustered in the ecology, ski, and tennis clubs.

The development of an ethnically diverse and ethnically defined student population was magnified when a decline in student enrollment in the district resulted in 1990 in the closing of Washington High School. The closing of this school, which served a predominantly Latino neighborhood of the city, precipitated tremendous political turmoil and a failed lawsuit against the district. The result of the closure was an expansion of the Madison enrollment area to encompass the entire area of Bayview west of the interstate freeway and extending along its length through Bayview. After the incorporation of Washington High students, Madison's *The Golden Bears* states that there were 1,783 students in grades 9 to 12, an increase of approximately 400 students. The student population was 32.8 percent white, 26.1 percent Hispanic (largely due to the student shift when Washington High School closed), 13.5 percent African American, 13.3 percent Asian, 11.1 percent Filipino, 2.4 percent Pacific Islander, and less than one percent Native American. The LEP population nearly doubled from spring 1990 to spring 1991. Close to half of the students in the school spoke a mother tongue other than English at home.

By 1993, *The Golden Bears* is still thick with documentation of sports and clubs, of spirit days and yearly events—and the rich diversity of the school is evident on every page. This year there are again hints of change. The Spanish American Club is now the Raza Club. There is now a combined Filipino and Asians United Club. There is an addition of an Afghan Club: "The Afghan

Club starts its first successful year here at Madison. The members of the Club are learning many brand new things about their culture.... The success of this year's Afghan Club will surely make an impact on the Club Scene at Madison and should help Afghan students become more visible for themselves and for the rest of the campus." A steady theme running throughout the book are references to the massive budget nightmare that has plunged the school into crisis. The opening spread reads:

> This year the students at Madison faced many changes. Due to budget cuts, class sizes increased, we unfortunately lost counselors and our librarian. Many teachers were transferred, but still spirits remained high and the Mighty Golden Bears united to make this year the best it could be.

And across the two-page spread in large bold letters it says, "The worse thing about the budget cuts is that we lost our counselors."

The second spread begins: "DIVERSITY. Diversity is not just a word, but a word that symbolizes the different types of backgrounds of teachers and students that we have here at Madison." And indeed, the yearbook shows faces of every color and names reflecting family heritages throughout the world. But it still does not tell the whole story. There are other realities as well. The lives of newcomer students, seldom involved in school clubs or teams and absent from the student identification photo sessions taken when school begins in fall, simply are not evident in the yearbook. Although the yearbook boasts an integrated and diverse social life, the pictures of student clubs begin to hint at a more racially separate campus. And behind the smiling faces of the *The Golden Bears* that shine out from the glossy pages of the yearbook, is a story that does not get told.

In this school, where no single ethnic group constitutes a majority any longer, where a common home language does not span more than half of the student body, where the birthplaces of students span the globe—an unprecedented diversity prevails. Students confront each other across languages and cultures, and school each other in what it means to be American.

Through their encounters we witness an illuminated version of the American system of stratification and exclusion through language, cultural, and racial relations.

CHAPTER TWO

The Maps of Madison High:
On Separation and Invisibility

In this task, you will think about how Madison High students arrange themselves socially. Throughout the school day, students find themselves in many social groups. It is your job to observe (notice) what these groups are, describe them, and try and understand why people choose to be part of the groups they are in. Begin by brainstorming the "types" of students there are at Madison. You will then work together to create a large map of the school campus, and draw the different groups onto the map to show the class where everyone is. You will also be explaining the map to the rest of the class when you have completed the project. You will each have a paper due which describes the different groups and analyzes why the school divides itself the way it does.

HISTORY TEACHER Lisa Stern had just finished teaching her classes a unit on prejudice, discrimination, World War II, and the Holocaust. She followed this with a new unit that we designed together to encourage her students to look at their own school with regards to how students group themselves. Assigned to four different cooperative groups, the classes were given the above assignment.

Stern's social studies classroom was housed in a temporary bungalow on the far edge of the campus. She taught one period a day of "sheltered" history for limited English proficient immigrant students, and two periods a day of "regular" history. Thus, through her door flowed alternately a wave of immigrant students, then a wave of "regular" students." She tried, through the materials she hung on her walls and through her telling each of her classes what the "other" class discussed and did, to be a conduit of communication between the two worlds.

The "rules" developed by each class were posted side by side. The sheltered class rules read:"No mean racism. No making fun of people's dress. Don't make fun of culture. No laughing at English mistakes. Try to learn about each other." The "regular" class rules read:"No put-downs. No personal attacks. Respect yourself and others. Don't talk when others are talking. Be good listeners. Keep an open mind. Say what you think." Handwritten definitions for "racism," "xenophobia," "prejudice," "stereotype," and "discrimination" hung on the walls.

Every day, every period, Stern stood at the door to greet each group of students as they arrived:"How'd it go this weekend with the job, interview John?" "Hey, Vivien, you're looking a little down are you okay?" "Saskia, what happened to your leg?" "Lucky, did you get a spot on the varsity cheerleaders?" As students filed past Stern into the classroom, they were surrounded by student work on the walls. Although recent immigrants are separated from U.S.-born schoolmates in the daily school program of "sheltered" classes and English-as-a-second-language classes through the student work on the walls of this classroom they confronted each other's presence.

On the day the assignment was due, students came to class with their maps. The "regular World History" sixth-period students rushed into the classroom and immediately began assembling their map of the school on the wall. One student looked over and noticed the maps of the high school that had been created by the class of immigrants. She whistled and then said loudly: "Jeez, you'd think we were going to a whole different school!" Her comment continued to resonate throughout the entire month of the project.

■　■　■

Lisa Stern's mapping project engaged newcomer students in drawing the "America" they observe and their maps became a backdrop talking about what they believe it means to be "American."[13] A contrasting map drawn by the "American" students became the vehicle to explore what turned out to be an intense process of racial sorting and unlocked a lengthy dialogue about how they find and define their racial identities at Madison High.

The Madison High that newcomers walk into is initially perceived by them as being composed of people of various national and language identities: Americans, Chinese, Vietnamese, Mexican, Spanish speakers, English speakers, etc. The journey they perceive they need to make to become "American," is to cross over into the English-speaking world and by taking that path, they believe they will become Americans. By adopting a new language, they believe they will be bestowed with a new nationality. Only during the process of that journey, they discover that as immigrants from Third World nations they also need to undergo a complex baptism of racialization into subordinated positions in the U.S. racial scheme.[14]

The school that immigrants enter is engaged in a major process that includes slotting them and others into their "proper" positions in a racial hierarchy. In contrast to the maps of newcomers the maps drawn by "American" students in the sixth-period history class were not about nationality and language. "English" and being "American" are simply taken for granted not mentioned at all. Instead their maps are laden with racial categories. The issue that they struggle with is a world steeped in racial meaning and full of divisions, which are monitored carefully through a process that includes labeling and judging each other as "wannabees" or "white-washed," as "knowing who you are" or "forgetting who you are."

A closer look at each of these illustrates how one feeds the other and how they work together to teach newcomers their place in America.

"CAN I BE AMERICAN AND STILL BE ME?"

The Madison High World as Perceived by Immigrant Newcomers
Within the first few months of my research at Madison, immigrant students had mentioned to me and I'd heard conversations that made reference to "taking off my turban." I couldn't make sense of that statement, particularly when it was from the mouths of girls, of Mexicans—people who had clearly never worn turbans. I understood only that the reference was about going too far in giving in to pressures to be American. Finally I asked a group of students specifically where the expression came from. The response was somewhat vague. They said that there had been some student who had taken off his turban because he couldn't take the pressure any more. Nadia, an Afghan girl, said, "It was about a kid going too far who gave up who he was under bad pressure from American kids. Giving up his turban and shaving his hair was going crazy."

As a teacher remembered it the boy's father took off his turban, too. In her memory it was a story of a family that leapt together into American society. Thanh, a Vietnamese immigrant girl, insisted the boy had committed suicide later. Jani, a Fijian immigrant, said emphatically "No, he hadn't committed suicide, he had done really well and graduated and gone on to college."

The story became symbolic to newcomers at Madison. The reference to "taking off the turban" is shorthand for succumbing to the pressures to cease one's foreign ways and to act American.

■ ■ ■

Although newcomer students are labeled as "ESLers" (short for the English-as-a-second-language classes they take) or "LEPs" (short for "limited English proficient") and are centrally focused on learning English, learning "English" increasingly comes to be for them, as it is for the "Americans" who label them solely in terms of their lack of English, a proxy or code word for a much broader concept of being "American." Teachers at Madison talk about the "language barrier" and the "language program" when they refer to the newcomer students. But these terms almost always encode deeper meanings of being foreign or being a limited American. The social world of Madison High described and mapped by the immigrant students is explicitly about nationality and language. But as they get to understand their new land, the labels they use to speak of their world (the labels of national identity, of the language spoken and religion) become intertwined with skin color. Skin color, religion, and language seem to define being "American" or not.

Their maps make this clear. The actual location of where groups hang out and proximity to the center of campus or to the margins of the campus seems symbolic of relations to school life. On their maps, most of the immigrant groups are either clustered on the edges of the campus, on the side of campus close to the Newcomer School down the street, or close by the classrooms of the teachers who provide the "sheltered" classes for limited English proficient students.[15] In contrast to the detailed group descriptions they are able to provide about the clusters of newcomer students, the students use only three categories for the rest of the social campus: "Americans," "Mexicans," and "blacks."

As the immigrant student groups made their presentations of maps to the class, the first category each represented was "American" students.

> Okay, the American students hang out in the middle of the school in the Quad.

> Americans like to be in the middle of things. They are here near the cafeteria. They dance at lunchtime, and everyone talks English.

Some used the term "American," however only to refer to white students. The rest of their maps were inhabited by students of specific national and language groups: Mexican, Chinese, Indian, Fijian, etc. "Blacks" are the one exception. On some of the maps, "blacks" did not seem to imply either a national or a language category. Only with black Americans did newcomers use racial categories. For others, "blacks" is one subset of "American," but the other subset is simply "American" with no racial or skin color reference made. They learn quickly that "whiteness" is invisible and is the natural taken-for-granted state of being American.

Their maps further described students in terms of the language they speak and their activities. Here are some examples:

> There is a category of Chinese students by the cafeteria—Chinese girls who speak Mandarin who like to go to UC Berkeley.

> Filipino students? We didn't find any! We didn't know about them!

> Vietnamese people who speak Vietnamese sit near the cafeteria. Those who only speak English hang out between A Hall and C Hall.

> There are two categories of Mexicans. The Mexican Mexicans who speak Spanish hang out near the tennis courts. The Mexican Americans who speak English and don't want anything to do with the Mexican Mexicans hang out in C Hall.

> Afghans who speak Persian are in B Hall and near the cafeteria.

> Fijian boys mix with American people, but the girls stay separate in front of C Hall. They speak Hindu language and listen to Indian music. Most people don't get it that we're Hindus but not from India. Kids here think we're just from India.

> The Blacks like to dance and do RAP music.

The maps done by the immigrant students in the sheltered class included great detail and many categories for immigrant students. In their descriptions we learn that "Indian girls" sit by a tree on the edge of campus; "Mexican boys that haven't been here too long" are identified by proximity to a fence. Girls cluster differently than boys. The description often had fine gender distinctions, such as "the Chinese girls group" or "the Hong Kong group of boys." Over and over during discussions of their maps, newcomers spoke of "same religion," "same language,"

NEWCOMERS' MAP OF MADISON HIGH

PLAYING FIELDS

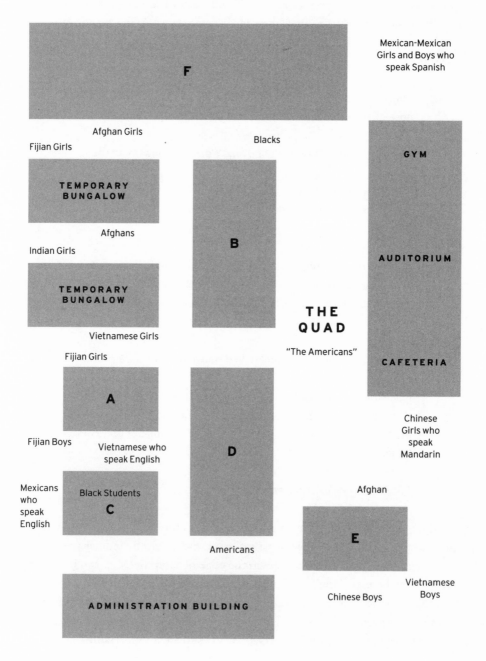

"same culture," and "same nationality" as the ways students cluster. Cecelia, a new-comer student who was chosen to present her groups' social map of the school to the class, explained in terms reflective of all the other groups:

> There are good Americans and the bad American kids. The bad ones are the ones who smoke and they stay separate from other Americans. Then there are the Chinese students who speak Mandarin. And Vietnamese students. Some of them speak Viet-namese and some don't. Mostly in this school it's the same lan-guage and same culture kids who hang out together. The Fijian boys mix with Americans, but the girls don't.

On all the maps, newcomers are shown at the edges of the campus. Stand-ing literally at the margins of the Madison High School world, newcomers learn and construct what it means to be "American," and where they fit into the structures of American life.

There are many paths to and aspects of becoming "American," though they all involve becoming English-speaking. And to listen even briefly to con-versations among newcomers about becoming American immediately illus-trates the tight connection in their minds among race, religion, and language as inextricable and often interchangeable identifiers that mark one as American or not American. For newcomers, the persistent question is whether or not the path to being American is one that is really open to them.

Nadira, a recent immigrant from Afghanistan, feels she could never be American. Not only her religion holds her back. By her definition, being American is impossible for her. In her way of understanding America, to be an American is one must be black or white.

> The rest are not real Americans. But the immigrants most of us wish to be American and try. And they become more and more like Americans. And they want to hang out with kids who are more American. But you can never really get there. We can speak English; we can wear the clothes. But we aren't the right religion; we aren't the same. You can't really get there.

This question remains even as they learn English. Consider the following comment from a Chinese immigrant boy who has been in Bayview since he was five years old:

> I mean I'll never be an American. I've got a lot of white friends but
> I have a skin barrier with them. And I can't even speak to a lot of
> my Chinese . . . like at my church . . . They all sit around and speak
> Chinese and I'm just sitting there and can't understand what they
> are saying. So, I'm not really Chinese and I'll never be white.

The point from which newcomer students observe learn about, and begin to interact with "America" is always from the sidelines. In Bayview, a Newcomer School was started ten years ago to serve the influx of immigrants into the high schools in the district. It provides initial assessment, basic levels of English-as-a-second-language instruction, and some bilingual assistance. Recent immigrant students in the high schools in Bayview spend half of the school day at the Newcomer School site across the street from Madison High and the other half of the day in English-as-a-second-language or "sheltered" classes grouped with other immigrants at Madison High. Their view of the other students and of the life of the school is truly a view from afar, a view from the margins of the life of the school.

The newcomer students who converge in the Bayview Newcomer School and the sheltered and ESL classes at Madison High have been in the United States for anywhere from one day to three years. They share the experience of trying to find their way and make life comprehensible in a new country, culture, and with a new language. As they seek to comprehend the world of Madison High, the topic of conversation often flows to the oddities of this new life and the difficulties of fitting in.

The newly arrived immigrants spend much of their time at school as careful observers of American ways, trying to understand and describe the culture, and sharing with each other tricks of survival in the United States. There are many such conversations in which the students continuously measure and judge their own behavior and that of their peers through a lens of how American one is and of how much has been given up to be American. Attracted, repelled, courageous, and afraid, the tugs and pulls of the daily decisions about "how American can I be and still be me" comprise a major focus of their lives.

Some of this focuses on general aspects of America. In describing Americans newcomers' views almost always converge in a perspective on American teenage life and society. They work themselves to a remarkable near consensus about what "American" teens are like.

Issa and Grace sit outside near the Quad each day at lunch and watch the action, sometimes talking about "what Americans do." Grace said, "I look at

American teenagers and their clothing and the kind of music they listen to and what they do with their free time. Girls wear beautiful clothes that match and new clothes, too. We just like to watch."

Clothing is a major theme in conversations of immigrant girls. Acutely aware when their own clothing does not measure up to American standards, they struggle with what might be appropriate to wear. Their American schoolmates are also concerned about clothing, and to some degree the concerns of immigrants about dress is an absorption of this most American behavior. But for the newcomers, there are distinct and unique aspects. On the social maps created by the newcomer students, dress and style were often used as key descriptors marking specific social groups. And the experience of being judged for one's clothing is one of the common early incidents marking a newcomer's entry at Madison High.

Amisha, a Fijian immigrant, recounts the shame and discomfort about her clothing and style at school.

> I don't wear jeans because my uncle is very strict and he makes rules for me. I was the only one from Fiji, and they were all Mexicans. I had to wear a long dress and my hair was tied up and no make-up or nothing. Everybody was saying to me over and over, "why do you tie your hair?" They were teasing me and talking about me. And I had lice in my hair and they teased me and teased me. And it was so embarrassing.

Gloria, newly arrived from Mexico, wore a beautiful serape on her first day of school. She describes the immediate knowledge that something was wrong:

> It was a beautiful serape that my uncle had given to me when I left home. It is woven green and brown and is very soft and warm. I was excited on my first day that I could wear it to school. But it did not feel beautiful when I got there. It felt wrong.

The first thing, Nadira, an Afghan immigrant said about what it is like being in America was about the clothes. "These clothes here in America are great and America is a comfortable place." The importance of clothing became clearer and clearer as Nadira and I got to know each other. The sense that American women can "be open to the world" in their clothing symbolized for Nadira a level of religious and sexual relaxation that both attracted and repelled her. Clothing spoke to her of the wealth and availability of many styles and of the opportunity for new choices. But she also commented critically on what she initially viewed as an obsession of Americans about judging each other's clothes and caring about their own. In all of these ways—being judged, making choices, and learning about what matters in the United States—clothing is a central theme in her perspective and experience of becoming American.

> Americans always change their clothes. It is the first thing they say about immigrants coming to this country like we are in dirty clothes. They say, "oooh look at her clothes." When I first came they made fun of us. That's why clothes are so important to me. Sometimes it is all they think about. A person is their clothes in America.

Later, when Nadira was trying to explain why she likes the life of an American teenager, again it began with a description of clothing.

> Here we are like, you know, free. We don't wear stuff on our heads like the big scarf in Pakistan. There is a lot of mujahdeen in Pakistan and Afghanistan. But here we don't have to wear the scarf. But it is not just that we don't wear the scarf. Here we are free, we can wear little skirts.

A surprise for many immigrant students is that coming to America does not make them American. And that within the United States there are distinct divisions and groups of people.

> I was surprised to see so many kinds of people here. I thought everyone would be the same, like on TV. But there are blacks and Mexicans. And they dress different and stay apart. I do not know how I fit in. I do not know who to dress like.

The fascination with specific styles of dress of various national and racial groups is not only about what makes them distinct but also about what marks group identity and makes movement between groups harder. The confusion over "how I fit in" becomes an issue in figuring out what new clothing styles to adopt when a newcomer shifts from their "foreign" ways of dressing to American styles. Making the wrong choices apparently opens a newcomer to ridicule.

> I have learned that all students in this school divide into many
> groups. Mexicans with Mexicans. Vietnamese with Vietnamese.
> Americans with Americans. And the American students don't
> like the immigrant ones and usually laugh at our dresses and
> sports and language.

The clothing is one clear marker of difference in the eyes of immigrant females, but it is also connected to another aspect of being American. If you dress American, it leads to acting American; it sends American signals. And American teens go out with boys. Nadira draws a line for herself. She can dress in comfortable clothes. She does not have to wear a scarf and that is freedom. She enjoys knowing that she could dress freely and comfortably. But she will not wear what she refers to as "little skirts." And she absolutely would never go out with boys. She explained "We can dress like this, but we are not allowed to go out with guys. If I dress a certain way, people will think I will act a certain way."

Illustrating the narrow band of acceptable style and dress related to female sexuality, Sandra, an immigrant from Brazil, has found her accommodations to life in the United States to revolve around clothing. But for her, standards of dress in the United States are not freeing, but require a more restrictive and less sexual expression than she was used to:

> I used to dress different, and people were treating me different
> because of how I dress and making fun of me. In Brazil, we wore
> short skirts and we liked to walk with our hips. Here girls dress
> like boys in long pants and shirts. If a girl puts on a dress they
> just talk about her legs. To me, that is the way girls are supposed
> to dress — to wear skirts and to swing your hips. Now I dress and
> walk like an American. My Mom asks me, "you don't like dressing
> like that, do you?" And I say, no I don't but I have to because the
> other way they're going to make fun of me.

"Making fun" of her it turns out was calling her a "slut" and a "whore." Her open sexuality made her an immediate target both for Americans and for the other immigrants with whom she shares her classes. She gave up dressing the way she believes "girls should," and along with it developed a sense of sexual caution that persists. Sandra does not trust boys in the United States at all and believes her safest path is to dress like boys, avoid dating and any situation of possible sexual encounter, and to retrain herself to walk without swinging her hips. "Here it means something different. Here it means being bad." Her strongest desire is to blend in, to be not noticed, and to avoid the pain and heat of the heavy teasing and visibility she felt as a newcomer.

For most girls discovering the acceptable standard of dress is one of the most immediately obvious requirements of life in America, along with needing to be English speaking. Dress, however, is just one aspect of youth culture.

When asked to describe American teen behavior (e.g., what do American kids do?), many newcomers answered in terms of music:

> Americans listen to English music and good songs and most of them listen to rap, especially the black Americans.

> Very few people listen to piano.

> They usually listen to music in the car and turn it up way loud so that everybody would hear them.

> Music is way loud.

> The music you listen to is part of who you hang out with. People don't listen to different kinds of music. Each group just listens to one kind.

And in a statement that again characteristically equates nationality with language and religion one boy said, "In my school Americans always listen to English music and never listen to other religion's songs because they hate that."

One general image immigrant students have about American teens is that they have fun, do not take things seriously, and are carefree. This comes up not only in describing Americans but also in conversations in which newcomers are measuring themselves and their peers in terms of degrees of Americanness.

> Most Americans like free time to get in their different groups and have fun. They always want to have fun. When I go to the library at lunch I never saw many American people there, except some. They go outside and have fun. I always see most immigrant people in the library because they sit and study there.

> They want to do good in school, and they don't have fun outside
> the library. But Americans want to have fun.

"Having fun" is associated with not taking school seriously. One cannot, in this view, both have fun and take school seriously. A Fijian newcomer said, "Americans want to laugh all the time. They like to be fun. In classes even, they try to have fun even when they are supposed to be learning."

And her friend agreed: "Americans have a good time. That's what they like. That is what is so important to them. They laugh and go places and have parties. Having fun is more important than anything else."

According to newcomer student reports, as well as the impressions of the staff of the Newcomer School, many of the immigrant families in Bayview stress the importance of schooling for their children. They believe strongly that going to school and learning English is the key to getting ahead. Prior experiences with schools differ widely among the immigrant students (from those with almost no prior schooling to those with strong excellent prior schooling; from those who are considered of adult age and have fought in wars and consider themselves finished with school, to those who think they have years of schooling ahead to get a professional degree). Regardless of their level of education, most seem to share a belief that school is important to their future. Almost all newcomers express surprise that American teenagers do not seem more serious about school. One student told me:

> I can't believe that Americans have very good conditions about
> education but they don't want it. Here is a opportunity where
> there are a lot of schools the government gives the money for
> and the country could have a lot of talented people. But some of
> the students don't want to understand that or think about their
> future. Their parents let them go to schools, buy them shoes
> and clothes and [give them] food money and just ask them to go
> to school, but [the students] take the clothes and money and
> just come to school like a habit and study nothing and cut class-
> es. They think it is good to "get away" with it.

"I FEAR I WILL BE LAUGHED AT."

The clearest warning sign to newcomers that they have made a mistake or are not accepted is hearing the laughter of their "American" peers. Laughter is watched carefully. It is not always clear to newcomers what the laughter means.

Is it a joke? Is it just fun? Is it meanness? There sometimes appears to be a nebulous line between the "having fun" kind of laughter that "Americans" are perceived as doing a lot and the kind of laughter that makes fun of someone. Carolina, an immigrant from Mexico three years earlier, looked back on the experience of having been laughed at and at her relief when it finally stopped. She wrote:

> Why do native born laugh at the immigrant students? Mostly I find that immigrant students feel badly about things that the native-born students laugh at—like the way the immigrants dress, the way they play sports, their language, which are concerned to me. I feel sorry for them because I used to be like them. Right now, I am not that immigrant. I'm happier. I do look different from what I used to. I learned the American ways and quicker than many other immigrant students. But in one way I don't act American; I don't think it's a good idea to go along with the native born by making fun of other people. And I have seen that situation many, many times. In a larger way, if the native-born people don't like the immigrants the native born don't give them a job or let them go to school, and how are they going to live? Instead of [discriminating against] the immigrants the native [born] should help them out so we all together could heal the world. I think the teachers should be very important because in class they could talk about racism, to teach their students not to discriminate [against] or segregate with other races.

Newcomers often fear the laughter, not only because they feel shame and humiliation, but also because they think Americans can be very mean and even violent. From what they hear and see on television, many newcomers apparently perceive Americans as being very violent. "Even before I came here I would see American television. Many times people get killed in the streets and fight. I knew it was a dangerous country."

They feel that the streets are not safe and guns are everywhere. This generalized perception about Americans becomes intertwined with immigrant experiences of being treated badly as newcomers. In both Lisa Stern's history classes and Garrison's science classes, we asked students to write about their first few months at Madison High as newcomers, and then discuss with each other what it was like. Their voices provide some picture of the difficulty of entry.

It is so scary to walk around the school and the street. I fear I will be laughed at and then someone will push me, just to laugh. You can't know when they just laugh at you and when it will be violent. So I am always scared.

The way we speak English is why the native people laugh at [us]. Another thing they laugh at is immigrants' and newcomers' clothes because they usually wear their own country clothes. Some laugh at them in physical education because they think that immigrant people don't know how to play games. I walk around school and see what kind of things people do, like how American people act and how they treat immigrants. I have seen sometimes American people say bad words and make fun of immigrants, and some of the things happen to me, too. I see what happens to newcomers at Madison if they won't have any English. Immigrant people feel bad when American students say bad things to them or make fun of them. In my physical education class, there was that Indian boy who had a big culture hat and American people were [making] fun of him. He couldn't take it anymore and [took] it [off] and cut his hair—and he don't even think about his culture in front of American people. I feel so very sad about this. American people always embarrassed us in front of everybody. Some of the meaning I take from these finding are prejudice is how we are treated.

The first couple of weeks was very strange for me at Madison. I felt very uneasy. Whatever I saw or heard, I used to compare it to our way. Sometimes I looked at the sky, clouds, and trees, and suddenly felt very sad feelings [rising] from very deep [in] my heart and I knew the feeling was about coming to a country totally 100 percent different from mine. My fears were, what if I won't adjust here and always feel this pain, or what if an American talks to me and I would not be able to answer them? And then would come the part that I hated the most, laughing at what I say. I could not understand why Americans enjoy to put somebody down and how bold they are. I still cannot understand this.

The words that come up again and again in the written statements of immigrant students about making their adjustment to Madison were sad, nervous, afraid, alone, and confused. The recurring themes were the racism and discrimination, and particularly the hurt of discovering that it is often "people from your own country" who "discriminate" against new immigrants.

The message immigrant students receive from the "Americans" is clear: "stay out of our way if you're going to be different stay separate in your corner. If you're going to be around us, be like us." The message is a deep source of stress and confusion for many newcomers. They recount experiences of their first days at Madison of mistakenly going up to other students and smiling or attempting to be friendly, only to be snubbed or laughed at. And they learn quickly they are safest and most comfortable in circles with other immigrants.

This reinforces the way American students think about newcomers. Many of them complain that "those foreigners just stick to themselves," or "they just want to hang out with others of their own language." This separation is particularly costly for the immigrant. They are cut off from opportunities for English language learning and from sources of understanding the complex culture they have joined. It daily reinforces their sense that "American" is a category that does not include them, and that America is not open to them. When they realize that they are marked as outsiders, they begin to turn to each other to figure out how to survive and cope in ways that avoid the laughter and teasing, that avoid violence and still do not cause them to have to act "too" American. Passing along to each other information about what it is safe to do and acceptable, and what will result in trouble, is one of the prime topics among immigrants. Their conversations also serve to monitor each other's behavior, and results to some degree in narrowing the choices a young person must make about his or her identity. Newcomers often end up limiting each other's solutions to the problems of adjustment to a new culture.

One day, just before a sheltered social studies class was about to begin, a Vietnamese immigrant boy held five others riveted with his explanation of American hand signals.

> In Vietnam, we had some signals like hold the hand and give to someone's face, it means I'll beat you. When I came to the U.S.A., I saw the Americans do some strange signals. I didn't understand them. I thought they were happy ones, friendly to do those, but little by little I came to know that some signals are not good. Then I decided to draw those pictures to give to my cousin

to remind or let him know these signals, so he will not be misun-
derstood or be stupid and smile at someone who is doing something bad to them. Some signals like "give me five" is okay. But
the middle finger and hold up your hand [are] not good. I feel
very happy when I figured this out because I understand and so I
will not do that to someone here. In my country it has no meaning. When you point to something you can use any finger you
want. But sometimes they do hand signals that are friendly, and
you have to know when to be friendly back. Some mean "keep
going" and some mean "how are you?" You have to be very
careful about hand signals.

"THERE IS NO EASY PATH."

Few newcomer students had things to say at first about what their teachers or the
school might do to help them adjust to a new school and culture. But it became
clear from their discussions that they identify school itself as one of the problems
that they have to learn to deal with. "Teachers talk too fast and don't have time for
us to ask questions when we don't understand." "We can't understand what is
going on." "We need more help with homework and to go for extra help when
we don't understand things." They say that they would like "more books in our
language so we can read about things that we don't understand in English." And
when a discussion in class directly asked them to try to imagine school approaches that might help, they began to dream of the way things might be. Their ideas
were numerous. Students who first come to Madison High should be put in
classes with someone they know or with a buddy who speaks their language.
Newcomers, they said, should have a map in their language showing where the
bathroom and cafeteria and classes are and maybe be given a personal tour on
their first day. Their final suggestion was that they should put together an orientation booklet for other immigrant students—and they did.

The orientation booklet is entitled "Newcomer Student Handbook." The
content ranges from visa requirements for enrollment in school to how the
school determines what classes they are placed in. It describes where to go for
help and how lunchtime works. The booklet describes student social activities
and what to do if you lose a book or an identification card. It tells where to get
a translator and how to open a locker.

When the orientation booklet was completed, the students looked at it
proudly. Then Zahira said, "This is great! If I'd had something like this when I
first came it would have been so easy!" Rosalia looked at her and replied:

"You're wrong. Nothing can make it easy. When our lives are torn from our homelands, there is no easy path. This book takes some of the rocks off the path, but it's still a hard path."

There are attempts to make it easier. Networks of family members and friends from the same homelands serve as guides, advisors, and key sources of information to newcomers about survival at Madison High. Although the school has no official counselors or supports assigned to newcomers, there are a few teachers who get to know the students in "sheltered" or ESL classes, who try to find ways to help immigrants with their adjustment to their new land. Their classrooms are places where newcomer students are encouraged to share what they are observing, learning, and experiencing as newcomers and immigrants at Madison. The teachers make themselves available as both sympathetic listeners and advocates for their immigrant students. Most free periods, lunch times, and after-school hours find the teachers meeting one to one with immigrant students.

However, that kind of support does not address the overriding sense newcomers seem to have that as hard as they try, they cannot "get there from here" at least without great cost and perhaps not even then. The greatest dilemma the immigrant students confront is whether all paths are open to them and how their skin color and language confound the problem of becoming an American.

"YOU HAVE TO STAY ON ONE SIDE OR THE OTHER.
IF YOU TRY TO BE IN THE MIDDLE, YOU ARE STONED FROM ALL SIDES."
Over and over in comments and conversations, the depth of feeling is evident as newcomers tried to weigh which direction they could and should head when facing the problem of being American. Said one Vietnamese boy:

> People ask me, why can't you be both Vietnamese and American? It just doesn't work, because you run into too many contradictions. After a while you realize you can't be both, because you start crossing yourself and contradicting yourself and then it's like math, when two things contradict each other they cancel each other out and then you are nothing. You are stuck as nothing if you try to be both. So I chose to be Vietnamese. I'm not sure I really could have been American anyway.

This was echoed by the comment of an Irani girl: "You have to stay on one side or the other. If you try to be in the middle, you are stoned from all sides.

You get hurt too easily. There are stones from all sides."

The sense of being caught in the middle, and of the vulnerability of being in the middle, is pervasive. It is made more complex because the "sides" are sometimes defined in terms of nationality, other times in terms of culture, still other times in terms of religion or race or language.

"We're from Mexico, and I'm seeing an American guy and it's the hardest thing not only because he's American but my parents feel I'll lose my racial customs like religion and dating and things like that."

Or in the words of a boy who had emigrated from Taiwan when he was still small:

> The one problem I have is that while I came here as a baby I'm obviously Chinese. But there's a language barrier between myself and my people because I can't speak Chinese. And I have a skin barrier with Caucasians. So the thing I have a problem with is sometimes I say to myself, why do you even try? And then my cousin just came from Taiwan and he's living with me. He's got his group of friends, but I can't feel at home with them either cause they don't totally accept me because I'm too American. And sometimes they ignore me because I can't speak the language. And I feel really left out. And I'm trapped in the middle. So if you ask me what I am right now, the only thing I can say is I'm just myself. That's the biggest problem I have.

Over a dozen times, while talking to students about how American they view themselves, I'd hear: "How could I be American, I have dark skin." "My English isn't good enough, I'm not really American yet." Which lines are crossable and which are not? For some immigrants, the barriers to becoming American feel particularly insurmountable because of skin color; for others, it is religion or language or the "open" behavior of American teens. But there is surprising clarity and agreement that to be American is to be English speaking, white skinned, and Christian. And there is little tenable ground for holding on to multiple identities or multicultures. As one remarkably perceptive and articulate young woman explained: "They won't accept you if you're not like them. They want to make you just their culture and if you try to be who you are, and try to be both American and yourself, forget it. It won't work. It's not allowed."

"SHE IS SO CHINESE, I CAN'T STAND IT."

Although this process is perceived as being imposed by outside forces, through the pressures and demands of Americans who refuse to recognize multicultural identities, in fact newcomers play a strong role in pressuring each other. As a result, there is enormous tension in their relationships. At times, they hold each other back, criticizing and lamenting those who "cross the line" or "take off their turbans." Or one person may be tolerant of a friend being more American on one level (e.g. dress and sexuality) but not on another. Each newcomer has to forge his or her own path, proceeding on a journey of becoming American, annoyed at those who would hold him or her back and uncomfortable with being judged when they move in directions that distance them from others. What might serve at one point as a support group, a place of comfort and acceptance, becomes at another moment a source of torment.

> My cousin embarrasses me so much. She just won't admit that she is here in America now. I can't stand the way she keeps talking to me in Mandarin. Sometimes at school she comes up to me and I want to pretend I don't even know her because she is just so—I don't know—like she won't talk English. I just try to avoid her. And she tries to tell me that I'm forgetting who I am! All we do is fight now. She is so Chinese, I can't stand it.

Changing who they are appears to be viewed by immigrants as a requirement of membership. It is a one-way process. They perceive their "American" peers as different than themselves, and often feel buffeted by the pain of how much they have to give up in order to be accepted by Americans. But it is quite clear to them that it is they that have to do the changing. What they do not quite see is the full extent of what those changes require. And they don't understand what will be "enough" to end the ridicule and resentment they feel from Americans at the school.

The newcomers are acutely aware that their American peers do not fully embrace their presence at Madison High. During one month the walls on Stern's social studies classroom held flip chart pages generated by her history class of immigrant students. These sheets listed "reasons we immigrated" and "things we think *they* think about why we're here."

REASONS WE IMMIGRATED:

To find work

Wages too low in home country

To get a better education

Not enough opportunity in our land

To have a better future

There were political problems

No jobs in my country

Economic opportunities

There was a coup

Escape war

Political freedom

To be with mother

THINGS WE THINK THEY THINK ABOUT WHY WE'RE HERE:

To take over

Think we want to be American

Think I'm a communist

We're trying to be better in school
   than they are

Fear we'll be higher

Think we chose to come—
   we didn't, we had to

They think US is better than our countries

We're taking their jobs

We bring diseases

We're nerds

It turns out they were quite perceptive about what American students think. One day in the "regular" history class, one young man leaned across pointed to that flip chart and said:"That's right, that's why they're here. They want to take over." He didn't "see" the list of the reasons they came; he only noticed and validated the accuracy of the second part of the list. And that one minute illustrated newcomers' lives in the world of the "American" student at Madison High. Their realities are invisible to the Americans in this new land.

CHAPTER THREE

We Make Each Other Racial: The Madison High World as Perceived by the "American" Student

THE DISCUSSION in Lisa Stern's sixth-period world history class began neutrally with students being asked to do a "quick write" introductory writing exercise using the prompt: "If it were up to you, what would you learn in high school that would be useful to you? What would you be studying?" They were then asked to share what they had written.

There were few affirmative answers about what might be useful to learn in school. Their responses were instead couched in accusations about what they are not getting and why. The discussion exploded into a general frenzy of voices. "Why do we have to learn the same thing over and over? Why do we learn about the past?" The anger was initially expressed as resentment that some students get what others do not.

> TONY (WHITE): If there's ethnic studies for one group, it has to be for all of us. It's not fair if the other guys get it and we don't! They think their culture is so important, well so is ours!

> MARVIN (LATINO): Yeah, but there is no ethnic studies here anyway, what are you talking about? No one cares at this school. They don't teach us nothing. Particularly us Latins.

> TONY, PERSISTING: Well, what if you wanted to learn about a different culture? It shouldn't just be Raza studies for the Latins. How come we don't have it for everyone? How come we can't study about white culture, too?

At this point, a student attempted to assert a class alliance, heading off the threatened racial split in the group and emphasizing how they are all treated alike.

ALFRED (WHITE): Knock it off, you know we don't get any kind of real studies at all because the school's too poor.

JEFF (WHITE): It wouldn't happen even if we tried. No one tries. No one comes together.

VIVIEN (FILIPINA): You said it, no one tries.

MS. STERN: You all sound so discouraged!

CLASS: YES

ALFRED: This school doesn't even have any money to spend on us.

TONY: We're getting NOTHING!

JENNIFER (WHITE): School isn't what kids want. If it was up to us, we'd never come up with a high school like this as what we want. We have to read *Lord of the Flies*, and the teachers don't explain it to us. They don't care if we understand it or not. They're just putting in their time. It's all a game. We're supposed to just put in our time, too—seat time. To grind us down. To learn that it's all about sitting still and taking it.

JEFF: A lot of stuff is just never even taught to us. And when we do read stuff, you don't get to discuss it. We don't get what other schools have. I know kids who go to other schools and they look down on us. We're the lowest. And we're supposed to think we're getting an education.

MARVIN: We come for the diploma. We want a diploma.

VIVIEN: To be able to say I finished high school. That's what keeps me coming. It seems like it's important, you know, to say that I walked across the stage, but then I think, say it to who? What does it matter?

MARVIN: We have to try to better ourselves. But we don't learn the stuff that helps to better ourselves. The students over in

> Oakland care. They had a walkout for ethnic studies. Here, no
> one cares. Our teachers are being laid off. The district don't care
> about us or what we think. All they do is get you down.
>
> LORA (AFGHAN): They should be encouraging us! All they care
> about is getting us out of their hair.

And in this moment of solidarity, the villains become not just the teachers or the administrators or the district, but the newcomer students who are viewed as perpetuating the belief that school is about getting ahead.

> VIVIEN: So for us, school is just, you come to classes and you just
> sit there. And if you sit there long enough, after four years they
> give you a diploma. After a while you figure it out—you don't get
> anything and you don't give anything. The only ones who don't
> get it are the ESL kids. People tell us, we should be more like
> them, we should try hard, we should study as hard as they do. I
> get so mad! They are so blind! They still believe. But sooner or
> later, they'll get it, too. We just don't matter.

■ ■ ■

The world inhabited by the "American" student at Madison High is every bit as intensely involved with "finding one's place" as the immigrant world; however, the arenas are not about being American, they are about "race" and class. The maps these students drew for Stern's social studies assignment were almost wholly racialized maps: almost every social group was labeled either by a racial identifier or the category "mixed race." There were two exceptions, which were labeled by school activities ("band kids" and "basketball players"), and a single undifferentiated group of "ESLers," a label referring to newcomers by their programmatic placement in English-as-a-second-language classes.

The descriptions they created for the school overall were largely American ethnic and racial categories, attended by great detail about the behaviors, activities, and common interests that mark these categories or distinguish sub-groups. For example, groups were referred to as "white skaters," "white smokers," or "white social outcasts." Many groups are also labeled by their geographic turf on the campus.

PLAYING FIELDS

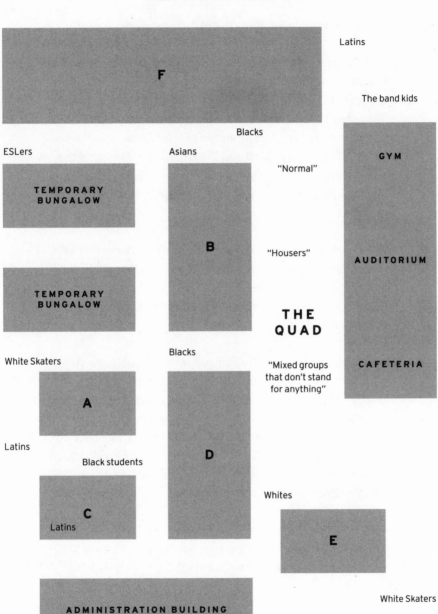

Latins

The band kids

F

Blacks

GYM

ESLers

Asians

"Normal"

TEMPORARY
BUNGALOW

B

AUDITORIUM

"Housers"

TEMPORARY
BUNGALOW

THE
QUAD

White Skaters

Blacks

CAFETERIA

A

"Mixed groups
that don't stand
for anything"

Latins

Black students

D

Whites

C

Latins

E

ADMINISTRATION BUILDING

White Skaters

Here is a collection of the descriptions used to label the maps of the "American" students:

There are two categories of "the White race" students:

By A Hall and sometimes by E Hall or the Portables are the white skaters who hang out in the sun. They are largely excluded by the school. They dress alike; they don't care what others think. They aren't exclusive or anything; they are pretty friendly. But no one really pays much attention to them. They listen to the same music (heavy metal and "alternative" music), and they hang where no one else will bother them. They stay out of the way, and hang in a place where the administrators are unlikely to come after them.

The smokers [who] hang out across the street are another kind of white student, bound together by their addiction. They don't hide it, they like the visibility. They don't apologize. They don't belong very easily on campus in other groups, so they hang out separate and distinct.

Mexicans stay far from the administration, close to the street so they can see their friends who drive by and stop for awhile. Mostly they hang out outside of C Hall at the street end or just inside the C Hall, down the hall from where black students hang out. The Latinos dress alike. It's just their style. They are considered very cool. Others feel excluded, not welcomed. Some of us feel nervous walking through C Hall. It's a lot of the East Gardens kids.

In the middle are black students, a big group of around twenty (mostly freshmen and sophomores) who kid around a lot. They seem to know each other from junior high.

At the other end are Filipinos and some other mixed Asians. Nicely dressed, baggy pants, beanies. These are "housers," they can dance. They are relaxed. They don't exclude other people. They are pretty popular.

D Hall is where the cheerleaders hang out. These are white and female. These are another kind of whites besides the skaters and smokers.

B Hall is for the "normal" kids who study. You know, just normal. There is nothing to say about them.

In the Quad at the center of campus is where blacks practice dancing. Nerdy kids hang close to the cafeteria, studying. It's a place of mixed races, who are pretty accepting. There aren't quarrels in the Quad area. There is a definite Asian group, but they are pretty accepting of others and friendly. People in the Quad are just normal people. They don't have a title or a place or one race. They don't stand out for anything.

Hardly anyone hangs out near F Hall—it's a place for loners.

Near the basketball courts, kids who want to play go. This is a mixed-race group behind the gym. It is mostly guys, but some girls come to watch them play. When administrators aren't around, they play craps.

The quiet band kids are near the band room.

These descriptions are rich in aspects of youth culture that are deemed important: the kind of music people listen to, how friendly or unfriendly the group is thought to be, how they dress, how they are thought of by others in terms of being popular or cool. And almost all have racial labels. The one group that is identified by where they live are the Latinos, who would have been enrolled in Washington High if it were still open. They are markedly not part of the "community" of Madison High. What is unclear is whether they themselves have taken on the badge of their East Garden neighborhood as a key identifier, or whether it has been a label given to them by those who consider them outsiders.

The Quad is the one area of campus identified as the turf of mixed groups. It is interesting that the words attached to these groups are terms such as "normal," "accepting," "don't stand out," and "don't stand for anything." In fact, the Quad is a rather large area and quite crowded. Architecturally, it is the heart of the campus. It is widely acknowledged as an area of social mixing between the groups.

And yet it commanded very little attention as students got into discussions about their maps and became engaged in describing the social world of the school. It is not that they deny that mixing across races occurs, or that there are some social arenas of the school life that are pretty "accepting and friendly." Rather, what holds their attention, what they feel is salient to talk about describing the dimensions of social life, are the separations, the differences of race and ethnicity.

LEARNING TO BE FRIENDLY, CAREFULLY

The sixth-period "regular" class argued at length about whether the campus is primarily a mixed-race campus of friendship groups, with a few groups who keep to themselves or whether it is a wholly racialized campus of separate groups who stay separate, with a few kids who mix. There was enormous tension in the discussion, and clearly heavy investment in how students might choose to view their school's social climate. Is it divided by race? Is it a mixed campus? Is it happily diverse? Is it tense and hostile? Is it all of these things?

Some students spoke of their fear of walking past or through the turf of other racial groups, an issue that came up in the descriptions they gave of certain areas of their maps. Some mentioned being hurt when rejected or put down by people or groups of races other than their own whom they tried to befriend. Others insisted that their friends were of all races and they get along great. It was a heated and tense discussion. Apparently, there were high stakes in the social representation of their world.

After a lot of discussion, the consensus seemed to be that the social life of the school was about groups isolating themselves by race. The students viewed the sharpest conflicts as between the Mexicans and blacks, with heavy rivalry between the groups expressed primarily through verbal exchanges and occasional fights. C Hall was identified as the tensest locale on campus, and in fact, a stabbing occured there early one morning as school was just starting because of a conflict between rival gangs. Most agreed that the sharpest separations occurred between freshmen and sophomores who are new to the school and are still finding their way. The longer people are in the school, the more they claimed to have found a way to live comfortably in and with the divisions, to be more skillful when walking through the turf of other groups, and to make friends across ethnic lines. As one student said: "It's a matter of getting comfortable with it all, and then learning the skills of how to be friendly, carefully."

> There is a lot of teasing here about being a wannabee. People
> don't want others to think bad about them for not being where

> they belong. They don't want people to think they are rejecting
> their people by choosing to be with others.

How complicated the rules of interaction are at this school! By the time students are juniors and seniors, they have begun to master the art of being friendly with people of racial groups different than theirs without appearing too eager as "wannabees" and without appearing to reject their own racial identity.

Most of the social maps drawn by the "American" classes simply did not have any mention of the newcomer groups on campus. Only two had any mention, and they both put "ESL kids" on their maps as a single undifferentiated category. Absent are the national or language identities. The only notice is of a group in terms of its programmatic place in the school, defined by its lack of English. When the absence of the immigrant students was mentioned to the "regular" history class and comparisons made between the immigrant maps and their maps, the sixth-period students acknowledged that immigrants were indeed present in the school and should be on the map. "We just didn't think of them," the group said in defense of their social map. Then they proceeded to add to their map the descriptions: "ESLers hang out over by the edge of campus near the Newcomer School." The category they used was a single "ESL" label, echoing the basic truth that newcomers are seen primarily in terms of their lack of English-speaking ability. One student said, "By E Hall is where ESL kids sit and talk. They don't connect to anyone else. It's their differences that bond them." And another added, "They hold on to their language. They don't even try to speak English."

As a follow-up to the social-map unit, Stern had her classes continue to focus on aspects of the social experience at Madison High. Among the assignment were small group-class projects, created to examine what it is like being a white student at Madison and what it is like being an immigrant student at Madison. A third was assigned the task of probing interracial or interreligious dating.

Stern was particularly interested in having a group of white students explore their own experiences and those of their white friends in attending a school in which they have become a numerical minority. Her concern stemmed from knowing the increasing activity of white hate groups in the community and their recruitment efforts at Madison High. From class discussions and student journal entries, when she had done a social studies unit on historical scapegoating and prejudice in which she had the class analyze hate materials, she knew there was an undercurrent of fear and anger among many white students in the school.

It seems like my white students think they have no culture at all, and it feeds a kind of targetless anger against things like Black History Month. I can't teach a curriculum that includes black history and Raza issues without somehow finding a way to address its impacts on the white kids.

She wanted to provide an opportunity, a safe and sanctioned opportunity, for white students to reflect and speak about their feelings. This new unit was a way to try to address that undercurrent. The assignment read:

EURO-AMERICANS/CAUCASIANS/WHITES

Your group, a group of white students, is charged with finding out what some of the racial attitudes of white students are at Madison. Each of you will interview about five students and you will pool your information to make general conclusions based on what you found. You should try to determine several issues that you think white students are concerned about, and create questions to get good responses. For example, you might want to ask white students how they feel about being called names that are related to the fact they are white. Because you, too, are white (or look white to others), chances are they will be a bit more comfortable opening up to you. Do not put words in their mouths. Let their answers be entirely theirs. A second aspect of the project will give you an opportunity to reflect on your own feelings.

QUESTIONS TO THINK ABOUT IN FORMULATING YOUR INTERVIEW QUESTIONS:

- what are the feelings of white students about being in a diverse school?
- what kinds of problems do they face as a result?
- what advantages do they see in the diversity?
- what general social issues do they feel threaten them as whites?
- do they think the school is racially harmonious?

It was, as Stern suspected it might be, controversial. One Latina asked, "Isn't that racism, Ms. Stern, to put people in a working group just because of their skin color?" But the white students wanted to do the project. And they defended with anger what they perceived as their right to be in an all-white assignment group. "You all get to have your clubs—the Black Student Club, and La Raza. We never get a club. For once, let us have a group."

The white students worked hard, as one student wrote in her evaluation of the unit: "We worked harder than we have ever worked on a social studies project. This just seemed so important. It was our one chance to let other people know what it is like for us. We wanted it to be good."

One strong pattern that emerged was the development of their own racial consciousness among white students.[16] In the midst of the intense racial sorting of the student body, white identity has lost its transparency for white students. They no longer are able to see themselves as raceless (a privilege associated with racial domination), but are awkwardly, painfully, and sometimes with great resistance developing a recognition of race for themselves. They are seeing themselves from the outside as a racialized person, as "white," "honkies," "crackers," or "oppressors"—the words others apply to them. A junior tried to explain this process:

> You know everything was fine before I came to Madison. In elementary school up to middle school, we were just all friends pretty much. Then you get to middle school and high school and WHAM, it's like you're white you belong over here, and you're black and you are supposed to act a certain way. Here, I'm a white kid. You know, it's something everyone says about other people—a way you describe people. You're white, like it's a big important thing about you. And you can't tell like if it's an okay thing and like they are just describing you, or like are they saying you're some kind of honky or bad person.

In the midst of this process, there is a crisis of identity among some of the white students at Madison. On arrival at Madison, they seem to find that for the first time in their lives they do not represent the majority. Despite the whirling demographic changes occurring in their communities, most residential areas are relatively separated by skin color. Students attend elementary schools in their residential neighborhoods, but as adolescents are combined into larger consolidated secondary schools; the multicultural reality of the city becomes apparent to them. School is the major public institution and public space where young people find themselves actually confronting this reality. As they move from elementary to middle school to high school, the white students see their numbers dwindle as the dominant group in their schools. This is not only their own experience as they move through school, but a perspective they have about the difference between things now and the way things "used to be" in the community before their time. Even though white students are still the majority among the academic classes of the Madison school system, many expressed anxiety or resentment at the increasing numbers of immigrants and Asians they perceive as pushing them out of their place in the academic hierarchy. The language used in Stern's sixth-period history class when students were explaining why they think immigrants come to the United States reflects the language they use in talking about being pushed out by Asians in their academic classes. It is almost evocative of the ways they talk about immigrants in general. Here is an example:

> They come to take our jobs, and they are willing to break their backs for shit pay, and we can't compete.

> These Chinese kids come over here and all they do is work and work and work and work, and all you have to do is look in the AP [Advanced Placement] classes and you'll see they are filling them up. No one else can compete anymore.

> They just want to take over.

Many of the students at Madison are working class, who look beyond their high school years with an apparent kind of cynicism, knowing they have little capital in the world and what little they have stems from being white and English speaking and native U.S.-born. Although some white students sit back in silence, giving no hint of their opinions, others express enormous anger over affirmative action and regularly voice their feeling of being discriminated against. They rail against the existence of ethnic clubs in a school where ethnicity is the major basis of club organizations on campus, and insist they should be allowed to have a European American club, but have little interest in actually organizing one. Only rarely a voice speaks up in support of changes needed to address inequities and discrimination against students of color.

"SHE'S BLACK AND I'M WHITE, AND THAT'S THAT."

Every one of the white students interviewed for this study is acutely aware of their white identity within the social world of Madison. But when they leave school, most move back to worlds beyond the school, where they believe their whiteness has no particular meaning. To them, school is the site, the place, the world that racializes them. School is the place they feel put down for being white, or excluded for being white. And school is the place they associate with being taught the lessons of racialism.

Several girls gathered to talk about the transition from elementary school to middle school, and the lessons of racialization. One spoke in tears about her best friend Rose in elementary school.

> We were so glad we were going to go to the same middle school. But something happened there. She's black and I'm white, and we just started having different friends. We'd still get together some- times after school, but not at school. I don't how it happened, and we never talked about it. But she ended up with all black friends and I ended up with all white friends. And I missed her, but never said anything. Now we're both at Madison. You know, I see her pass by sometimes in the Quad, but we never stop to talk, and it feels kind of awkward. I used to cry about it, but now I'm used to it. It's just how the world is. She's black and I'm white, and that's that.

In Lisa Stern's social studies class, white students were outspoken about their discomforts. Jeff writes in his final paper on the unit on white experience, echoing what I heard over and over from white students about how localized at school the experiences of whiteness have become for them:

> I don't like to talk about racism, and don't like that Ms. Stern is making us to find out about things like races at Madison. I never think of myself as white any place but at school. I don't like racism but there is nothing I can do, it is everywhere. We just have to learn to put up with different skin colors and cultures. These folks aren't gonna disappear. I'm proud to be a Euro- American even when dummys try to discriminate against me. I mean, what do they want me to do, change colors? People at Madison think in terms of race all the time. But out in the world, I never have to think of myself as white—only here.

Jennifer, as a white cheerleader, is safely ensconced in one of the few social settings of the school in which white students still predominate. After asking

twenty white students what it was like being white students at Madison High"
Jennifer explained:

> I liked the chance to talk to white students and find out exactly
> how they feel about being white in a diverse school. I mean,
> we talk to each other all the time, and people make remarks
> or comments sometimes, but we don't really talk about this.
> We don't think of ourselves as white until someone makes
> us think of ourselves as white. I was shocked! And I was sur-
> prised at how honest people were when I interviewed them.
> It turns out that inside, all of us at school know we are white
> and feel that it is this big thing. But we never talk about it to
> each other. When I interviewed them, none of them liked the
> idea of an unqualified black getting a job over a qualified white.
> But when asked how they felt in a school with lots of races
> and cultures, there were a lot of different and mixed feelings. It
> boggles my mind how differently people feel about the same
> situation! It really disturbed me that kids in this school would
> join the KKK. I thought the KKK only existed in the South in
> the 1800s, not here in Bayview now, not in my school. When I
> dug deeper into these kid's thoughts, I found out their parents
> were also racist. But it's like, you know, if they [the blacks] are
> gonna make a big deal about us being white, okay, we will too. I
> think a big part of the whole problem is how kids are raised and
> their upbringing. It's our parents. I wonder if things will ever
> change. I don't even think assemblies or anything about racism
> make any difference. It's all in how we see each other. We make
> each other racial.

As the white students' projects evolved, many of their comments in small
groups focused on defending the right of white people to feel angry for the
position they are thrust into. Here are some excerpts from these conversations:

> As long as there is special treatment for some races, there will
> be angry people who don't get special treatment and it will
> cause major problems. You can't stop anger from people who
> don't get fair treatment. (Jesse, a white student talking about
> affirmative action)

Very few whites are really racist here. But most of us are upset about the way whites are constantly stereotyped. We feel like we are being forced to pay for the sins or mistreating that were invoked by whites a great many years ago (none of the kids here were even related to anyone who was around when there were slaves; our families came to the United States after slavery was over). And we are always getting threatened by other races. They have too many things to help minorities, like affirmative action. And they deserve them, but so do we. How come we don't get any help. (Lisa, white)

Education doesn't help one bit when certain races pass along a 200-year old hate. Most of the reasons why people hate each other is because lots of whites just hate blacks because they are black, and there are lots of blacks who just hate whites because they are white. It doesn't make sense, maybe, but hate is strong. There is a lot of tension that most people pretend not to see so they can figure there isn't a problem. They are living in a fantasy world. Things have been done to me because I'm white, and I have gotten to the point where if someone pissed me off really mad, I would have the guts to blow their brains out. I'm sick of it. Sick, sick, sick. Yes, I'm white. And I'm proud of it. (Mike, white)

For these students, trying to define areas of commonality and similarity and to dispute the notion that they have privilege is complex. They see a kind of class commonality, and do not see racial privilege. They have no historical perspective to help them, and little current information that might mitigate their stances that "racism was back then, this is now and we're in the same boat." Much of the conversation revolved around "being in the same boat as they are," claiming similar class positions, or feeling discriminated against, and disputing the existence of white privilege. Here's an example taken from a comment of a white boy who is a junior. "My old man doesn't have the money to send me to college either, so how come I can't get any help and a black kid can."

Few of the white students feel they are getting much help in "getting ahead." In particular, they talk about not getting help to go to college, not being able to get into college, and not being eligible for financial aid. Most are struggling. A class solidarity with students of color at Madison seems obvious to them. Their privileges as whites are invisible. The majority of their references to race were about black–white relations. Interestingly, most of the discussion about getting help, about being in the same boat, about comparisons to other groups who "get help" is in reference to blacks. The complaints, the anger, the hurt of white students is aimed at black students when it comes to "getting help." They simply believe that blacks are getting something that whites are not, and it is not fair. Their anger at immigrants has a different tint.

The comparison to "Latins" was rare. In fact, despite the large numbers of Latinos in the school and community, somehow Latinos seem irrelevant in the analysis and comments. The comparison to "Chinese" or "Asians" was often in terms of anger at being pushed out, but not felt as unfair. There may be resentment that these groups "work so hard," but their rewards were generally viewed as earned privilege, reasonable rewards. These groups were viewed as doing so well academically because they work so hard. The bitterness is expressed in terms of "they want to be better than us."

"IT'S RACIAL, PURE AND SIMPLE. THERE ARE SOME KIDS WHO MAY MIX HERE, BUT MOSTLY YOU STAY WITH YOUR OWN KIND."

One's social capital at Madison in the world inhabited by "Americans" is measured and conferred in terms of one's identity. Crossing the line socially and one's style (dress and behavior) are heavily monitored by the students. It is not that students do not cross lines to have friends of different racial groups or even to date. In fact, there are plenty of mixed-race friendship groups. The campus is dotted with such groups. But unless these friendships are rooted in activities such as the band or sports teams, such mixing becomes noticed, commented on, and tempered by a lively discourse among peers and between students and their parents. The formal activities appear to provide a rationale or reasonableness about the mixed-race associations—but cross-friendships outside of the context of such formal activity seems somewhat in need of explanation or defense. Students talk pretty unanimously of the tension with regards to who your friends are, how you dress, and the racial appropriateness of those choices.

It is most often the peer reactions that dominate their concerns. For students of color, there is little that is as hurtful or as threatening to their sense of identity as being labeled "white-washed." "White-washed" is used a lot in passing conversation. One Latina explains: "If you don't speak your own language, you are white-washed—you have forgotten who you are."

"White washed" refers to talking white, acting white, wishing you were white, getting good grades or "being in good" with the teachers. Movement toward white behavior or white groupings on the parts of many students is carefully monitored by others and viewed as clearly objectionable, disloyal, and forgetting who you are. It is not universally true that all students engage in this kind of monitoring. But it does appear to be the norm. Those students who "mix" or "don't care how others want them to act" tend to be defensive about their positions and often cite being put down by others.

For students of color who are more culturally identified with another nonwhite group, the monitoring term is the label "wannabees." "Wannabees" is regularly used and sometimes refers to specific subgroups of students, e.g., "those girls who smoke cigarettes and hang out near C Hall are a bunch of Latin wannabees." These words have power. Apparently, no one wants to be labeled either white-washed or wannabee, for they connote lack of authenticity. Underneath these terms, lies a host of issues such as loyalty, resistance to white cultural domination, and fear. This seems to be particularly true for Latino and black students. For example, Trina, a Latina senior who has a mixed group of friends, explains: "My sister hangs around *cholas*—you know, wannabee *chola* types. She's said stuff to me like, you're a white-washed Mexican, just look at your friends. I want to smack her."

Aisha, a black student, said:

> Either you're a black person and you're hard, or you're white-washed. I've been called white-washed because I don't hang around just with black kids. Some of the black girls here don't like the way I do my hair (straightened). I'm supposed to have hair up to here with tons of grease in my hair and talk like I'm from the ghetto. I wasn't brought up like that, but there are a lot of people here who think that's how I ought to be.

Developing armor against the hurt of these charges becomes an important survival tactic for students who chose to still cross the lines. Sandy, a senior who has been buffeted back and forth through periods of sticking with black students and periods of venturing out into mixed groups, explains it in the following way:

> There is a lot of shit talking, but as you get older if you're a stronger person you can get over it. People say "You're not really black." Well, guess what, I'm always going to be black; my skin is black. The world treats me like I'm black. But since I don't act "black," then they say I'm not. I'm blacker than half the people at

this school. I know more stuff about my history than they do. But they say, you don't have hair up to here and you don't have five earrings in your ear and lip gloss all over your face, so you're not really black. I try to shrug it off, but it gets to me. I get it from both sides.

And Andrea adds:

Me and my sister are two different people. My sister is really into the black thing. She's a sophomore and younger than me. We walk down the hall together. I keep to myself. I won't say any- thing to anybody unless they say something to me. But Stephanie is out there. If someone looks at me wrong, she'll go up to them and say, "What the fuck are you looking [at]? Don't touch up my sister." I'm older and she is younger, but she's like out to protect me. She's the one where if any shit even threatens to come on, she's the first one to say, "Don't mess with her because I'll kick your ass." She's out there. And I'm more the white sister, the one that will keep to herself and not start shit with anybody. She's more defiant, more extreme, more black.

Patty, also African American, has a Latino boyfriend. They don't hang around with anyone else at school. She says, "I hear this all the time. You don't have a black boyfriend, you're not a black." For white students, the charge of being a wannabee is the strongest epithet. It is akin to saying "go back to your own kind."

And yet, for many of the students, hanging out with kids they identify as of their own culture, as sharing the experience of skin color, also has deep positive meaning. Their choice to be together is a choice of preference—of friendship that often has a history in their community and in elementary school, a choice for the ease and recognition that comes from sharing a code and culture. There is comfort from shared experience, a protected shelter against the racism and prejudices of others, as well as pride and loyalty. Raul, a tenth-grade student expresses some of this:

It's racial, pure and simple. There are some kids who mix here, but mostly you stay with your own kind. It's important to know who you are and be true to who you are. Some kids are

wannabees, looking somewhere else instead of standing by who
they are. Me, I'm proud to be Latin. I feel good to be with my
Latin brothers.

And thus, the social life of the school is created around racialized groupings and maintained through an active system of monitoring. "Finding your
place" and "staying within your own group" is generally viewed by students as
a positive value. It is about loyalty to one's people and knowing who you are.
The students who are the proponents of these values contrast them with "losing who you are," a process they define as living in a racist society that would
deny them that identification. They view their strong group identification as
resistance to forces that would make them invisible or denigrate them. Time
and again, in discussing these racially defined social groupings, students would
become defensive. Robert, a black junior, explained:

> It's not about not liking other people. It has nothing to do with
> who you are, it's about who I am. We gotta know who we are and
> feel pride in that. I'm black, and that's me, and I don't kid myself
> about it and I won't let nobody keep me from myself. I'm black
> because I claim it!

And yet, they construct narrow boundaries for themselves and others, limiting the multicultural possibilities inherent in a campus and community that is
so diverse. The friendships lost, the cross-cultural understanding and learning
that might have been gained, the connections that might have been possible are
foreclosed. The many students at Madison who are biracial or multiracial cannot embrace their full humanness, but rather are pushed to choose one part of
their being for their social identity—or find it chosen for them.

**"THERE IS WHAT WE ALL SAY, THAT NO ONE IS PREJUDICED AND WE ALL GET
ALONG—AND THEN THERE IS WHAT WE DO."**
For the students presenting their maps and discussing these social issues in
Stern's classes, each discussion eventually focused on the different versions of
the social maps and on the seemingly crucial issue: "How separate are we?"
This led to an examination of how students learn to perceive and find their
way around a diverse and complex social environment.

The class puzzled about the kind of survival and coping skills they had to
develop to make their way through the subtle divisions of the campus:

People getting along here depends on everyone pretending they're okay with each other. It's death for it to get around that you're prejudiced against another group, or that you're not willing to be with your people. You got to find a way to be with your own people, but not let it seem like you're doing it because you don't like any one else.

Everybody at this school seems to talk to everybody. We don't hang out a lot with each other, but we talk to each other. You talk to everybody but you hang around with your race. If you look once, you can see everyone talking to each other. But if you look again, you see that they walk in and out the door with their own race—people the same as them.

I knew we had all kinds at our school, but when I really started looking when we did our map, I was surprised. I didn't realize the number of groups that are out there. It was pretty overwhelming. I think most of the time I try not to notice too much, and I stay in my own part of the school.

The "trying not to notice," the "staying in my own part of the school," and the "surprise" students report when studying how divided the social maps were posed a crucial contrast to the depth of understanding they in fact all seemed to have exhibited about the actual divisions on campus. What is allowed to be noticed and remarked on, what is safe to perceive and articulate, does not seem to match the actual experiences of most students. The social-map activity began with brainstorming in the classroom when students were first handed the physical map of the campus. Most groups immediately filled in the maps and had to be admonished to take the time to "look around" and check their initial perceptions. They knew well what the divisions were on their campus. Yet, the students proffered "surprise" at what they found. I began to understand the complexity of a social world in which what students experience and what they are safe in articulating are quite different.

In the course of the discussion, students developed a theory that the more diversity there is, the safer students are because of two reasons—there is not any one dominant group that can get away with "getting down" on others very easily. For example:

[If there was] a huge amount of Latins at this school and a small amount of white kids, then the Latins would feel superior to the

whites and the Latin kids would more likely make sure it was
true and they wouldn't let the whites get in their way. It would
lead to more hate and fighting. A huge amount of whites, and it
would be just the opposite.

The other aspect of the theory is that with so much diversity, with so few
of "your own kind," you just have to learn to watch your own back and not
ruffle anyone's feathers. Either way, they agree that a lot of diversity pushes kids
to keep a lid on acting out their prejudices. This is what it means, they say, to
learn to live in a diverse society. They also noted that the larger the group, the
more likely it is to act exclusive. This is how they explained that the three
groups they view as being most exclusive are blacks, Latins, and ESL students.
These three groups seem to them to have the numbers that allow for exclusiv-
ity. The newcomer students would, more than likely, be startled and surprised
if they could hear this explanation of their social separation. The social
predicament for students becomes having to hang out with others like themselves, but appearing to do so for reasons other than not liking other groups.

This student–developed theory of intergroup relations sharply contrasts
with the faculty's view, which generally posits that intergroup relations became
more volatile and dangerous with the increasing diversity of the student body.

The formal discussion only continued for two class periods. But the issue
remained alive in the class for many weeks. Students in Stern's classes regularly
write in reflective journals about things that arise for them from their work in
the class. Students wrote a lot about additional thoughts on the mapping project. A tenth grader, an African American student (who wants to be a sociologist), wrote:

> The thing that has been most disappointing to me as I did this
> research is that I found more groups consisting of all one race
> than those groups that have more than one race. Does this
> mean that most people like to hang with others of the same
> race? Before doing this research I believed what we all say, that
> Madison is a great diverse place and we're all mixed. I didn't
> think I would find many groups of just one race in areas like "ter-
> ritories." But I found that some races do have their own areas to
> be away from the others and it really bothers me. Why do the
> Mexicans have to hang in C Hall, and why do the whites hang in A
> Hall, and why do blacks hang in B Hall? This feeling that they

have to have their own area and give people who don't belong there bad looks causes problems. Tension will start building up, and it also causes a problem for those who are outside of these groups because they feel uncomfortable to walk past them. If we all keep pretending we don't notice it, we just keep our discomfort inside and things stay calm. But it makes you kind of crazy.

Jennifer, on completing her social mapping project, was deeply disturbed by what she found:

Maybe it is better if we keep believing we are all mixed. Maybe it is better to just not see what I saw when I did my social map. There is what we all say—that no one is prejudiced and we all get along—and then there is what we do, and that shows how separate we keep ourselves by race. . . . I think we have to try hard to not see that because it hurts. I think down deep we all really know what's up—that we're a divided school.

Another student, a white eleventh grader, wrote:

Before I did this project I didn't think that many groups of people hung out with their race. I just thought people hang out with their friends. I just thought our school was filled with different races and we [are] all mixed, and people had all kinds of friends. At first when I started looking around at the groups for this project, I noticed that some were the same ethnicity. Then I noticed that almost all were the same ethnicity. It's not like we choose to be with our own race, but that's who we are comfortable with and have things in common with, and then other kids see us and they don't approach us so it gets more and more rigid. Other people don't come up to us, and so we stay one race. It made me really uncomfortable to see how separate we are.

The separateness of racial and ethnic groups is usually peaceful at Madison High, at least on the surface. Most, who remain in their own groups, are careful not to get in the way of other groups. And those who choose to "mix" do so in their own section of the school or keep it relatively quiet. The system is kept in place not by open hostilities or threats or the physical protection of turf through intimidation. It appears to operate more as a social system of pressures on individuals to place themselves and to stay placed. But sometimes, the underlying tensions explode.

Madison sits in the neighborhood where the headquarters of the Ku Klux Klan for the entire county is housed. Nearby high schools have had some incidents with literature from the Klan, graffiti on lockers, etc. The little post office on the corner near the school is the mailing address for the South County John Birch Society. Although there have been no incidents directly attributable to these organizations, the presence of white resistance to the demographic changes in the community is evident among some of the white students at the school. The presence of white hate responses appear to be generally confined to occasional comments made by a few individuals. There have been bottles thrown at the buses of immigrants arriving at or going home from the New-comer School as they pass by Madison High, reportedly by white students. But on one occasion it was Mexican Americans aiming at Afghan immigrants.

The "recently arrived" versus the "been here for a while" immigrants versus the native borns is a tension described by students in each of these groups. All of this is couched in terms of intense competition, a sense of eroding opportunities, and of being crowded and invaded by others who have an unfair advantage. Many native U.S.-born students feel that "immigrants are given everything"; many Latinos feel that newly arrived immigrants are pulling them down.

In Stern's sixth-period class, some of this resentment was voiced in the context of broader working-class anger, a sense of resignation, abandonment, and lack of future resulting in anger at those who believe in the American dream (as they believe the recent immigrants do). The anger and sense of being abandoned was very close to the surface in the discussion. Students cited the budget cuts in the district, the growing class sizes, and the lack of counselors as evidence that they do not really matter to the adults in the community. They talked about the bad reputation that Madison has as the "lowest" high school in the district. Some spoke of an assembly on colleges where a counselor reportedly told them even if they get all As, it would not mean anything in terms of getting into college because they will be competing against students from "good" schools.

Student anger gets acted out in two direct ways: noncooperation with school personnel and rage at the newcomer students who "still have dreams," and who view schools in terms of freedom and mobility. The noncooperation shows up in the slouched, passive postures of students sitting in classes with little response to their teachers. It also appears in the minimal amount of effort put into homework.

The rage is evident in different ways. As one boy in this class said:

> Sometimes I see them [immigrants] with their backpacks and
> their books, studying so hard and I want to knock them in the
> face. What makes them think that studying so hard is going to do
> them a damn bit of good. They try so hard it makes me sick.
> School hasn't done a thing for any of us.

As "Americans" look across at the newcomers in their midst, the anger is partially about immigrant groups who achieve success in the school, and part of their anger is aimed at newcomers for reinforcing the ideology that academic achievement is a product of individual motivation and effort. That ideology is fundamentally the dominant view that teachers project, and "American" students view their newcomer peers as collaborators with teachers in perpetuating a belief that pins the academic failures of students back on themselves.

The rage at newcomers for "still believing" is one of the dynamics that serves to wear down immigrant students. They feel the resentment against them and many come to understand that holding to a belief in hard work and making it in the school stands in the way of being accepted by their American peers. From their early perceptions that "they think we came here to be better in school than they are," to the social exclusion from the social maps of the school as long as they continue to "hang out" with others of their own language and national group, to the daily brushes with the anger of established resident students, immigrants learn that the choice is between continuing to live at the margins of the map or becoming more like "Americans." And becoming more like "Americans" may mean changing their relationship to the academic system of the school, an academic system that is to an extent racially arranged. In making the transition to life at Madison High, newcomers face tremendous pressures not only related to the language they speak or the racial identity they adopt, but also in the relationship between those choices and academic success. It is easier for students who are Asian or white to find their way into the higher tracks of the school. It is harder for newcomers who become Americanized as Latinos or blacks to make their way out of the lower tracks to which they are relegated.

Academic achievement is not just a product of intelligence, self-perception, and effort. There is an institutional reality that provides groups of students with different resources, different encouragement, different curriculum. And it results in tracking some groups of students into futures with far more opportunity than others. From the moment kindergarteners enter school, the expectations of their teachers and the degree of effort and resources available to them make an enormous difference in their attachment to school and what they learn. Students who are in classes where a teacher speaks their language are far more likely to learn social studies, science, and other subjects than students who cannot comprehend what their teachers or texts say. In this country, in far too many schools, resources and expectations are meted out differently to children of color and white children, and differently to poor children and middle-class children. By the time they arrive in high school, students already have a well-developed sense of whether they are "smart" or not, whether teachers will like them and encourage them or not, whether they like school or not. But high schools also play a role in the continued tracking. Madison High, like most high schools, has three academic tracks: college preparatory, regular, and skills (for "remedial" students). Ninth-grade English teachers determine which social studies track a tenth-grade student will be put in. Once in a track, the curriculum students receive is different, leading to different futures.

Of the thirty-two Latinas (immigrant and U.S.-born) who spoke about wanting to go to college, twenty-nine told of seeking advice from a school counselor. When they expressed interest in college, they reported being told versions of "you aren't college material," "you don't have the credits," "you better consider the community colleges," "you don't have a prayer of getting into a four-year college," or "don't bother." In fact, some of the young women do not have the required courses they should have had by this point because of lack of information. All, however, were hungry for help in planning for future higher education. Six of them spoke of individual teachers who were actively encouraging them to go to college, and trying to fill in and provide some college information because they believed the students could do it. At Madison High, where counselors' time is tremendously scarce and generally devoted to those who are obviously on the college-bound track, individual teacher advocacy is the essential avenue to college information for language-minority students or those who are not already into college-bound tracks. A severe fiscal crisis in Bayview schools resulted in cutting almost all counseling from Madison High, to a .7 position for the whole 1,800 student body. Here, the presence of the few young teachers committed to immigrant and LEP students makes a difference. One of these teachers spoke triumphantly:

> Hah! I was so happy when Gloria got into CSU. I'd worked with her for hours on the applications and financial aid forms, and encouraging her and encouraging her and encouraging. And then, you should have seen the counselor's face when I waltzed in and told her that

Gloria had gotten into Cal State. She nearly fell through the floor. She had told Gloria she didn't even think she would make it through high school. I said, she made it through, no thanks to you!

During one late afternoon session with Lisa Stern and Rebecca Garrison, two teachers who see themselves as active advocates on behalf of immigrant students, the two spoke at length about the intertwined phenomena of race, ethnicity, social class, and academic level. They also spoke of the silence about this relationship among the faculty. Stern said:

It's like you're fighting against this enormous monolith. The teachers protect it like crazy, the students keep it going. You know you see this tracking going on, and people don't see anything wrong with it, or they just want to keep it the way it is. How can you justify that? It's beyond me.

Students in the "high" college-preparatory classes and students in the "low skills" classes (classes for students who need basic skills and are considered "remedial") feel a sharp sense of identity tied to those placements, according to Garrison. The sharp boundaries are both academic and social.

They are really their own group. Every time you try to move one of the skills kids into regular or college-prep classes, they won't do it. It's hard enough convincing them they can do the work academically, but there is something else more powerful that holds them back. They believe they belong there. They've been convinced. And they believe they belong with the other kids who are there. They feel like they'd be so socially isolated if they were moved out. They want to stay with their friends. They want to stay where they think they belong. Last semester I moved Trina, a really bright African American girl into a college-prep math class. Her grades were high; she really could do the work, but she couldn't take it in other ways. She came back to me and begged me to put her back in the skills class. She said, I hated it there, we don't speak the same language.

It is not that there are no African American students in the college-preparatory classes, although their numbers and proportions are distinctly less than in the skills classes. African Americans comprise 16 percent of the school, but only 7 percent of those completing the A-F requirements that prepare them for college, and only 5 percent of those in chemistry and physics (laboratory sciences required for admission to many four-year colleges and universities) (California Basic Education Data System 1993). But there are other distinctions that mark the divide. As Garrison describes:

> In the college-prep classes, the African American kids group by themselves. I think that is true of all levels, but actually at the college-prep level there is less friendliness. It is a very competitive and clique-y track. The atmosphere in skills classes is really a lot friendlier. Kids are more accepting and curious about each other. If you come into skills classes, you find friends really fast. And the discussions are great. There is a relaxation about skills classes. Everyone knows they are at the bottom together. There is no competition. But at the college-prep level, it's competition for the top. It gets fierce sometimes.

Garrison and Stern ponder what holds students together at the skills level:

> I think about these things every day now that I'm teaching a skills class. It's really interesting to watch them willfully accept it all. Even if I grab a kid and say, "You, you have potential" or "You're really smart, you could do the work in college prep," they don't want to see themselves any place but where they are. There is a sense of alienation they share. They identify ambition and behaviors of ambition as a sellout. They don't want to fail, but there are certain things they know they'd have to do to be successful and they reject them. I think on some level it's fear and distrust. Fear of trying again and being put down—fear that if they let themselves believe the door is open and it just gets slammed in their faces again, it'll be unbearable. They reinforce each other. And it's a powerful bond. And its scary to realize the terrible power that teachers have to create in students a certainty that they belong at the bottom.

For the black and Latino immigrant students to break through these patterns requires enormous resolve and a willingness to pay high prices to jump from the skills track into the college-preparatory track.

Juanita Sanchez is one of these students. She came to my attention as one of the seniors in the Madison High School yearbook class that I sometimes observed. She went often to Ms. Stern, the yearbook sponsor, for advice and the two spent a great deal of time trying to steer through the mazes of college applications, interviews, financial aid forms, and Scholastic Aptitude Tests (SATs), which are required for college admission. After witnessing one of these episodes, I asked Juanita to tell her story.

Juanita spoke of a childhood of changing schools and being bounced between homes, each with different cultural influences, different messages about who she was and what she could accomplish, and different lessons about independence, attractiveness, and her class and educational future. She was born in Mexico and came to Bayview with her Mexican parents when she was young. Though moving often between living with one of her divorced parents, by middle school she found some stability living with her grandparents. Juanita began to closely identify with the Latino neighborhood in which her grandmother lived.

> I was going to the same school for a long time. We lived in an apartment where I had a lot of friends. Our neighborhood was full of kids. Everybody was Hispanic. There was hardly anyone white. A few Filipino, but mostly Hispanic. And we fit in finally. My sister looks white but she is still Mexican inside. We were home. We were with other Hispanics and we had someone to take care of us.

These were the middle school years. Juanita felt at home and proud as a Latina. But this changed when she entered Madison High and was placed in classes and tracks with few Mexican Americans, and her neighborhood friends were separated from her at school.

> I was so scared to be a freshman that someone would throw me in a garbage can or something. And I wasn't in classes with other Latinos. I couldn't figure out why. My friends were in the skills classes. They were smart, but somehow, that's where they were.

In eighth grade, Juanita had taken placement tests and was told she should be placed in sophomore English and history classes. At first, she was sure it was a mistake. The freshmen year was hard. Mexicans at Madison High, according to Juanita "were at the bottom." She missed her friends and was uncomfortable in the classes where there were few Latinos.

> I started to cut [school] a lot with my friends. It was the only way I could see them. And I had to reassure them that I was still their friend even though I was in higher classes. Heck, I had to reassure me! I didn't want them to think I was stuck up. And I couldn't see them after school. I have the strict Mexican way, which means you can't have boyfriends until you're eighteen, you can't wear makeup—you know. It was strict Mexican ways for my grandfather. I wanted to go places with my friends and my grandfather was like, you can't. He's the kind of person that everything has got to come from the past. You can't move on. He was back in Mexico in his head. And he tried to keep us in Mexico, too. That just doesn't work here.

Juanita started to forget about school, and just "hang" with her friends. Her grades dropped and by sophomore year, she was back in "general track" classes with her friends. She recalls her dad as the only one who would encourage her to pay attention to her studies. He would say, "Keep your head up high and be proud of yourself. Your sister is beautiful and she will have many men falling for her, but you're smart, you're intelligent." Juanita looks back on that and thinks perhaps that is what saved her, because she took it to heart that her survival would rest on being able to "make something of myself."

> I knew I wouldn't have men to take care of me so easy, so I would need to take care of myself. And I wanted to prove to my family that I was worthy. So I was in a war with myself. No one except me and my dad cared about being smart. All my friends hated school. But I knew there was no future for me if I didn't make it on being smart. I wasn't pretty, and I saw what being a weak woman did to my mother. But I was Mexican and didn't like the loneliness of being the only one of my friends to do well in school. And I didn't like the way I got looked at by teachers who kept thinking I couldn't be able to do the work in the hard classes.

Juanita tried to turn over a new leaf in her sophomore year. Ms. Stern was her history teacher and Juanita loved that class. For the first time she felt a teacher believed in her. That same year she met her boyfriend, and credits him and Ms. Stern for her staying in school. The older she got, the more her grandfather wanted her to stay home. He did not know she already had a boyfriend and was very concerned that she might become involved with boys. Juanita had to sneak to see Miguel, but she felt he was her lifeline. He was a senior, and although he encouraged her, he was not around school after that year. Ms. Stern had Juanita rescheduled into college-preparatory classes for the second half of her sophomore year. The racial dynamics of school achievement became even more difficult for Juanita after that.

> I was in honors classes with a bunch of Chinese people and a bunch of white people and one black girl. Ms. Stern scheduled me into the honors classes. She says, "You're too smart. I'm going to put you in higher classes than they schedule you for. You can write very well, you speak well and have a good vocabulary; you work hard and you have a lot of important things to say." I was all worried. "I'm not going to know anybody." But she kept saying, you'll make friends. She was wrong.

Juanita recalls that on the first day of her new classes, she was asked to check her schedule card in each class to be sure she belonged there. "It's like they believe you can't do it. It was awful. I started to doubt myself again. It gets me mad [that] I let it get to me, but it did."

Despite an ideology among most teachers that achievement is a product of effort, the disproportionately large number of Latinos that fail in the school ends up confirming their suspicions that it must be, in the words of one teacher, "a cultural thing." A host of damaging mistruths and stereotypes flow from that: Latinos do not value education, Latinos do not work hard, Latinos do not aspire to be much. And those who fight against it, like Juanita, have to stand up to expectations that she does not belong. She described the situation: "It's like, are you sure you are supposed to be in this class?" She felt as though students and teachers alike were looking at her as if she was in the wrong place.

> And they would be like, you got Latin blood in you, don't you? Like I was a weirdo or like they had never seen any Latin person in their classes and they couldn't believe it. And one day in Ms.

Kramer's class we had to write a composition on a role model. And one Chinese girl next to me goes, can I read your paper? I go, sure. So she reads it and her eyes were getting real big. I go, what's wrong. And she says, you're smart! I thought you were going to be a dumb person in this class. That did it, and I got all hot and said really loud, "You're very ignorant. You're the one that's supposed to be smart and you should know its not just one type of person that is smart. Anybody can do honors class-es if they apply themselves. They've just got to want to learn. It's not about nationality. The Mexicans in low classes just don't try. They get sick of trying and getting put down again. They just look around and say I'm gonna get a diploma and cross that stage and get a job and get married and have a family, and they don't see why they should try. But they're smart and don't you ever again think Mexicans aren't smart.

It was hard for Juanita, but she began to love going to classes despite the social isolation. She could not believe how much she was learning. She worked harder than she ever had before and felt very excited. She said: "I learned every day something new. It was like, oooh, I can't miss a day." Juanita still has some Mexican friends from her middle-school days, but mostly her friends now are Filipinos. She explains: "At school, I hang out with Filipinos because it's more okay to be into school with them. You can carry your books and they don't has-sle you about it. It's okay.

But the pain associated with separation from her Latino friends runs deep. As Juanita says: "I wasn't sure you can really be Latina and be in college prep. I guess I kind of crossed over into some other identity. But it burns inside me. I know all my friends could've done it, but they were pushed down."

Juanita was accepted to the University of California at Berkeley, but did not have the money to pay the tuition and support herself. She was surprised by the deluge of college catalogs that came to her unsolicited, "probably because of my high SAT scores." But without scholarships or grants, her plan is to get some kind of secretarial job and save money to go to college later. When Juanita told me this, she began to cry.

I keep getting this feeling that I'm going to work and I'm never going to go back to school. I was going to go to work and then go to school at night, and it's like, now that I don't have the money to go right now. I'm scared that what if I have to keep putting it off and putting it off til I'm thirty and still in the same job and nowhere to go. And that's what I'm really scared of. And sometimes I look at Mexican women who are all middle aged and have all these kids and I wonder if any of them thought once that they were going to make it. I wonder if any of them had a dream like me. And I wonder if I'm going to be like them, never having gotten to where I want to go.

Going to college requires a desire to do so, a belief that it is an appropriate goal, academic preparation adequate for gaining admission, and information about admissions processes. For Juanita, as for many students at Madison, none of these come easy. Because budget cuts in the district eliminated almost all counseling positions (leaving just a single part-time person for the entire student body of almost 1,800), counseling advice about colleges ends up being channeled through a few large assemblies, brief daily bulletin announcements of key deadlines, and the particular relationships students forge with teachers who will be their advocates. Most of the information and teacher support comes through the honors classes at the school. Students who are not in those classes do not realize there was information that might have helped them prepare for college until it is too late.

Juanita ended up in honors classes, and she benefited from the help of Ms. Stern to get through the array of applications, SAT tests, and procedures of college admissions. She had a father, a boyfriend, and a teacher who believed in her dream and supported her, and still she found it a massive struggle. Juanita had to struggle with the social isolation of being a Latina in a academic track where few Latinos end up, she had to face down the prejudices of teachers and students who believed that as a Latina she did not belong, and she had to combat her own self-doubts. And in the end, Juanita felt she had to cross into a world that left her community behind.

For Juanita, academic achievement and the pursuit of her academic dreams were never divorced from her view of the future as a Latina. Believing she did not have the sexual capital of good looks as defined by "white" standards, her expectation was that as a female, her only hope of making it would be through her "smarts." But she also often looked around at the Mexican women she knew, and feared and rejected their futures as her own. Looking around Madison High, she also felt that given the numbers and dispersion of Latinos in the various skill tracks of the curriculum, she would have to beat tremendous odds to make it. She knew, she witnessed, she felt the viciousness of a racialized system that pressured to keep her in her place as an undereducated Latina.

Her journey and the journey required of newcomers involves learning and then accepting or fighting their place in the racial order—to accept it has a high price, to fight it has a price as well. Madison High is highly racialized and students who do not fall into those racial categories and the academic placements, which are thought appropriate, remain at the social margins. Immigrant students in this scheme are denied the richness of their many national and language identities, existing solely as an undifferentiated ESL category on the maps drawn by the "American" students. And the newcomer immigrant students look across from a perspective of a world divided by nationalities and language groups, where "American" is synonymous with "white" and English speaking.

Stepping back, the end product of the two maps is actually a closely knit social system in which conforming to American racial categories and giving up distinct national and non-English language identities and groupings are necessary to be recognized as part of the school. For newcomers, this process of confronting "America" and coming to understand what is required of them consumes them during the first few years. It is a complex process that begins with the disenchantment that learning English will be enough.

CHAPTER FOUR

Learning the Language
of America

IN LINDA O'Malley's English-as-a-second-language classroom, students sit in a large u-shape, clustered by language groups—Spanish with Spanish speakers, Farsi speakers together. Vietnamese with Vietnamese speakers, etc. Late in the year such clustering is no longer required for communication, because most of the students by then have some basic English-speaking skills. But it still makes a difference in their comfort levels, O'Malley feels, if they sometimes can work in groups in which they can use their mother tongue, their strongest language. So, although students are mostly asked to speak in English for this class, when they are working on small group projects, the teacher lets them speak their native language. She explains:

> Misunderstandings are so common because even though they know the English words they want to use, when those same words are spoken by someone else with a heavy accent, they can't hear it. If I really want them to be able to discuss something, it works best when they can speak as fully as possible and understand as much as possible of what each other is saying. It makes it easier for them to share ideas, but also it is the only place in school where they are allowed to use their language. I think just to hear their own language and to feel it is allowed makes for a different sense of relaxation and "being here" in the classroom.

On this particular day, the groups are doing small group projects and speaking their native tongues. The room is filled with the excited voices of students planning presentations in Farsi, Tagalog, Spanish. A boy knocks on the door of the classroom, bearing a note for the teacher from the principal. He crosses the room to give it to her, and on his way back out the door says very loudly, "Where am I? Doesn't anyone know how to speak English? Is this some kind of foreign country?!" The class is noticeably silent. When they begin to resume their conversations, it is subdued and in English.

■ ■ ■

According to formal school policy, court law, and program design, the educational task of becoming American is viewed as a matter of becoming English speaking. The role of the school in Americanizing immigrants and addressing issues of national origin is viewed as a matter of taking non-English-speaking students and making them fluent English speakers. The program at Madison High and the teachers in it label and serve students expressly in terms of their English language fluency and language group. This reflects the politics beyond.

No other aspect of immigrant adjustment to life in the United States receives as much programmatic attention or generates as much political focus and controversy as the matter of language. Politics has intervened despite both common sense and research that established that students learn best in a language they can comprehend, and a research base on second-language acquisition that has shown that literacy in one's home language is the best basis for developing literacy in a second language. The use of a child's home language in schools has become a politically charged idea. Current public demands to assimilate immigrants more quickly, as well as demands to keep them out because of fear that this nation cannot absorb more diversity, both center largely on issues of proficiency in English. Framed in demands for strengthening English as the common or only language of the nation, legislation and initiatives throughout the country have focused on the need to demand allegiance to and use of English as a requirement for those living in these United States.[17] English has become the major public issue in the socialization of immigrant children in the United States.

Learning English is a fundamental requirement for acceptance and participation in an English-taught curriculum and English-dominant social world. Teachers, immigrant students, and native U.S.-born students alike, all agree that to be American, to be part of the fabric of Madison High, one must speak English.

The goal of becoming fluent English speakers appears to be embraced by all newcomers. There was no ambivalence or hint of negative judgment I could detect associated with adopting English as one's language. It is a border all seem to want to cross as soon as possible. The pressures appear to result in newcomers desiring to become full-fledged English speakers as soon as possible. They are surprised and often discouraged then by the contradictory pressure to become English speaking and the many roadblocks to developing that proficiency, and the many barriers to becoming English literate. They and their families are saddened by the discovery that comes too late, that becoming English fluent usually is accompanied by a loss of home language use, fluency, and development.[18]

Because, in their first few years in the United States, newly arrived immigrants are enrolled for one half of the day in the separate Newcomer School across the street and for the other half day in classes designed for limited English speakers, newcomers are formally separated from English-speaking schoolmates. The social dynamics of the school include many English-speaking kids rejecting, putting down, and freezing newcomers out of social involvement with the English-speaking social world. Although the courses designed for LEP students are a vast improvement over the way things were done even ten years ago, where no special supports were in place to help immigrants access the curriculum, the institutional arrangements at Madison High still provide insufficient English language development and still prevent access to a full academic core curriculum. The result is that Madison is a world in which those who are not English speaking are precluded from learning the English that they know full well is necessary for acceptance and success in U.S. society. And because being English speaking is viewed as the central key to being American, most newcomers attempt to abandon use of their mother tongues while on the school site. The language in which they can express themselves, the language through which they can understand the world becomes banished.

With all the focus on and anxiety about immigrants learning English, few appear to recognize that the efforts of the school might mitigate this goal. Placed in special classes designed to address their lack of English proficiency, immigrant students are separated from English-speaking schoolmates. As a result, their access to learning the language and becoming part of the English speaking world is severely constrained. Put down for use of their mother tongues, and with no supports for continued development of their home languages, immigrant students not only fail to develop literacy in their native language, but begin to lose it. With that loss, they also sever ties to their families and homeland cultures. Unable to converse with grandparents, unable to read the literature from their homeland, unable to write to friends and families back in their motherland, they lose a rich and important connection.

"IF YOU DO NOT SPEAK THE ENGLISH RIGHT, YOU CANNOT BE AMERICAN."
In answer to the question, "Are there ways in which you feel American?" Mandy, an immigrant from Taiwan, once said emphatically, "Of course not! If you do not speak the English right, you cannot be American." In the initial understanding of newcomers, becoming English speaking is the same as becoming American. For almost all immigrants coming to Madison High in the first few years of their transition to the United States, learning English is a central and major issue in their lives.

Learning English is not easy. The prevalent attitudes that most immigrants encounter is far from accepting of accented and flawed English. Common attitudes of exclusion toward students whose English is not fluent is far from the "safe" effective environment necessary for language acquisition.[19] Being laughed at for incorrect English, being teased for heavy accents, and having difficulty finding their way when they do not understand and do not feel free to ask for clarifications of English, are daily occurrences for most immigrant students. One student described the overwhelming experience:

> I'd get so tired, my head would hurt. All day, I sit in classes and hear English, English, English, and try so so hard to understand, but I do not understand. I was afraid the teacher would call on me. I was trying to hear a word I knew. I was trying to figure out my science and my math. In the morning time it was better. I'd think, today I will understand. But by lunch my head was hurting, and I felt despair. By the last class in the day, I couldn't even listen anymore—it was so hard. I just sat there and nothing made sense.

They are in many ways suffering from "language shock." They need to learn English, they want to learn English, but there are also limits on the opportunities to learn and practice English.

Madison, like most high schools in California, has an English-as-a-second-language program. The newly arrived immigrants begin their ESL sequence with the lower-level ESL classes taught at the Newcomer School. They continue when they achieve intermediate levels of English fluency in higher-level ESL classes taught on site at Madison High. Together, the Newcomer School and Madison provide an ESL sequence that compares well to other high school ESL programs in California. However, a common weakness in Madison's program as well as most high schools is insufficient attention to writing, to reading comprehension, to academic vocabulary. Oral fluency and comprehension are achieved—students eventually learn to speak and understand basic English—but the skills needed for academic participation and success at the high school level are not sufficiently developed. The problem is not just this. Although the school provides five periods of ESL levels 4 and 5, the school needs more sections than are currently offered. ESL is only one component of a comprehensive program. It should address the learning of English. But learning all the other subjects a student needs to learn requires a different kind of support. A student cannot learn social studies, math, and science if they cannot understand the language of the teacher or the language in the textbook. It takes three to seven years to become sufficiently fluent in English for academic learning. During these years, students need instruction or support in their home language and what is called "sheltered" instruction, in which teachers use visual cues, check on comprehension, work on vocabulary, and assist in bridging the language gap. This is where the Madison program has the most trouble. It is short of bilingual teachers who might make academic course content comprehensible and accessible to the LEP population while they are in the process of learning English more fully.

The school is, according to a Newcomer School analysis, short twenty-eight needed sections of academic courses taught in either the students' primary language or in sheltered approaches.[20] Of the sixteen that are offered, six are taught by teachers who do not have training in providing sheltered instruction. Thus, immigrant students are divided into their own classes, paying the prices of separation without gaining the benefit that such separation might offer and without the help that they need. At Madison High, LEP students receive insufficient formal English language development and are placed in many academic classes that do not address their needs for comprehensible instruction. The lack of trained teachers and the lack of sufficient offerings severely cuts down their access to schooling and curtails the development of English. And for immigrant students, a lack of English language fluency not only precludes them from access to the core curriculum, but is a social stigma as well. Immigrant students regularly express frustration about not having the English needed to participate fully and comprehend what is happening formally in school.

Some spend long hours desperately trying to unlock the secrets of English fluency. They carry dictionaries to look up every word they cannot understand in their English textbooks. Most newcomers appear to consciously make themselves students of English speakers' behavior, spending lunchtime on the fringes of the activity on campus, listening and watching carefully and trying to absorb what it is that Americans do and how it is that they speak.

Others simply retreat into social groups with others of their same language, or cluster in social groups with other newcomers where some baseline social English allows them to communicate superficially, and then float by in classes without really understanding what is going on or what is being said, hoping that good behavior will suffice for passing the course—frequently, it is.

"YOU CAN'T UNDERSTAND ANYTHING, AND YOU CAN'T SAY ANYTHING."
For immigrant students at Madison, a sore and painful arena of their transition is the embarrassment and rejection they feel because they are not fluent English speakers. As Helen, a Chinese immigrant, explained:

> The kind of things [for which] American people laugh at immigrants, are their ways of talking in English. Because like Chinese people talk different ways of English that Americans couldn't understand. They make fun of the English and laugh at them. They pretend to say the same words that Chinese people say and make it funny and tell other Americans and laugh together at us. Immigrant peoples are very embarrassed in front of American people. It is because of the English.

And Samiya, a tenth grader, added:

> If I want to fit in the American way I have to talk like American people in English all the time. If I talk Dari ever, they make fun of me. But they make fun even when I talk English. I learn to shut up.

The need to learn English is not only to avoid ridicule, but also to be able to understand fundamentally what is happening around them and to be a participant. This is a struggle. A young woman from Mexico explained:

> I felt very bad at Madison. Everyone was talking in class and their English was better than mine and they had friends. I also was surprised because students [were] rude to their teachers, which didn't happen in my country. Sometimes they were very rude but the teacher didn't do anything. I wished I could go back to my country. I thought my teachers and other students here were so lucky because they could talk their native language at school. They don't know how it feel when one lives

in a strange country. You can't understand anything and you can't say anything.

This sense of loss for not being able to understand what is being said begins the first day of school. Padma described her first week at Madison High, after immigrating from India.

> I felt so nervous. I was so shy when I came here. I didn't know English so I have problems. I didn't know anybody in this school, and I am so alone. I didn't know where the main office [was] or who is the principal. I didn't know where is my classroom. I was scared and afraid. In India we didn't have to change clothes in p.e., but here we have to change clothes. It is all so different. I thought, if only I could speak English it would all be okay.

Huan described the invisibility.

> I remember all the classmates make fun of me because I couldn't spoke English. I felt very upset because I didn't have no friends who can help me with my work, and it was very hard for me to understand the teacher. The teacher didn't see me. I felt I wasn't there at all.

It is not only a desire to understand that drives these young immigrants to want to learn English, they seek also to adopt the behavior and make the sounds that would not give them away as foreigners and result in being excluded. Even those who are considered fairly English fluent by academic standards used by their teachers find it difficult to master the slang of their American peers and to overcome the accents that mark them as different. In classes, the English that is spoken is a classroom English. Cut off from much interaction with English-speaking peers as they sit in their sheltered classes or attend the Newcomer School, many newcomers hear the English of the youth culture only as they walk through the campus, but they cannot understand what they are hearing nor participate in the peer banter. As a Vietnamese student, Lanh wrote:

> In other countries they speak a language and it is all the same. But here in America, slang words are used everywhere by the students and most of all especial here at Madison. Even the teachers do not

use these words. Firstly, let's start with the American students. They are using slang words...everywhere. And sometimes when I was there, I don't even understand...what they are talking about. They all, "hey dude, wuzz up?," and I think it means... "How are you doing?" Well it sounds a little weird but anyway we have to learn to use them because here at Madison if you don't use them, then people will make fun of you. In some other ways, the American kids usually say: "uh huh" or "get lost." Well, I got very confused because it does not make any sense at all. And besides the American kids, the immigrants student also try to say slang words like "hey, gals, what's up with ya?" and things they heard from the American kids used to say. They do this because they don't want others to laugh at them by not knowing the new style that the natives know. I don't know how other people feel about those slang words from the American kids, but for me, I'm really interested. It is weird and cute, but I have to study it hard. No one teaches it and it is not in the dictionary.

Learning a basic vocabulary and rudiments of English is step one. Finding American teenage friends who will converse so the new language is used in context and finding friends who will explain the slang is step two. The commonly expressed desire to "find an American friend" is not just mired in a desire for companionship, but also in a desire to have the means of learning social English. Mandy spoke about her wish to find an American friend:

Sometimes we tried to talk to them to learn more English, some of them helped us, and some of them just laughed and made fun of us. Sometimes, most when you have an American friend talk to you and be friendly and be nice to you, you feel really happy. But most, when you walk on any street or walk through a group of American students, you hear them say something or they pick on you or they throw something at you, and they do it because they think you don't understand English and speak English. They think we don't understand their message because we can't understand the words they use. We understand. They tell us by how they act that they don't want us.

Shirley, the eldest of three children from Taiwan, is the person in charge of her household. The children were sent to the United States for their high school education. It is Shirley's responsibility to see to it that her brothers and a cousin get up in the morning, have food on the table, and go to school and do their homework. She is a competent seventeen-year-old, full of concern for her family and willing to be the head of household. She is also a serious student. Her biggest worry, though, is how to learn English herself and to help her charges learn English. All attend Madison High and assume they will be returning to their homeland when they finish school. It is important to them to learn English, both for the capital it will give them on their return to their homeland, and also because they are lonely. But learning English is problematic. None have American friends, so Shirley has tried to get a tutor to come to their house and help them with English.

> How can we learn English if no one speak it with us? No Americans speak with us. A friend would be best, but it is a puzzle. If you don't speak English you can't have American friend. So how do we learn English?

On the advice of her teacher, Ms. Meyer, Shirley has posted an advertisement for an English-speaking tutor at the local community college. She is waiting for a reply.

For most of the students, one of the transitions they make as they move between their home and school, is the switch in language environments. Their families are not English-speaking. The world of school is English-speaking. There are no bilingual classes at Madison in which their home language is used, and only the ESL class and the Newcomer School provide a space where they can sometimes speak in their native tongues. Socially, their native tongue would be the language of choice, but the proximity of English-speaking students and the fear of being overheard and laughed at is a deterrent to using it more often. In the sheltered classes, a particular form of English is the language of currency. It is an English that is so heavily accented in a variety of ways that students often can't understand each other even though they are all speaking English. Ms. O'Malley has mentioned this often in explaining to me the importance of her voice in her classroom as the only real English-speaking model.

Without strength in English, newcomers rely on help from friends who speak their language and seek places where it is safe to use it. The Newcomer School offers a respite from and contrast to the anti-native-language attitudes of Madison High. Many immigrant students speak in glowing terms of how important the Newcomer School staff and classrooms are to them because of the relative comfort and ease they feel about using their home language. "I like it at the Newcomer School. Mr. Moreno speaks Spanish to me, and Ms. White is so patient and always lets me speak Spanish or English, even if my English is so bad."

In addition to the Newcomer School, there are some places certain newcomer groups have found at Madison where they are safe to use their own language. Dorothy Meyer's ESL classroom is a place where the Indian girls can hang out during lunch. They can speak their language and they can listen to their music, away from the sting of being laughed at by American English-speaking students. It all started during Ramadan, a holy season, when this group of girls were fasting and needed some place to be during lunch time, away from all the lunch eaters. Meyer, on learning of the traditional fasting, had invited them to come to her classroom. The practice has continued for years. For this group of students, Meyer's classroom is a place where they can be who they are. Similarly, some other immigrant groups have managed to find a place on the campus under the sheltering wing of the few teachers who have befriended them.

In these few classrooms, in the Newcomer School, the students appear to appreciate the ease of not having to monitor the language they use, of being free to use whichever language makes things most comprehensible, and of being free from harassment. But the desire to be English speaking and accepted by Americans, and to avoid the sting of being laughed at or put down are powerful incentives. They not only become English seekers, these students abandon their mother tongues relatively quickly, becoming English preferers. The students seem immune to the messages that adults at the Newcomer School attempt to get across, that bilingualism is an asset and is something students should strive for. It appears that very few immigrant students put any premium or value on continuing to develop their native tongue. Perhaps they take it for granted. Perhaps they do not understand that lack of use leads to atrophy. Perhaps they do not know the wealth of literature and tradition and history that could be theirs by strengthening their literacy in their mother tongue. Or perhaps it is simply too great a load to try to develop literacy in two languages at one time. They appear to be aware of the pain and difficulty of standing between two languages and most respond to that pain by emphasizing a transition to English and leaving behind their mother tongue. As Concepcion, an immigrant from Mexico two years earlier, explained:

> I sometimes don't have Spanish words anymore for the feelings
> I have here, and I don't yet have English words for them either.

Or I can't find the English words that explain what I know and
have felt in my Mexican life. The words don't work for me. I have
become quiet, because I don't have words. I don't even try to use
my Spanish. I only wait until I know my English.

The discomfort of being "outside," the trouble of not having the
words to express themselves, the frustration with being laughed at for use
of their native tongues, all result in a determination of most immigrant
students to try to learn English as quickly as possible.

Even if students were to develop their home languages, there is no program which supports that task. Even for those who might need instruction in
subjects through their home language because they are not yet proficient
enough in English to comprehend the instruction taught in English, the program does not exist. Unlike some schools and districts, Madison High sidesteps the issue of primary language instruction. There is no official policy in
either the school or the district about bilingual and home-language instruction. Newcomer School teachers and administrators repeatedly speak to the
high school principals in the district about the need to hire bilingual teachers
to offer the primary language instruction that is necessary to provide educational access. Throughout the district, people respond that they are making
every effort to provide "appropriate instruction." The rhetoric, the official
policy, the verbalized discourse about services for students who cannot
understand English enough to learn in English is heavily influenced by the
fact that there are legal mandates requiring the provision of such instruction,
and by a political atmosphere opposed to it. For years, Bayview has been
under pressure from the California Department of Education Bilingual
Compliance Division to make some progress toward "remedying the shortage of bilingual teachers." Yet, little progress has been made. The political
issue is not confronted directly, but offhandedly. The general tenor of comments by mainstream teachers and administrators is reflected in the comments of this administrator:"We have so many different languages here that it
really isn't realistic to try to find teachers and offer primary language classes in
all those languages. It just makes more sense to teach them in English."

These comments pose a kind of common-sense stance but display
ignorance of the processes of second-language acquisition and learning.
They are often followed by some reference to the need for a common language and the need to promote faster learning of English. Here are some
examples from teacher and administrator interviews:

> Anyway, the sooner they learn English, the better. That's really the most important thing we can do for them. Get them into English as soon as possible.
>
> I'm not really sure our resources would be best put into bilingual teachers anyway. After all, what they really need is English as soon as possible. I think we're holding them back if we put them in classes where they can fall back on using their home language.

When the point is not argued in terms of common sense, or a defense of English, it is argued in terms of practicality. In one meeting with the high school principals, I heard one make the following comment in frustration when the Newcomer School coordinator spoke up again for priority hiring of bilingual teachers.

> Christ, don't you know there is a shortage of bilingual teachers in this state? We can't get the applications or qualified folks. Get real. We couldn't get the teachers even if we wanted them.

In some sense, the principal is right. There is a national shortage of bilingual credentialed teachers—in California, the teacher pool provides only half of the bilingual teachers needed. Furthermore, Bayview salaries are low compared to other districts in the region. Because of the persistent fiscal crises in the district, hiring is usually done at the last minute. The rare bilingual teachers certified for secondary single subjects are already hired and placed elsewhere. But the "even if we wanted to" clause gives him away. In all of these responses, it is also evident that there is little understanding that when primary language instruction is not provided to LEP students, it means that they are being denied access to an education. A student who speaks no English and is given instruction *only* in English, is really being given no instruction at all.

Repeatedly, the Newcomer School and the sheltered teachers at Madison make efforts to "educate" the administrators and department chairs about the role of primary language instruction in providing access to core curriculum. The message apparently is not heard. If anything results in action, it tends not to be appeals about student access to instruction, but references to potential lawsuits or compliance violation reports. Meanwhile, instruction continues only in the majority language of English, preventing the one-fourth of the student body who are immigrants limited in English fluency from fully acquiring educational resources and content.

"SHELTERED—THAT'S LOWER, RIGHT?"

The program designed for the immigrant students, which is supposed to address the "language barrier," tends to be some sheltered content classes and English-as-a-second-language classes for those at the lower levels of English fluency. With the exception of physical education and an occasional elective class, most of these newcomer LEP students remain with other LEP students through most of their school day. The attitude of other students in the school quickly permeates these classes. They are stigmatized.

On the first day of Lisa Stern's "sheltered" world history class, she introduced herself and said: "This is a sheltered-content world history class." One of the students called: "What's sheltered?" Before Stern could answer, another called out: "Sheltered, that's lower, right?" She tried then to explain that it was not "lower." The textbooks are the same, the content is the same. She *showed* them the stack of textbooks from her "regular" world history class to try to convince them that the curriculum was the same. But the students would not believe her. It seemed confirmed in their minds that classes for "LEP" students were "lower."[21]

It is not only this incident that drove home to me how thoroughly it is believed that classes to address language issues are stigmatized. In the first weeks of a semester, six Chinese and Vietnamese students reportedly switched out of the sheltered class. Interviewing the students later, I found out that they had been told by friends, cousins, the "grapevine," that it wasn't good to be in sheltered classes if they wanted to get in to a college later. The grapevine in their community was trying to protect them from being identified as LEP and being "trapped" in LEP classes. Perhaps as a result of trying to escape the stigma, these students ended up being denied needed support and help in language development. Or perhaps they were right and they saved themselves from being identified and held back in ways that would track them away from college and academic success. At Madison High, there is no real way to know. The school does not have a data system that would enable anyone to track LEP students by the courses they opt for and to trace their academic success. It is one of the ways that the data and monitoring system contributes to the invisibility and silence about the ways in which the school sorts students.

Madison High does offer one Spanish for Spanish speakers class for those who want to develop literacy in their mother tongue. It is offered because a foreign-language teacher (the Spanish teacher) wanted to offer it. It exists only because like other courses for LEP students, there is interest on the part of an individual teacher. From a program perspective, from an institutional point of view, home language is neglected. In fact, few of the students taking Spanish for

Spanish speakers are immigrants. It is a course more often taken by U.S.-born students whose home language is Spanish but who are English dominant. Furthermore, as linguists have pointed out, teaching a minority mother tongue for a few hours a week in a school where the majority language is the medium of education may be psychologically beneficial, but represents only therapeutic and cosmetic support rather than a basis for language maintenance and development.[22] And there is little mention that literacy in their home language might be an essential way to introduce them to the writers, history, and literature of their culture. Thus, throughout most of the school native language use is not allowed except for the English speakers. To be taught in one's home language remains the privilege only of those whose homes are English speaking. In the sheltered classes and ESL classes and the Newcomer School, however, there is permission to use the native language. Only in the few bilingual courses offered at the Newcomer School is there actually promotion of minority languages. Of the newcomers in the district, only a few Spanish speakers are literate in Spanish. In the fall of 1994, out of a total of ninety-five Spanish speaking students, sixty-two fell at or below the tenth percentile on the SABE (the Spanish version of the California Test of Basic Skills test). There is no evident effort to encourage or prize bilingualism or biliteracy. And in the social atmosphere in which students' use of languages other than English is looked down on, the result is a school campus experience that is highly "disabling."[23]

As an example, Nadira is moving farther and farther away from the young woman she might have been had her family remained in Afghanistan. Having immigrated at age thirteen, she is already forgetting her Farsi, she can no longer read or write Farsi, and she can only read and write in English.

> I used to read when somebody sent a letter. I used to read it but now I can't. I've forgotten. Sometimes my Dad is sad, and he says to me, "You have forgotten your own Farsi."

At home they speak some Farsi. But Nadira's younger siblings speak only English. This is deeply troubling to Nadira and her parents.

> We are trying to teach them (my younger brother and sister) more about the Afghan religion, and my parents are very strict. Sometimes we think we should speak only Farsi at home, but they turn on the TV and it's English, and my sisters and brothers speak English most of the time anyway.

Nadira has also become increasingly troubled at how quickly she has lost her Farsi.

> I never guessed that this would happen. My language was part of me. I wanted so much to be American and to speak English, but I never knew I would lose my language. I feel so sad. I used to think about maybe going back to Afghanistan after the war. Will I get my language back?

"SPANISH IS OUR LANGUAGE, MAN. YOU GOT TO HAVE SOME PRIDE!"

Newcomer Spanish-speaking immigrants feel the same sting of hostility and embarrassment about using their mother tongue as their immigrant peers from other language groups. However, a different campus dynamic exists among U.S.-born Mexicans about speaking Spanish than exists among other languages.[24] In the last six months of the fieldwork for this study, a change in political climate was occurring among the Mexican American and Latino students at Madison High. Organizers from La Raza clubs at the nearby university involved several dozen Madison High Latino students in study groups in issues of language and culture. This became the seed of a budding Latino student movement at the school. Many of the Washington High students who had moved to Madison from their largely Spanish-speaking community hold on fiercely to their language as a badge of loyalty and connection to their culture. In the C Hall corridor where Latinos hang out at the school, Spanish is sometimes spoken both as a means of communication and as a symbol of cultural visibility, pride, and ownership of turf. Although some Latinos there continue to put down newcomers for speaking Spanish, others can be heard speaking with pride of Spanish. I overheard one student admonish another (although I did not hear what prompted it). "Spanish is our language, man. You got to have some pride in it. Don't let anyone tell you it's no good."

Demands from a Latino student walk-out in the spring and discussions of the Latino Task Force, which was established by the school district following the walkout, made clear that for Latino students, improving the schools' attitude toward and support for the Spanish language was a key element of what they wanted to see changed. They called for the hiring of more bilingual teachers and a greater number of rigorous courses taught in Spanish. They requested the use of Spanish literature in their courses. And in describing the conditions they wanted changed, they wrote: "Some teachers say: don't talk Spanish here, we're not in Mexico, or It's rude to talk Spanish.

For the newcomer immigrants from Mexico and Central America, the status as newcomer still brings with it a desire to be English speaking as quickly as possible and, for many, a deep shame about their home language. To be accepted as American means they first have to shift from their home language to English. But for an increasing number of Latinos and Chicanos at Madison High, a kind of reversal of the shame process is beginning

For most immigrants, including the vast majority of Spanish-speaking immigrants who are yet untouched by the Latino student movement, the requirement remains that they must be English speaking for participation socially and academically in the Madison High world. English-speaking proficiency eventually comes; English fluency and literacy do not. There seems to be no hint of newcomer students judging each other for having "crossed a line" as they become English speakers, or chastised for forgetting who they are because immigrants stop using their home language. The transition to becoming English-only speakers is an uncontested aspect of becoming "American" and appears to be the one aspect of becoming American that immigrants continue to believe that they can achieve without question.

The intense desire to be accepted and be able to participate in their new land results for almost all newcomers in becoming English speaking relatively quickly. As they become English speaking, immigrants participate more and more in the social world of Madison High. But the level of English speaking required for social participation is not sufficient to participate or succeed in high school courses taught only in English. The program continues to provide insufficient English language development that is necessary to participate fully and succeed academically. Attitudes and social pressures are maintained which negate and weaken immigrant ties to their mother tongue. These patterns reinforce the stereotypes held about language-minority groups and limit their paths to participation. Despite stereotypes held by U.S.-born students and teachers that immigrants crowd out native born students and outdo them academically, the reality is that very few get the preparation they need and the language development required for success.

Newcomers cross the threshold and do become English speakers but not usually full English participants in the academic system. Still, they achieve the conditions of that original social compact they understood would result in acceptance. Is becoming English speaking sufficient for newcomers to be accepted as Americans? With all of the overt and conscious focus on English as the dividing line between foreigners and Americans, between "them" and "us," it turns out that in the life of newcomers at Madison High, a complex weave of other transitions and changes are expected and required for citizenship. And as newcomers face these expectations, they learn to question their original assumption that if they learn English and work hard, they will make it in this new land.

CHAPTER FIVE

To Find Your Race and Your Place: Race Tracks at Madison High

IT IS the end of the school year in the ESL level IV class. This group of students has been together for two periods a day all year long. Sitting in small clusters arranged by primary language group, they face toward a big u-shaped opening in the room to watch each other's oral presentations. There is a large cluster of Spanish speakers, a large cluster of Chinese students, three Vietnamese, and six Farsi speakers. Sandra sits alone, the only Portuguese speaker in the class. She has almost never spoken up in class when I have been there. The point of this assignment is to give the students more practice in speaking and making oral presentations and in arranging content into logical sequences. Today, it is Sandra's turn, and she chose to do her presentation on Brazil, her homeland. She has prepared many visuals. Sandra pins a drawing of the flag of Brazil on the board and around it she arrays pictures of Brazil she has cut out of magazines. Finally, she posts two cardboard displays. One says "The Sorrow," depicting the poverty in the streets of Sao Paulo, and the other says "The Beautiful," showing pictures cut from *National Geographic* and travel brochures of the countryside of Brazil. She begins by saying.

> I am Brazilian. I am not black, I am not Latin, I am not white, I am not Mexican, as many of you think. I am Brazilian. I make my presentation about Brazil because I love my country and because I don't want you ever again to think I am not Brazilian.

> Here every culture wants to be with the people from their culture. And people see me and wait for me to be with my culture. But I don't have one here. Some see my skin and think I am white. They think I belong with white culture. But the whites hear me and think I am Latin. They think I belong to Latin culture. I do not belong anywhere here.

Sandra's presentation is riveting. Unlike most presentations that are accompanied by a fairly constant undertone of people talking, everyone listens. Her voice is strong as she tells of growing up in a very poor village and coming to the city to live with her grandmother. She tells of Carnaval and happy days with her grandma. She speaks in somewhat awkward English, but with passionate eloquence. Sandra tells of the Sorrow of Brazil as its poverty and what she characterizes as the meanness of the government. She then describes the beauty of the land. As she does so, tears begin to fall from her face and she stops talking.

The teacher gently asks her if she would like to take a few minutes' break before finishing. Sandra shakes her head no, and then talks through her tears about the enormous homesickness she feels. She describes the color of the hills and the smell of the air. She ends her presentation with the words: "I love my country. I dream about it every night. I hope to see it again. I have no place I belong here. I do not belong with Latins; I am not at home here. The whites do not accept me. I am the only speaker of my language. I am Brazilian!"

The teacher is about to voice some kind of response but is interrupted by Hanh, a girl from Vietnam, who says: "Sandra, I too dream of my homeland which is beautiful, and where people knew who I was. Now here people think I am Chinese. At home, they knew who I was." The rest of the class period students speak about their homesickness and the way the smells and colors and breezes and sky are different in America. They do not speak again of the problem of racial or national identities.

■　■　■

As newcomers become aware that fluency in English is not the only requirement for being accepted in their new land, they experience pressures to locate themselves on the "racial map" of Madison High. This requires figuring out the peculiar meanings of racial categories in the United States and doing so while these categories are the focus of intense negotiation among American teens. It is one of the crucial steps in Americanization to be socialized into the racial categories and processes of racial formation that underlie our national patterns.[25] A task for each immigrant is then to be racialized into the U.S. system of race, a social order highly structured by race. For immigrants encountering this system, the question becomes, where do I fit?

In this dilemma, Sandra feels deeply alone. Like many other immigrants, she has become a careful observer, a sociologist of the social landscape at the school. As she realizes the extent to which the school is racially and ethnically defined, the fact that Sandra is the only Brazilian leaves her without a "place."

For the first year in the United States, Sandra resisted the racial categorizations she felt were being forced on her. In Sandra's emerging understanding of U.S. racial categories, there are whites and blacks, Asians and Latins. She is unacceptable to the whites because she is an immigrant, she is unacceptable to the blacks because unlike most immigrants at the school she is white-skinned. She is clearly not Asian, and so by default she is Latin. Two years after Sandra's arrival, she was beginning to identify herself in American racial categories. Sandra aligned herself with the *cholas* because it solved her problem over clothing and style (she felt her looser and more sexual clothing would stand out less, and she would conversely also have more freedom to dress in jeans and flannels to hide her sexuality if and when she might choose to).[26] She does not speak Spanish, and so her path is to somehow become less visible by blending in with the *cholas* and Chicanos, many of whom also don't speak English but who identify as strongly Latin. At Madison High, the *cholas* are mostly English speaking and mostly U.S.-born Latins. Sandra is one of only a few newcomers who have found a home among them. In describing to me the *cholas*, Sandra says (noticeably using a new kind of English that was unfamiliar to her even several months before): "You know, the home girls—the Chicanas from East Garden, the tough girls. I can wear short skirts and tight blouses and they don't say nothing. I can wear flannel shirts and baggy pants. It's no big deal to them. I'm cool."

These changes in Sandra took place over an almost two-year period. For a brief moment, the status of immigrant newcomers allows for a kind of non-racialized identity. They can remain simply the ESLers." But the pressure to align, to be defined racially within the American system of racial categories creates an unsettling persistent force. To not be racially ghettoized is to not enter into American society. And the definition of U.S. racial categories is often too different from the racialized systems of the nations from which immigrants have come, is far too rigid, formalized and narrow for the identities of most immigrants, or has stigmatized connotations that the immigrants prefer to avoid as long as possible. The categories are constituted through a limited set of skin color demarcations and sets of behaviors and alliances. Black and white are understood as the basic American races in the eyes of the students at Madison High, and beyond that, brown and yellow complete the spectrum. It is basically a four-category system, despite the fact that there are many mixed-race students at Madison, and the majority of the immigrants do not fit well into this racial schema. Theoretically, these are conditions that might erode the racial-meaning system. And in the amount of concern expressed by newcomers about not understanding where they fit and feeling discomfort about making themselves fit, there is in fact a counter-discourse with respect to the racial categories. There is acknowledgment that they would prefer an identity system that acknowledged more fully the complexity of their national backgrounds.

But it is highly unsettling to hold to this counter-discourse, for not to be able to define one's race is not really to exist on the social map of the nonnewcomers. There were few categories on the nonnewcomer social map that were not racially explicit. And to figure out where one belongs, where one is "supposed to be," or where one chooses to align, is tricky. Is someone a real Latino or a white-washed Mexican? Is a person a "wannabee" black or a real black? These questions pursue and haunt the social system of youth relationships at Madison. The students engage in an explicit discussion about authenticity as they work to understand and then to monitor the racial system. Figuring out where people belong in this racialized system is not just a matter of skin color. Sandra's skin is light but she comes from South America and speaks English with an accent, and so is considered by most as Latina. Marta is Mexican American but "acts white" and hangs out with white girls. I heard her referred to by one group of Latinas as "not a real" Latina but a "wannabee" white, a failed Latin. She did not "act" Latina. There are distinct sets of expected behaviors that mark belonging to a specific racial category. The process of finding one's place is fraught with tensions and resistance.[27]

In the early months and years of immigration, most newcomers simply do not see, and then begin to observe only the racialization of American life, placing themselves outside and continuing to hold on to identities and definitions that are national, linguistic, and religious. They resist internalizing the U.S. racial definition of themselves, despite being treated by others as if they were already racialized into categories of black, brown, or Asian. In the process, their schoolmates, their teachers, and society's inability to see and understand the distinctions in identity they themselves would make (e.g., Guatemalan as compared to Mexican as compared to Salvadoran) pull them into the broad racial category of Latino or brown that lumps together nationalities and ethnicities. The schema makes only a slim allowance for newcomers to be nonracialized. They can be simply newcomers, ESLers. But there is impatience at how long one can remain there. Newcomers themselves begin to understand the high price of invisibility or remaining outside in a no-man's-land of nonbeing. The requirement of racial identification is very strong.

The invisibility and nonstatus of immigrant newcomers present both a minicrisis of identity for immigrants themselves, as well as for others who do not know how to "place" them. One of the benefits for newcomers of clustering together with other immigrants is permission to avoid being racialized at least for a while.

How one is defined (both by self and others) depends on the density and recognizability of one's group. Sandra was Brazilian, but this was not a recognizable or meaningful category among her peers or even many of her teachers. She tried identifying herself as South American, but that too was meaningless. Eventually, she succumbed to identifying herself as Latin. This process of the necessity of giving in to broad pan-ethnic identities because of the refusal and blindness by others to accept national or linguistic identity as being an equally important category as race is viewed as a U.S. cultural obsession. In Bayview, this is also supported by conscious political mobilization occurring within the Latino community. There is emerging at Madison a kind of pan-ethnic Latin identity accompanied by the activism of the Raza Club. This new dynamic form is being prompted and promoted by the Latino activists who are part of a larger statewide student movement. This is not equally so with the development of a pan-ethnic Asian identity. This year, there was the emergence of a Filipino and Asians United Club, but Asians still appear more often to be able to retain separate national identities such as Chinese or Vietnamese.

"WE ARE ALL LATINO. WE DON'T MAKE A DISTINCTION. WHAT'S MOST IMPORTANT IS FOR US AS RAZA TO FIND THE COMMON THREADS."

In the spring of 1994, Latino high school students throughout California were organized by La Raza clubs on college campuses to confront the problems of exclusion and lack of responsiveness to their needs in schools. Their strategy was a combination of leadership development, organizing boycotts, and walk-outs. Edith was one of the young leaders of the Latino student walkout and boycott at Madison. Educating her Latino peers to be aware of their connection to each other was one of her major goals. She was well aware of the separation and tension between U.S.-born Latinos and newly arrived immigrants from Mexico and Central America. The boycott sought to emphasize issues that cut across newcomer and longstanding U.S. Latino communities. Although the agenda was inclusive, the actual participation was not. And in an effort to forge unity, the student leaders sidestepped direct discussion of the issues facing immigrants as newcomers. Some of this was a political choice related to holding together a coalition—but it was also rooted in ideology. Edith explained:

> We don't call attention to immigrant issues because we don't
> like to think in terms of immigrants at all. We don't use the term
> "immigrants." We are all indigenous North American people
> who have been colonized and borders drawn across our lands.
> What you call immigrants are people who cross the lines that
> colonists have made. We are all Latino. We don't make a distinc-
> tion. What's most important is for us as Raza to find the com-
> mon threads, the things that matter to all of us, first or second
> or fifth or tenth generation.

For the student leaders of the boycott, as well as for many who joined them, there were sharp contradictions and fissures over how much to identify with and relate the issues of the boycott to the specific concerns and problems facing newcomers. Whether it was the result of these contradictions or something else, few immigrants felt included or involved in the boycott. The pain of their exclusion and humiliation at the hands of other Latinos, people who they perceived should have been their allies and countrymen, was very deep. It was one of the strongest themes in the comments made by newly arrived immigrants. "Why do other Mexicans laugh at me and won't talk to me?" U.S.-born Latinos understood only too well the need to differentiate between themselves and immigrants. This is not only a pattern among the high school students at Madison, but is reflective of politics in communities throughout the nation as the anti-immigrant backlash began to be articulated in the past few years.

Evangelina, now a senior at Madison, reflected back to two years previously when she arrived in Bayview as a newcomer to the United States from Mexico:

> It hurt. I still feel the hurt from when other Mexicans wouldn't
> help me. It was like they felt shame because of me. But now, I have
> friends who have lived here all their life through. The same ones
> who try not to have to be around newcomers. And I ask them,
> why? And they just make fun. I think they make fun because they
> are afraid that someone else will think they are also newcomers.
> There is such a long journey you have to make from that first day
> when you arrive in the United States. You think your journey is
> over, but it has just begun. And no one who has gotten through it
> wants to be reminded that was once them. It is like they cut them-
> selves off from their own heart. I won't do that. I try to help all the
> immigrants when they get here, because I still remember.

Many of the U.S.-born Latino students struggled to define a Latino niche that was not immigrant, to clearly differentiate themselves from immigrants, and to insist that they are Americans. But others were trying to make the bridge. This was made more difficult, however, because socially and institutionally the two groups do not overlap. And often they do not share a language. Edith feels this is one of the main challenges she faces in bringing together a united Latino student group. She knew that the broader they could make their Raza group, the more power they might wield in gaining attention to their needs. Their demands were for more Latino counselors and teachers, La Raza studies courses, and Spanish bilingual classes. The student leadership of the boycott felt that these demands addressed the needs of immigrants as well as native U.S.-born Latinos. However, the immigrants generally did not support the boycott nor did they attend the La Raza Club meetings. Pizza, special announcements did not seem to work. Furthermore, the student leaders discovered they had quite a task to convince the general membership of the La Raza Club that they should identify more closely with the newly arrived immigrants. Edith explained the dilemma facing the leadership of La Raza at Madison.

> It is a matter of helping everyone learn our history, and seeing we are one people. Before the border was drawn across our land, we were all one *raza*. We can't let the border that they drew continue to keep our people apart. But other students don't know our history. They don't understand this. That is why it is so important that we get La Raza studies at the school. And the immigrants don't understand that we are on their side. It is like the La Raza Club has to become a bridge to reunite our people.

For Edith, as for other leaders of La Raza Club, a strong sense of a Raza identity has largely been forged outside of school. She labels herself a "true Latina," born in Nicaragua, living in California, proud that her life crossed the borders. Statewide, La Raza youth leadership conferences that pull together high school leaders have been a strong source of development for Edith and her friends. A local Latino community family service and counseling center provides workshops on youth leadership and serves as a base of support for the emerging Latino student movement. Meetings planning the boycott were held at the center. These Latino community structures have been important to provide a sense of pride, place, and vision for the youth leaders. Veronica, a young woman very involved in the boycott at Madison, explained how involvement in one of the conferences sponsored by an off-campus group inspired her:

> At the Raza Day conference, I was just so inspired! They showed videos of the Chicano movement and I didn't just want to sit and watch it, I wanted to live it. I wanted to be that movement. I was just out of my chair and I came right back to Madison fired up to get kids involved. We ordered pizza to get kids to come to our meetings and then would have speakers there about our history and our identity. You don't hear that history at our school. And when you do find out, you're surprised. But you are also angry that you didn't ever get it before.

The speakers they brought in included Latino students from the nearby university who were involved in organizing students from other high schools as well. They explained to the Madison students that their attendance at school produced money for the school district and that their attendance was a tool they could use; they had power. During this time, a small group from Madison went on a march to Sacramento after Cesar Chavez' death. It was here that Lisa, another student leader, met Dolores Huerta, the Latina labor union leader and one of the inspiring leadership voices of the farmworkers and Latino rights movements. Lisa invited her to come address the rally after the Bayview walkout.

On April 22, the Latino students from Bayview and surrounding school districts walked out of the schools and staged a rally before presenting their demands to the superintendent. The theme of the walkout was Brown Pride. As Edith explained, "we wanted people to know we are not a gang, we are La Raza." Students who walked out were asked to trade in their red or blue rags (handkerchiefs/headbands used to denote gang affiliation) for brown rags. They all felt it was important to show that they were united for this one day. Lisa described the march:

> It was so beautiful. It was so great. I couldn't believe it. I was all pumped up, and jumping up and down. My brother thought I was crazy. I looked out and was blown away at how many kids showed up. We were all wearing our brown rags. No one could stop us. I just knew it. We marched to the school district office and then to the park. We were alive. We were awake. We wouldn't let no one tell us no. We wanted an end to the discrimination, an

end to things like getting in trouble and bullshit for using our
own language. We wanted to get our history, we wanted bilingual counselors, and we wanted college information that other
students get.

As excited as many of the Latino students at the school felt, others did not
share their positive view. Some of the other students in the school felt the Latinos were just having a lark. Several teachers spoke out about how it was divisive
to "make education an ethnic, political thing." In the faculty lounge, a common
comment was that if students cared about their education, the best thing they
could do was to go to school rather than boycott. When the Latino students
wanted to do a show at Madison High during lunch time on Cinco de Mayo,
they were told by the principal that they could not. The administrators feared
that it would stir up tension between African Americans and Latinos at the
school. Rebecca Garrison, a teacher and advisor to the La Raza Club, was
called into the principal's office and asked to account for what part she may
have played in allowing the boycott plans to develop. The principal made it
clear that from that date on, he needed to approve any outside speaker brought
into the La Raza Club.

Despite the fact that the Raza leadership wanted to include immigrant
students, it was difficult to make it happen. Edith saw this as immigrants' choices to separate themselves and stand apart. However, the problem is more complex. Culturally, experientially, U.S.-born Latinos and newcomer Latins have
some differences. Many immigrant students at Madison have a stronger sense
of connection to teachers and gratitude to the school than do their U.S.-born
Latino peers. They do not perceive themselves as lacking access in school or
failing to be treated well. They hold on to their belief that school is their route
to success in this new land. To join in criticizing the school or critiquing the
curriculum for its shortcomings was felt as impolite by some, ungrateful by
others. Incurring at times the wrath of their non-newcomer peers, the newcomers who spoke about the boycott tended to feel thankful for the public
schools and uncomplaining about their experiences there. Explained one
Mexican newcomer who had been approached about joining the boycott:

Yeah, I knew about the boycott. My cousin wanted me to go to
the meetings, but it didn't feel right. And I would have been in
trouble if I went on the march. I didn't want my teachers to feel
bad that I was saying my school wasn't good. I didn't want them

> to think I am a troublemaker. And I don't know. I like school. I
> think it is fine if only all my teachers give me more time to
> answer a question and are patient with me. But it's not right to
> criticize your teachers.

This difference is evident even among the adults. During a contentious and difficult teachers strike in the district, it was the immigrant teachers at the Newcomer School who would not join the picket line, causing a deep rupture in faculty relations that has yet to heal. Similarly, few of the immigrant students at Madison were supportive of the Latino student boycott and walkout.

In general, the adults at Madison High who let their opinions be known responded unfavorably to the boycott and to the growth of the La Raza pride movement at the school. In a district administrators' meeting shortly after the walkout, the associate superintendent encouraged the site administrators to prepare for a meeting with Latino student leaders that would occur the following week. The conversation focused on trying to identify which students were really responsible for the boycott: "Okay, are they your students? Whose students were the real leaders of the walkout?" One spoke with cynicism about the students:

> All they wanted was to get a day off [from] school. I don't think
> we should dignify it by even pretending to take the demands
> seriously. We tried having a Chicano studies course before in the
> late seventies and early eighties, and let me tell you, we can-
> celed it because enrollment kept dropping and finally it seemed
> we didn't need it. Those kids didn't really want to study. They
> didn't want to work. They wanted a class where they could just
> sit around and talk about being Mexican and feel good. But
> when they found out they had to read books and write papers
> and work, they weren't interested.

The content of the demands, the seriousness and passion of the students in taking a political stand were trivialized. Nonetheless, because of the widespread press the students had received and the support of community groups, the public demonstration pressured the district to set up a Latino Advisory Council that included some students.

In addition to the direct activism around the La Raza Club, Latino students do receive support from a few teachers. Garrison, who advises La Raza club, is one supporter. But there is another teacher at Madison that the Latino students consider theirs. Roberto Guerrero is a social studies teacher who served for one year (until budget cuts ended the position) as a part-time counselor for Latino students as well. He speaks Spanish and was one of the teachers who came from Washington High, so he was known and could communicate with the parents of Latino students. He is known as an advocate and supporter of Chicano students at Madison, and purposely chooses to put his time and effort into this group of students.

Some limited teacher support is thus present for immigrant students, including those from Spanish-speaking nations. Some limited teacher support is available for Latino students, including both U.S.-born and immigrant. And there is a precarious program for limited English speakers, though no significant bilingual program. There is some significant overlap between these three ways of categorizing students and their needs; but there are also some clear differences. Many Latinos are language minorities, with needs for bilingual education. But some Latinos are fully English speakers and do not know Spanish. Most bilingual students are also immigrants. But many immigrants are not Latino, and not all Latinos are language-minority students. There is an undercurrent of a political tug and pull between how these overlapping needs and populations should be viewed, how support should be mobilized, and whether they should be viewed as ethnic related or immigrant related. There is particular tension, competition and confusion between matters of Latino education, immigrant education, and bilingual education.

Recently, the superintendent established several task forces to "advise" the district administration of educational needs of specific groups. A Latino Task Force was created (partially in response to the student boycott), with funding to enable them to institute some programmatic supports for Latino students. One project was started in the district to focus on immigrants, and it included a cross-district Advisory Committee on Immigrant Issues (with private foundation funds, no district funding). A Bilingual Task Force (separate from both the Immigrant and the Latino Task Forces) was also established, with no funding from either the district or a private foundation. The districtwide bilingual coordinator position was abolished. At first, each of the three entities were unaware the others existed. Until slowly, some of the crossover membership began sharing information with others. A search ensued to figure out which jurisdiction seemed to be the more powerful position from which to push the district to be more responsive to issues of language and culture in the schools. The three planning and advisory entities remain separate—testimony to the unsettled frameworks for viewing ethnicity, culture, language, and immigration issues.

There was indication that the political preference of the school district was to address needs through ethnic identification and to downplay matters of both immigrant education and bilingual education—perhaps as a result of the larger political climate of increasing attacks on both immigrants and bilingual education. It was less clear how students were negotiating their way through the minefields of identification during this time of shifts.

What constitutes a pan-Latino population? What is an immigrant need? Do Brazilians and Central Americans and Mexican newcomers and Chicanos belong in a single category either as immigrants or as Latinos? With what implications? The process occurring within Madison High and Bayview reflects national trends toward broader racialized categories; and works against the national specificity in the identities that immigrants bring with them. The process is not, however, without fissures and conflict for the students themselves.

Most of the newcomers at Madison appeared temporarily to resist the process of racialization into large broad racial categories. To them, Americanization into these categories is the abandonment of hope that others will see and accept them in their full national, religious, and language identities. It feels like an annihilation of self. Some hold fast to their national identities ("I am Guatemalan, not Latino") and simply resist identifying with or grouping with others in the ethnic/racial categories. They choose marginality as a means of resistance. They choose to remain off the social map, to remain "foreign," and not give in to racial categories. But within two years, very few of the students followed in this research maintained this stance.

Those who belong to nationalities that do not easily "fit" the U.S. racial schema, and whose cultural and community responses to immigration seem to result in more traditional behavior, are most freed from this racial imperative. Specifically, Afghans and Fijians seem to maintain their distinct national identities. However, for most, their choices regarding social accommodation appeared to include acceptance of a particular place in the racial hierarchy of the United States. And regardless of the time frame, for certain racial groups that process appears to be accompanied by giving up their immigrant belief in the "American dream"—that hard work will pay off in academic success and mobility. Here, there were distinct differences in the racial paths. Those on the Latino "race track" more often gave up the immigrant ideology and belief in school success. Their peer group at Madison seldom appears in the college preparatory classes, has the lowest rate of school attendance, the highest rate of disciplinary referrals for truancy, the lowest grade-point averages, and so on. Assimilation into Latino life at Madison brings with it social acceptance among peers, but is not a model in the eyes of the teachers for "making it" or being "included" in broader academic realms.

> I used to work hard at my studies. When I first came here from Mexico I was a good student and every day did my homework and worked hard. That's how a lot of the kids who just come here do it. But I don't know, junior year I just wanted to be with my friends and lighten up a little. I finally felt comfortable with lots of friends at school, and school didn't seem so important to me anymore. I loosened up, I guess I got more American. It's not like school doesn't matter. I mean most of my friends hang in at school. But I used to think that you get your high school diploma and that's how you get ahead, and if I worked really hard I'd get really ahead. Now I see that's not really true. Everyone pretty much gets a diploma if you just keep coming to school, and so what do you get for working harder? A diploma is a diploma. It's good for a job at Pizza Hut. I've just lightened up. I have more fun now. Most of my friends are like that.

Students change in where and how they place themselves and are placed in this racial system.

> You know, when you get here you want to fit in and be like everybody else and find your way. You are [with] one group or another. Then you calm down. You can start being friends across groups, but it's from the security of knowing where you belong. You have to go through one stage before you get to another. After a while once you're established, you can begin to see people just as people. You know who you are, so you can branch out.

This is part of learning "the ropes" of how to "walk through this school." Some newcomers become immersed in the racial separation of the school, but still hold to or return to friendships forged during their initial newcomer days when bonds were developed among those who stood at the margins of Madison High. For many, however, the institutional sorting powerfully separates them as it directs them to different racialized futures. The high academic classes are filled disproportionately with white, Vietnamese, and Chinese students; the "skills" remedial track is filled disproportionately with Latino and African American students. One Afghan student looked back on the friendships she had with other newcomers in her first year at Madison:

> At the Newcomer School and in sheltered [classes], lots of nations and religions and types were friends. We still stayed with our own country people, but we were friends with other kids. Now I don't see most of them anymore. We're in different classes so we don't get a chance.

Newcomers become more and more part of America as they learn to find their place in and to negotiate this system. Suana spoke of the urgency of developing these skills almost immediately after immigrating. She thought, in her own words, "it would be a new world. [But] it was hell."

> The first thing is that people over here are very different and they have lots of races. At home, everyone is equal and you are treated the same. But here, they treat you different. If you even look at students they say, "Why are you looking at me like that? You don't like my kind of person?" And I don't know how to say to them that I am just looking at them like a human being. I've had problems like that at school. I don't know why. I can't change them. I think my skin looks white. Or some people think I am Spanish. There is no place I belong. Here, people are more separate from other kids. They just want to be with the people from their culture. Kids here don't want others to get in their culture because they always speaking their language, and sometimes you don't understand what they're talking about and they don't want to talk in English. I had to learn to figure out what is okay and what is not okay, and then I had to find a group to belong to and stay there.

Says one senior, a Latina immigrant student, looking back on the last two years at Madison:

> Eventually you get used to being around different races. You have to. You go to school every day. You can't be fighting every day because he's black or she's white. You just have to get used to it and accept it. That's the environment, and you have to

> adapt—get along with everybody and don't start stuff. You have to be a little more careful because you don't want people to think—because they don't know you, how you act is what they think. Most important is the guys you're with. You walk once with a black guy and everyone is all, oooh, she's got jungle fever.

Says another student:

> We are forced to interact with one another, and that's good. We have no choice. We have to go to school here and they have to go school here. And you learn how to make it work so people don't kill each other. These are skills for the world. To find your race and your place, to make peace there, and then you can get along with everyone else.

Part of that negotiation and learning is learning not to speak openly of or acknowledge the process. Generally, this system seems to maintain itself relatively undisturbed. The administrators, teachers, and students alike speak about the relative peace and calm of intergroup relations on campus. Immigrants themselves learn to acknowledge the "diversity" as an overall fact, but not the tension or sorting or intense monitoring that occurs.

Making a place for oneself and finding one's race are central to student life at Madison. Newcomer students develop conscious skills for interaction, careful ways of behaving, and habits of monitoring their own and each other's behavior as they engage in this process. Some protest along the way and balk as they switch identity from a national identity to a racial one, but these protests do not seem to gain any support. Perhaps it is because these social processes alone do not explain the racial imperative and separation at the school. The process of identification and separation is not solely conducted by the students acting on each other. It reflects the politics and practice in the larger community and a specific though "unseen" racial sorting of the school program. The schooling process itself segregates, excludes, and discriminates. This is an overt manifestation of a racial project at the school. But it is heavily denied and hidden. The newcomer students only see the social process among peers and do not seem to recognize the big picture. The social separation and the academic tracking are part and parcel of slotting students by skin color, language, and class into their places in a hierarchy in the world. Their belief in individual effort clouds their ability to see this sorting project.

CHAPTER SIX

Love and Marriage:
How Young Immigrant
Women Negotiate the Terrain
Between Two Cultures

IT'S LATE spring at Madison High. Student activities are picking up, as the clubs focus on intensive fund-raising for their end-of-the-year trips and parties, and the proms are just around the corner. Part of this spring tradition is a major musical production of the Show Choir, a highlight of the entire school year. This year, the theme of the show is love and marriage, and the cast is preparing for a two-night run. Classes are invited to fill the cafeteria as an audience for the dress rehearsal. On the walls of the cafeteria are banners and poster announcements of the upcoming prom. In a wonderfully staged production of costumed acts, students belt out song after song of American love tunes. On the stage, a cast of mostly African American, Filipino, and white students bring the audience to its feet with musical numbers. They sing "Memory," *Oklahoma,* "Get Me to the Church," *Porgy and Bess,* music that is, according to the choir director who introduces the show, "homegrown in America." It is a startling reference to me, aware that most of the students on the stage are also "grown in America," in contrast to the many immigrants who people the audience.

In the audience, I notice a group of Fijian and Afghan girls sitting together. It is a sober enclave in the midst of much enthusiastic hoopla. While the school campus vibrates to the themes of love and marriage and proms and dating, I am struck by the contrast that must exist for this group of girls who are not allowed to date and who struggle at the crossroads of Christian and non-Christian worlds. The young Hindu and Muslim women face traditionally arranged marriages in the midst of the heavily romance-oriented American teen culture, struggle with the contradictory values between the freedom of young American female teens and their cultural respect for parents' rights to make important decisions impacting the rest of their lives. One girl is biting back tears, and the others reach over to pat her hand. I guess this interaction is related to Corinne's impending marriage. She has just found out that a marriage has been hastily arranged for her to a man she has never laid eyes on, and that the wedding will occur in a month. She will leave school and move to San Francisco to live with him. Her schooling is over. Her adult life as a wife is about to begin. The marriage was arranged in response to a scandal that had just occurred. One of the group's close friends, also an immigrant, had been caught kissing an American boy. The outraged guardian, whose responsibility she was, beat her and forbade her from seeing him again. When the girl told her favorite teacher and showed her bruises, the teacher was compelled by law to bring the incident to the attention of the vice principal, who reported it to child protective services. The word spread throughout the immigrant community. The next day, the girl was sent back to her home country.

Other immigrant parents, fearful that their daughters also might be becoming involved in dating, cracked down heavily on their daughters' activities. One was being married off posthaste. This small group of eight girls hang tightly together these days. It seems to me now that they are clinging to each other. They argue over whether Siona had gone too far in actually dating an American. They argue over whether the uncle was justified in sending her back, and wonder what Siona's fate would be and whether they would ever see her again. They are afraid yet a little in awe of Corinne's quick ascent into adulthood and marriage and are buzzing with questions about what her husband will be like.

During the intermission, members of the choir walked up and down the aisles selling "Love grams" (messages the choir would deliver to whomever a student specified, with Hershey kisses and a rose). This was used as a fund-raiser for their trip to Disneyland. A choir member approached the group of girls and asked: "Anyone special you want to send a love gram to? A secret sweetheart?" Corinne burst into tears, and her friends closed in around her.

■　■　■

For the young women at Madison High, the conflicts and struggles about coming of age as immigrants in the United States and bridging the expectations of two cultures is strongly related to how they negotiate their gender roles. On what feels to many newcomers to be a one-way journey toward narrowly defined "American" ways and away from one's home culture and language, there is terrain for negotiation. All become English speakers, though only a few are able to develop literacy in the home language. Most adopt U.S. racial identities and become integrated into the racialized social life of the school, dropping their primary national, language, and religious identifications (at least at school)—but not all. Most find that their English language fluency and racial identification mark them for a specific academic track in the school; however some defy these expectations. One of the primary arenas in which there is "wiggle room" for weighing and making choices about these paths into America, was the negotiation of gender roles.

Negotiating the terrain among their cultures is expressed in terms of sexuality, marriage, dating boys, attachment to school, and clothing. Issues of freedom and independence from parents as well as from potential husbands all mix with the lure of a culture of romance and the best guesses about whether an ideology centered on mobility and independence through school success can be trusted. They face the challenge of uncertain futures along several interrelated dimensions: home responsibilities, motherhood, wifehood, and the world of work. In all of these areas, and the cross-sections between them, school is a key site in the negotiation of immigrant women's identities as they try to understand their gendered options for balancing the costs and rewards of movement along any of the Americanization continuums.

High school years are fundamentally about the transition to adulthood, and a key piece of that transition is learning appropriate roles as women and men. This research focused primarily on young immigrant women. Recent literature on immigration has found that girls experience their adjustment to the United States differently than males. They exhibit significantly lower self-esteem and especially high depression rates the longer they are in the United States. It is also found that although boys chose to identify either in terms of their homeland or as Americans, girls hold to hyphenated identities, indicating a different sense of bridging two cultures.

For many of the young women in this study, becoming "American" clashes with their homeland cultural expectations. Coming of age in the crossroads between two cultures, they seek ways to broker the tools and values of each culture to create a path into adulthood that feels possible and maximally comfortable. But this is difficult. The prolonged adolescence that America confers on its young seems to have granted many of them a precious and time-limited period of freedom (or potential freedom) and postponement of marriage. Although most immigrant girls are more restricted in comparison to their American-born peers, they seem to experience their high school days as relatively free.

Schooling is generally taken seriously. There is a general belief that school is the vehicle for getting ahead in this culture. And for most of the immigrant girls, the worth of an education is closely tied to the power it will give them in marriage, by forestalling marriage until schooling concludes, by having their earning power become a powerful bargaining chip in the marriages they face, or as a fallback from these marriages that may disintegrate in the crossfire of differing cultural values. But the information available to them is inadequate. Some face the uncertainty of not knowing for sure if and when their marriages will be arranged. Few understand what the future careers they envision for themselves entail in terms of schooling or planning. They say, for example, that they want to be doctors and nurses, while they fail to take the courses they will need to achieve these professions, and without knowing how many years of schooling it will require.

It is not only the experience of immigration that shapes these responses. Religion and culture are key factors. Thus, the Vietnamese or Chinese girls handle the dilemmas differently from Mexican Catholic girls, and the young Hindu and Muslim women still differently.

Meanwhile, each hears the clock ticking in terms of cultural expectations about marriage, having children, and assuming adult female roles. The young women are unsure if or when their parents will expect, allow, or arrange their marriages, require help in assuming responsibility for siblings or arrange to send back to their homeland to help with family responsibilities there or to begin a process of traditional marriage. Unsure whether they have a few months or many years, these young women talk about both the uncertainty of their tenure at Madison High and of being outside of a decision-making process that is unclear to them. They do not feel safe about whether the independence they see available to their American peers can be theirs and at what price. During this interim, they struggle with each other over the ethics, the consequences, and the dilemmas of "becoming like American girls."

THE PLEASURES AND PRICES OF FREEDOM

One of the first things immigrant girls at Madison High will say as they describe American teenager girls is "they are so open" and "they are so free." These concepts, "openness" and "freedom," occur again and again in the contrasts made between an Americanized person and a newcomer. Most of the girls are simultaneously judgmental about these characteristics and are drawn to them. Jani spoke with pride about how much more open she is now, and how she would never be able to go back to Fiji and fit in any longer. But she expressed her disapproval at how American girls will talk about their problems openly with anyone. Thanh enjoyed telling me that she now talks to boys and that she never would have done it back home in Vietnam. But she would not, she insists, go out on a date.

Most of the girls have limits to their movement and behavior. These limits are imparted by tradition, culture, and fearful parents who wish to protect their daughters in the midst of a new land that is viewed as both violent and seductive. Almost all the newcomer girls go straight home from school and remain inside until parents or older relatives get home. Few are allowed to go to school dances or after-school activities.

Time at school then becomes a precious social experience. Schooling is viewed as a place to engage in social activities that are constricted outside of school. For this reason, most of the girls I interviewed loved going to school. They see their friends; they taste American social life (through observation if not participation). To them, the home becomes restrictive in one way, and a safe, protective familiar shelter in another. But it is school that opens up new and different worlds and possibilities to them, and it is school that is their window on America.

This is a strong contrast to the way many of the U.S.-born students talk publicly about their high school time. They tended to speak of school as a kind of prison and could hardly wait for the final bells to ring to release them. It is in the after-school hours when they get to live and enjoy life more fully.

The dilemma for immigrant girls arises when they realize that the social life within classes and the school day is only a limited version of the social life their American peers enjoy. Hanging out with friends, going to parties and dances are a kind of forbidden fruit which combines a relative openness about sexuality and relationships with boys, and a freedom of movement. To some, it feels like freedom from the restrictions on the lives of girls and women placed by their cultures that they begin to view as unreasonable. For others, the freedom and openness of American girls represent a loss of values and control. Most seesaw back and forth. And so they test the waters constantly: should they try to step out or should they remain within family and traditional limits? Would their parents know if they danced with a boy during a noon-time dance in the Quad? Would their parents find out if they went to a boy's house after school? Would it be bad? What price would they pay?

Several strategies become part of daily survival for some of the foreign-born female students. One such strategy is lying. Many of the girls lie in order to protect themselves from the judgments of family or friends. In discussions with the girls, they insist that the issues of freedom of movement and openness in relationships are really the rules for girls and not for boys. One day Jani was describing this by contrasting her parents' expectations for her with that of her brothers.

> Girls are really controlled more. If a girl got married to another race, she can't protect herself. And her parents and family wouldn't be there. Boys they don't worry about.

Rosalyn had a boyfriend her parents would not approve of, and she would regularly sneak off to see him. She desperately wanted to be an American girl and wanted her parents to give her more freedom than she had in Fiji. But she hated herself for telling them lies. Once she was caught, they stopped trusting her at all. She felt she had to make the difficult choice between continuing to be the good daughter and remaining part of her culture and doing what she wants. The latter choice she knew could carry a high price. She explained:

> I will not have a family if I do what I want. I would never see them again if I made decisions against them.

> There are two ways. To be American, it is okay to lie to parents, it is okay to wear American clothes, it is okay to have argument where you never would before, and it is okay to be with your boyfriend. To be Fijian, you follow your family ways.

In the eyes of many newcomers, lying to one's parents was a way to handle this split between home culture and American culture, and the morality or necessity of lying came up again and again in discussions among the immigrant girls. Lying is relatively easy to get away with, because most immigrant parents do not have full information about expectations, practices, or daily rhythms of the U.S. school day and social world. However, although lying seems to offer the girls some protection, lying is thought of by them as a step toward Americanization. It appeared, in fact, to be an American as well as an immigrant pattern. Witness this female student who is Filipina but American-born:

> My parents are very Filipino, like strict. You know what I'm talking about? They're just typical Filipinos about the boys I hang around with. Like I can't have a boyfriend until I finish college. And my dad sometimes doesn't like the ways I'm dressed. Like if its a low top, he'll say, come back in here and get dressed. I mean, I can't go out with my friends unless they really know that person. They're really strict. . . . We always argue because, see, I have a boyfriend, so it makes it worse—and he is Latin, so that

> makes it really worse. My Dad had a fit and said they think my
> education is more important and they are afraid I'll run off with
> my boyfriend. I explain to them that it's not like that, but they
> don't believe me. So now they think I'm not seeing him, but I am.
> We all lie. We just have to.

Shani, an immigrant, tried to describe why it is that some girls choose to "play around" and then to lie to their parents.

> The girls are playing around now because it is their only chance.
> Here in America, we hear about love all the time and we all want
> it. We see TV. And wish that was our life. So some girls play
> around. And then they have to lie to cover it up. They can't let
> their parents down by admitting what they are doing. But that's
> not me, and I tell my parents that I would never act American
> that way. But they are afraid. They are afraid maybe they don't
> know me anymore. Maybe I am like those other immigrant girls.
> Still I understand the girls that do it. We are left out because we
> choose to honor our parents. We don't get to be part of the fun.

Some of the tension was between girls who viewed the protection of family and dependence as keys to survival and those who experienced their family as constraining their survival. The girls would speak in hushed tones of the specter of abusive husbands and whether or how they would escape such a marriage. Some viewed their families as essential safety nets, given the uncertainties of marriage. Others felt that pressures from their family would lock them into unhappy marriages. They argued about whether single women have enviable freedom or are frighteningly vulnerable. Movies, television programs, books, friends feed an ongoing discourse about the apparent pleasures of freedom and the vulnerability of independence. Television, in particular, has great defining power. Staying at home in the afternoon and evening hours after school, they watch television. They learn English from television and they learn a version of life in the United States. That version is heavily saturated with romantic love as the centerpiece of a woman's life. School is the primary terrain in which they are involved in social life beyond that of their family and newcomer immigrant communities.

To most female newcomer students, school is a zone that offers a measure of both freedom and independence. Their attachment to school was related to this fact. But what at first appeared to be posed as a choice in their fantasies of the future—between stepping out as independent Americanized women or being true to their cultural and religious backgrounds along with staying within the home and the duties and responsibilities to family and husbands—all become quickly muddied in the reality of life in the United States.

"I HELP. THEY IN TURN WILL HELP THE FAMILY BY DOING WELL AND GOING FAR."

Few immigrant families in Bayview appear to make it economically without the mother as well as the father working outside the home, often for long hours and at two jobs. Increasingly, women need to be wage earners whose involvement in worlds beyond the immigrant home and whose economic leverage alter the patterns of authority in immigrant families. It is not only the mothers, but the teenaged girls who often have to work outside the home. In order for a family unit to make it, they have to depend on children for part of the support. This is the economic reality of immigrant working-class life in the United States. Families often expect and need their adolescent girls either to care for siblings and the home because the mother/wife is working or to go to work themselves in order to contribute to the economic support of the family.

Pani, an Afghan immigrant, is the eldest child in her family her parents expect different things from her than they do from her younger sister and brother.

> My parents need me to work at the cleaners where my mother also works. I go three days a week after school. I also try to do my schoolwork. But my brother and sister do not work—just me. I am the oldest. We want them to be able to just study and not have to work. As the oldest, I do both.

The older siblings are more often needed for financial support, and in some families it is expected that the older siblings will sacrifice for the younger siblings for whom "American" solutions and futures are more possible and more acceptable. Guadalupe, a young woman who emigrated from Mexico with her mother and three brothers, explained:

> We came because my mother wanted us to have a good education and to have chances. I wanted to be a teacher, and I dreamed I would go to school and go to college and return to my village and be a teacher. That was the dream. That was my

> American dream. But it is hard here. My mother works so hard,
> and I work, too. I am so tired from working that I stopped going
> to school. It has to be that way now. My little brothers are smart,
> and they still go to school. I will not graduate, but they will.

Shirley is a Chinese immigrant and the head of household. She and her
two younger sisters were sent to the United States to get an education. Shirley's
role is primarily to be the caretaker. She complains of having to be up at day-
break to make breakfast and lunches for her siblings and get them off to school.
She collects them after school, gets them all home, and cooks dinner and cleans
up the house before she can even begin to think about her own homework.
She explained:

> It doesn't matter. I don't like to clean up all the time, but it is the
> way I help my family. I don't do very well in school, but my sisters
> will be able to concentrate on their studies. They will do well and
> go to college. I help my family by being sure my sisters are taken
> care. They in turn will help the family by doing well and going far.

For many of the immigrant girls, the hopes for their own futures are set
aside as the struggle for family survival in the United States demands their
time, energy, and focus. As they begin to see that the American dream may not
work out for them, it becomes deferred to younger siblings or to the next generation. A fair number of them came to accept within a few short years in the
United States that those futures will be perhaps for their younger siblings or
their children. Most accept this as their role and contribution to family. They
associate the pursuit of one's own future as distinct from responsibility for siblings or family, as a peculiarly American pattern. However, despite many con-
demnations of the lack of sense of responsibility "American" girls have toward
their families, almost across the board, these young immigrant women's reflections on raising their own children led them to say that when they are parents
they will be more lenient and less demanding of their daughters, less fearful of
American ways, and allow their children to do things in a far more American
and independent way. But they also express hopes that their children will learn
to be responsible to the family.

Although many parents need their children both to work and be active in
American society, they watch carefully and fearfully that they do not lose control over their children. And for their daughters, that potential loss is often in

the arenas of sexuality, dating, and inappropriate marriage. A father spoke of his concern about his daughter:

> Leticia is a good girl. She is a good daughter. In Mexico, I could leave her at home with her grandmother and she was okay. Here it is different. American girls do things different. Leticia wants to be like them, but she doesn't see that those girls have lost their values. They dress like they want the boys, and they don't go home to their families. I tell her she has to come home. I tell her she cannot wear clothes that show her stomach to the world. She tells me this is not Mexico and doesn't want to listen to me. I am afraid what will happen to her here. I am afraid she will go too far.

When has a daughter gone too far?

It is different for different families. For example, Lupe was sent back to Mexico to live with her aunt after her father discovered she had a boyfriend. He felt she was too young. After several fights in which Lupe's father insisted that she stop seeing her boyfriend, and Lupe refusing to do so, the decision was made. In another family, Ronita was sent to live with relatives in a smaller community in California, where it was felt there were less undermining influences. The precipitating incident was that she talked back to her uncle, and the family felt she was becoming too American. Maria was sent back to live with her grandmother in Mexico when she reached fifteen because it was felt that keeping her in the United States was risky as she reached dating age. The decision was made by the grandmother and father together out of concern about preserving her Mexican culture and religion. Siona was sent back to Fiji when she was found to be dating an American boy. She was immediately married off in an arranged marriage, "before it is too late," as her uncle described the decision. "Going too far," and "crossing the line" are defined almost solely in terms of sexuality and dating.

There are girls of all cultures and religions who adopt American behaviors and choose to turn their backs on traditional values. But generally, different patterns are evident from different national and cultural groups. Vietnamese, Chinese, and Afghan girls almost all seem to accept limitations on sexual behaviors, keeping fairly separate from the boys and focusing in school primarily on their studies. There seems to be less interest in dating, less effort to mimic or adopt American teen behaviors. At Madison, it is the Fijian Hindu girls who most express the desire for boyfriends despite the religious values to the contrary. There is wide variation among the responses of the Mexican immigrant girls.

One of the fears shared by many immigrant and U.S.-born parents is of unwanted pregnancies with unmarried daughters. It is a concern that mixes the knowledge of foreclosed options, with the desire to protect daughters from the shame most cultures bestow on young unmarried pregnant women. The measures of how vulnerable and how much in danger a daughter really is of getting pregnant differ, however. One parent draws the line at conversations with unfamiliar boys. Another allows dating and unsupervised socializing with boys, but stops at allowing them to go into each other's houses. One mother sighed:

> I send my sister along with Maria when she goes on dates. She knows I won't let her date without someone from the family being with her. She thinks I'm old-fashioned, but I have to look out for her. She gives me that look, but she minds me. She is a good girl.

Another tells of her own experience, and the determination to protect her daughter:

> I was young, too. I let my feelings run away with me. I was so much in love, and I was silly. I didn't listen to my mother, so I had a baby. I went to live with my grandmother. I cried every day because the boy didn't talk to me after that. Here in America it is harder. The girls and boys run wild together. I don't want Sonia to make a mistake. So everyday she has to come right home from school. No chances.

In some of the families studied, the decisions over what is regarded as having gone too far and what the family needs to do to protect the daughter and family unit itself are difficult ones, and are often not made by parents alone. The patterns sometimes included cross-national family decision making. The decisions about where kids were to live were made based on two axes: what's best for the child and what is needed for the family.

In some families, it is not simply a matter of whether dating is appropriate, but who one dates. Soraya's father is Mexican and her mother Hawaiian.

> My dad sometimes says, "you're not a real Mexican," or he'll take off a black rap I'm listening to and say, "put on something

Mexican." I'm proud to be Mexican, but just because I don't listen to Mexican music all the time, he'll put me down. He's set on me seeing Mexican, speaking Spanish, having a Mexican boyfriend. That's being a real Mexican, I guess, to him. But it hurts me when he says that. He puts me down because I don't know Spanish very well. He says I'm just a white-washed Mexican. But I think what it is really about, is he wants to keep me a pure enough Mexican so I will marry Mexican. That's what matters. That I marry Mexican and have Mexican babies. That would be carrying on the family in the way that he cares about. And it's because I'm a girl. I don't think he cares so much about my brother. It's about the babies.

Judging from the long discussions among immigrant girls about the issue, it appears that many parents are particularly concerned about female children and dating. There is apparently a hierarchy of acceptability within many immigrant families according to the girls and their assessment of what their parents allow in crossing the race or ethnic line in dating. Their teachers also perceive it this way.

For example, two teachers talked at length about immigrant girls and the important dilemmas the girls bring to them for advice related to dating. Linda O'Malley explained that if a Vietnamese girl brought home a black guy, it would be the ultimate step over the line. Lisa Stern added, "dating out of your race" as an expression is almost always a code phrase for dating black guys. It would be a lot more acceptable if the girls were dating Filipino or white boys. Stern feels there is almost always a hierarchy of how immigrant parents look at who is datable. Often, any boyfriend outside the "culture" was viewed as a threat. This is apparently related to viewing girls as responsible for passing on the culture through their children. So it is their daughters' marriages and potential grandchildren that parents are most concerned about. One father explained:

We are Mexican. I want my daughter to be American, too, but she is Mexican in her blood and her bones and I don't want her to forget that. When she has children, they will be my grandchildren, and the children of our people. I want them to speak our language and know our culture. But if she marries someone who isn't our culture I would welcome him, but I would always feel sad and that something is wrong because the children. It just feels like that to me.

Although most of the immigrant girls feel they would follow their parents' values and honor their parents' feelings by marrying "our own kind," they are less willing to agree that that implies one must only date one's "own kind." But the parents are worried, evidently. As one Chinese mother explained:

> I think if Sylvia gets used to being with boys from other cultures, she will begin acting more American. If she acts more American, she won't make a good wife for a Chinese man, and it will be harder for her to find a Chinese man who will want her. I don't want that to happen. I want her to have a good marriage.

Immigrant girls struggle with how to respond to their parental and familial expectations, despite spending their school days on a campus that is heavily saturated with romantic love. The yearbook alone makes this starkly clear. The emphasis on couples, proms, and love runs throughout. The ads in the back are filled with photos of couples and promises of eternal love. "Alex, our love has grown for three years, and will last 4 a lifetime!" "Adriana, babe, I want to thank you for our relationship. I know it will last a lifetime." "Claudia, only you can love me the way that you do. You are the only one for me, forever." In a section on interracial dating, one young man writes: "I think interracial relationships are good because you could be missing out on the true love of your life by limiting yourself to your own race. I know this because my girlfriend is Filipino and I'm Mexican. I know I'm glad I didn't pass her up because there's no one I'd rather spend my whole life with." Throughout the school, interracial couples can be found. They face some resistance from friends and family, but it is a normal enough occurrence at this school.

SCHOOL AND THE FUTURE

Most immigrant students make a connection between being in school and getting ahead. What "getting ahead" looks like is less clear. Why did the girls think they were in school? What did they view as their end goals? What did they think their future would hold? What does school have to do with it? For most of the girls, the inevitability of marriage is relatively unchallenged. But the relationship between schooling, future jobs, and those marriages are cloudy, and immigrant girls feel they must prepare for multiple options. There is virtually no place within school where these interrelationships are acknowledged, and yet it is a major issue about which these young women think and frame their decision making and views of the future.

Almost all of them talked about wanting a good job and wanting to be able to support themselves. They knew that they would need to be able to work as a matter of survival. But it was not only economic survival they were concerned about. Many spoke of marriage as a state of isolation and constriction. Continuing their schooling was a means of staying connected to peers and social life. When schooling was over, a job would support that connection. When asked what kind of work they want to do in the future, they dreamed of being nurses or doctors, flight attendants, or do some kind of work "with people." But the plans were vague. Few had notions of how long such schooling might take, how to prepare, or whether their schedules and credits in high school were leading them in those directions. Their mothers work in dry-cleaning shops, canneries, or sewing shops, or they clean houses. On television, they see women in a variety of careers, but get no hint of what the preparation or career path looked like. Television also failed to give them a picture of decision making that weighed marriage, family relationships, cultural concerns, and career.

Nadira faces an arranged marriage like many other Afghan, Pakistani, and Fijian immigrant girls she hangs out with. Cooperating with the arranged marriage for Nadira is about showing respect for her parents. To say anything to her parents about what she would like in a husband would have been tantamount to questioning their wisdom and authority. "You can't talk. You can't ask, how is this guy? You can't say, I'd like to marry this other guy. We have to respect our parents to pick for us."

The marriage, she believed, would take place after she graduates from school. Nadira was not looking forward to marriage. In Afghanistan, she would already have been done with school and married at an earlier age, although she was a little vague and confused about when the marriage really would occur in this, her new life in America. One time, she said she thought it would be soon. Another time, she said she thought it had to do with finishing school and that she would be able to go to college and then get married. On yet another time, she thought she would be married at age eighteen. At any rate, it was unclear to her when her parents will choose to marry her off now that they are living in the United States. And she believed it is one of the things she could not ask, because it would show distrust of her parents. Thinking it over, Nadira decided she wanted to go to college and become a doctor, partly because it requires many years of schooling and that might stave off marriage.

She knows her husband will be chosen from among her relatives, although the first few times she spoke about this, she was very guarded when discussing it. Once she asked if it was acceptable to marry cousins in America. She thought it might not be and that she might have to lie to cover for the fact that it is an uncle's son she would probably marry.

Nadira's ambition to be a doctor was not only about staving off marriage. She also felt that Afghanistan would need doctors because of the war, and she wanted to go back and help her people. Long after many of her friends gave up their plans or desires to go back to their native land, Nadira still held to her feeling that she wanted to go back. In fact, for Nadira, having decided that she preferred to view her future back in Afghanistan freed her from many of the painful pressures her friends were feeling about trying to become more Americanized. Nadira did not have to worry about being accepted as an American. Her future would, hopefully, be back home, where her national identity, her language, her traditional ways would suffice. The decision was not in her hands, however. In fact, an arranged marriage is fine for Nadira. She trusts that arranged marriages will work out as well as any and looks forward to the security of a marriage arranged between two families who are committed to the relationship. Her concern, however, is that with so many unanswered questions and so little control of her own about the marriage, she is unable to see any aspect of her future clearly. She expressed this dilemma often:

> I don't have any idea what he will be like. Will he make me stay
> home? Will he drink? Will he be nice to be? Will he encourage me
> to go to school? I can't plan anything. I know my parents will pick
> someone they think will be a good match. But I also know you
> can never tell about a man until you are his wife. Will our future
> be in America, or will it be back in Afghanistan?

Nadira and her friends regularly talked about what their future husbands might be like, and the terms they used were related to "modernity": "Maybe if I get a modern husband he will let me go to school and have a job. Then I won't be home all the time serving my father-in-law."

Shani's mother was already talking to a potential husband, a man from Pakistan who was twenty-eight and wanted to marry her when she turned eighteen in a few months. Shani objected:

> I don't like him. I mean, I saw him once when he came to talk
> to my mother and he looks old, and he calls and tells my mother
> to force me to get married with him. I tell her no. He is too old
> for me. My mother stopped talking to me. She said, if you don't

want to marry, fine, do whatever you want. You've become American.

Her vision was that if she married this man, her freedom would be over. Her life would not be in her own control, and he would (she was convinced) be a traditional Pakistani husband. After this fight with her mother over the marriage, Shani became determined to get a "good" education.

If you have education, you can get a better job. If you're married, it's difficult if you don't have an education, because you have to stay home and look after kids and you never can say anything. If you have an education, you can have a job that is worth something, and if you earn money, your husband can't say so much to you. And if you don'the have a husband, you can take care of yourself.

Corinne had been sure her parents would wait to have her married until she was done with school. But one day she said, with a puzzled look:

Here, I get good grades but my parents say I need to get married now anyway. I'm seventeen and a half years old, so it's time. I didn't expect it yet. I thought they'd let me graduate from school, but now all of a sudden I find out I have to get married, and then it is up to my husband if I go to school.

Corinne's attention then focused on trying to find out everything she could about the man she was marrying.

I don't know what to do now. I am all messed up. My dreams and plans are all messed up now. I just don't know what kind of person he is inside his heart. I have to wait and see, and it is so hard. I am tormented.

Her parents told her only that he did not drink, he did not smoke, and he worked at the local airport. She had been told that he likes modern girls and that he does not care if she is modern, as long as she cooks and does housework. But this was all hearsay. She was not allowed to talk with him. She heard all this from her father.

> I didn't want to. I cried a lot. I cried and my parents got angry
> with me. I am very scared. My parents keep saying, don't be
> afraid, because we are with you. I am just going to do what they
> say. But my heart doesn't tell me what to do. I beg them, please
> let me graduate first. But my parents won't listen to me.

Corinne found his phone number, but could not call him.

> I'm a girl, and in my religion, the girl should be below the husband.
> So I can't call him. He should be calling me to say hello and to ask
> me my thoughts. But he doesn't call. I am waiting. Every day I
> think, please call me , please call me. But I cannot say anything.

The man was given Corinne's picture, but she had no picture of him. The man had come to a big celebration of the ending of the Ramadan feast at her aunt's house. He saw Corinne and called her father and said he wanted to marry her. Her parents went to his house, and one Sunday he came to her house. He seemed fine to her, but she did not realize that arrangements might be serious yet. On the day after Corinne's friend, Siona, was caught by her uncle kissing an American boy, the parents made the final deal with this man to marry Corinne.

> In our religion, we have to listen to our parents. I would like a
> nice husband who would work hard in a good place, who would
> earn money and take care of me, who doesn't drink. But I don't
> think it's my time to get married yet. It is too young for me. I
> want to be a nurse, and that is a two-year course. Then I would
> marry whoever my parents want me to. But they say, no, I have
> to do this now. They are concerned about other Indian girls here
> who are running away with their boyfriends. So they want me to
> be married fast. I just hope he is a modern husband.

Part of Corinne's resistance was fear of a husband she didn't know. But part of it was related to cutting her schooling short. She said she was too young and too inexperienced and did not have a way to earn a living. Economics were at the heart of her fear, but it related to the degree of power she felt she would have in marriage. The models she saw around her in America demonstrated that immigrant wives have to work. Their worth to their husbands was related to being able to earn money as well as cook and clean. Her father held down two jobs ("He tells us,'I'm sweating for you, so you must do what I say'"), and her mother worked as a presser at a cleaners. Corinne intended to appeal to her new husband by talking about economics and impressing him by how thoughtful she was about money. She was seeking to create some wiggle room for herself in what she feared would be a closed trap of a marriage.

> I'll tell my husband that I don't want kids right now. I need to fin-
> ish my school so I will have a way to earn money. Maybe when I
> am twenty-eight I will have children.

Corinne's dream was to have a good job and some money before she got married. Yet, she knew that it would not happen that way. Nonetheless, she was determined to try to hold firm about not having children for a while. There was no question in her mind that she would go through with the marriage. It would be unthinkable not to. During a long session with Ms. O'Malley where Corinne had been crying about having to marry so soon, the teacher had sug-gested that perhaps Corinne did not need to go through with it, and Corinne was indignant:

> In our religion, we have to think of our parents first. It would
> kill them if I ran away or disobeyed them. It would dishonor
> them greatly. My children will be Muslim, and they will be raised
> to be Muslims. For me, I couldn't marry someone who wasn't a
> Muslim. I will do it the Muslim way. And I would never go against
> my parents!

Corinne was not alone in her concerns. Besides hoping for a "modern" husband, the girls generally tried to strategize a way to bring in good money as a way to generate some power and leverage in a marriage. "If I can earn money, maybe he won't abuse me." The thoughts of jobs were always in the context of the leverage and release it might give them from potentially constricting mar-riages. They did not feel as if they had control over whom they would marry, so they tried to control the nature of the marriage by using jobs and earning power and social connections as leverage. To some degree, any kind of job might help. But the likelihood of attaining the kinds of jobs they wanted to get is in fact very slim. The particular difficulty many of these girls faced as immi-grants in the crossfire of cultures, is that their tenuous relationship to school (from being marginalized programmatically at school) kept them separate from the sources of knowledge and power that might help them attain the careers they want. Maintaining their cultural integrity meant cutting them off from education and the sources of mobility within the educational system. The girls experienced this as a tear between responsibility to family and cultural integrity on the one hand, and pursuing their education on the other. Even among those who believed they were pursuing college and a career direction, few had the resources or information or academic preparation that would allow them to get there.

For Maria, the plan was to go to college and to "get away." Continuing education, for her, was a vehicle for escape. Maria said she would live at home and commute to college at first, but then go live on campus as soon as she could get away from home.

> This is how it is. My parents work. I have an older sister who is nineteen and goes to school and has a job. She's barely home. And I have two brothers—they are boys of course, so they don't do anything. So all the work is on me. Maria, cook dinner. Maria, clean the house. Maria, Maria, Maria. I want to get away. I'm going to move out and live my own life. I'll get a good job. Someday maybe I'll be married and have kids. It's scary. Maybe when I'm twenty-seven or twenty-eight. But by then, I will have a way to support myself in case I need to. Then I won't be dependent on my husband.

But Maria was not taking courses that would lead to admission to a four-year college and did not have job skills that would qualify her for any but a minimum-wage, entry-level job.

Juanita wanted desperately to go to college, to escape the future of her mother, who she saw as trapped in dependence on men and dependence on sexuality as the magnet that draws men into taking care of her. Juanita became convinced as a child that she would not be able to rely on attractiveness and would therefore have to "make it on my smarts," and that dependency on men is fragile and dangerous. Jani laughs at all this conversation about the dangers of romance, or the importance of having ways to take care of yourself. "Have fun while you can, and stop all this worrying! A boy is going to fall in love with me, and I'll be just fine. Love is coming my way, I know it."

In the minds of most of the immigrant girls, though, further schooling and employment are keys in their thinking about the future, but marriage, romance, domesticity, and jobs are interrelated. They see jobs as a way to maintain some independence and control over their married life. Financial autonomy would provide them worth in the eyes of husbands and would be necessary for them to stand on their own, as well as protect them from some potential abuse. Work outside the home would also keep them connected socially. Many of the immigrant girls viewed the culture of romance with a combination of wishful belief, cynicism, and pragmatism. The immigrant girls appeared less willing to believe in romance than their native-born or more Americanized peers.[28]

The immigrant students in Madison High, particularly the Indian and Afghan girls, stay in school to some degree as a way to push back boundaries of traditional expectations of them as women in a way that was acceptable and legitimate. Mora, for example, is actually nineteen. She is the oldest in the family, although according to school records she is seventeen. Her grandfather purposely "messed up my age" when she enrolled in school, so she could get a full education. When the junior high discovered the age gap, they wanted to promote her to eleventh grade, but she said no. Partly, her family wanted her to be able to stay close to her younger sister in order to take care of her in school; partly, they wanted to be sure she would be educated. Mora says she feels young anyway, as if she were sixteen. And she likes the forestalling of adulthood, marriage, in particular. She says:

> I am sixteen in American years. I feel sixteen and I live the life of a sixteen-year-old. But I am nineteen in Afghan years. At home, I am expected to be nineteen. This is one of the ways I am two people—both Afghan and American. But I'm so happy to be able to be sixteen in America, because I have more time to be free.

Mora was part of the friendship group that included the two young women who were suddenly married off. Although Siona and Corinne's sudden marriages were deeply unsettling to the rest of the group, most continued to believe that their own parents would not marry them off until "we are done with our schooling." The immigrant family's desire to "make it" in America is closely tied to developing their daughters' earning power and schooling. Thus, it is a good investment in their children's futures to let the daughters stay in school longer, as long as there is no perceived risk to their cultural and religious purity and no danger of the devastation of unwanted pregnancies. This requires constant monitoring. The girls were well aware that the degree to which they "cross the line" into unacceptable American behavior (particularly related to dating) could jeopardize their entire career in school. They might be attracted by aspects of the culture of romance and social life related to that culture, but many were also cautious.

Even some of the U.S.-born girls, aware through family experience and increased exposure in the media to the rates of men abandoning their families, to wife abuse and to divorce, still did not seem to trust the culture of romance. A high school diploma would help them get jobs that might bring them some independence from their domestic life, so schooling then is not only a way to get credentials for employment, but also a way to increase one's independence as a woman. However, they differed markedly in their willingness to accept that schooling beyond a high school diploma would have any payoff for them. Immigrant girls, as they have more and more exposure to American teens, appeared slowly to begin to doubt the payoff. It appeared that the longer they were in the United States, the less sure they were that schooling was the path to economic independence.

One day, four Mexican immigrants described Americans by seizing on the notion that having fun and being openly sexual is related to seeing education as not very important.

> American girls—they fool around in school and have fun. They don't have to be serious. They don't want to be serious. Education is not so important to American girls, because they can just be as open and sexy as they want. It's being sexy to guys that they care about—that's what they think will take care of them in life. They [are not] serious about school, because why should they? They think a man will take care of them.

There is plenty at school that would convince them that this is the case. In a remarkable debate, they began to postulate which path had more security to it: being sexual so that a man will take care of them or being serious about school. They assumed that these are mutually exclusive paths. Girls that focus on being fun and sexual simply do not also become serious about school, and the reverse was also assumed to be so. Somehow, they perceived this as a matter of choice of direction. Jani and several of her Fijian girlfriends chose sexuality and fun, but were heavily criticized by the other girls.

References to school and its relationship to marriage, work credentials, and future paths were common during the discussions of the girls. But it was never a direct reference to school as an institution that played any active role in helping them address their concerns about uncertain futures. Madison High offers child development courses, but little other vocational preparation for girls. Immigrant girls seldom enrolled in the Regional Occupational Program (the formal vocational program) or in vocational courses. Despite the fact that many of the girls spoke of wanting careers as doctors or nurses, there was a gap in the science classes available to immigrant students who have limited English proficiency and sparse enrollments of girls overall in the laboratory sciences. Thus, there was little in the formal program of the school that prepared girls for their likely roles as breadwinners, or for the desired professional roles (such as nurses and doctors) they dreamt about. Instead of any programmatic or formal school advisement or training for the future, peers played a crucial role in defining issues of future schooling and of gender appropriateness for immigrant girls. The girls spent hours discussing issues of dress and sexuality, relationships with boys, dreams and attitudes about marriage, responsibilities to and the security of family, and the importance of maintaining their cultural values. For the immigrant girls, there were two strongly opposing peer group concepts of appropriate future gender roles: the romantic lover where attractiveness is key, and the respectful, dutiful wife/daughter.

The books they most often chose to read from the shelves in the ESL classroom were romantic teen fiction. One day, in a social studies class, Jani was reading a book instead of doing her social studies writing assignment. She passed it over to Nadira and said: "This is a great one, I'll give it to you when I'm done." The book was entitled *He Loves Me Not*. The back jacket read:

> Alison has never had a boyfriend, or even a date. She works hard
> and has no time for anything except school and work. When she
> meets Ted it looks like an impossible relationship. Still he asks
> for her phone number, and Alison begins to hope that maybe—
> just maybe—her life is going to change.

Asked where she had found that book, she reported that Ms. O'Malley, the ESL teacher, had recommended it to her. Linda O'Malley stocks her shelves in the ESL classroom with romantic fiction because it is the most often requested genre by girls. She tries hard to find titles with which to stock her bookshelves.

> They love to read romantic novels. I'm just happy to give them
> anything in English they love to read! Getting them reading in
> English is one of my main goals.

Even without the novels, television drives the message home. But there is yet another way the immigrant girls were infused with romantic notions. The teachers in the sheltered and ESL classes were mostly young, female, and single. They also spoke openly about their lives to their students. Lisa Stern gave occasional updates to her classes about her love life. The girls were fascinated. Stern views this as being a "real person" to her students, and as giving them some view about American life. On the final pages of the class journals, Stern invited her students to write her a summary letter about what the year was like and any thoughts for the future. Several of the girls mentioned Stern's love life. "Good luck, hope some of your dates work out this year!" "I'll miss hearing about the ups and downs of your love life." "Hope you meet a great guy!"

Similarly, on the wall of O'Malley's office hung several photos of her with her boyfriend. Throughout the school year, her ESL classes followed the course of the relationship breaking up and making up, and were tuned to the phone calls that occasionally came from Sam apologizing for a fight they had had the night before. On several occasions, flowers were delivered to the classroom for O'Malley from her boyfriend. The girls relished hearing O'Malley talk about this. And she believed it was good for them to hear about an American-style relationship and the efforts to make it work for her as an independent woman. The result for the immigrant girls was that two of their few primary adult female American role models were young women in pursuit of romantic love. Yet they were also working women, a fact that did not escape notice and mention of the immigrant girls. Once, after a rose was delivered to the ESL classroom for O'Malley from her boyfriend, Sofia shared her musing about independence, romance, and settling down:

> I don't really think Ms. O'Malley will get married, do you? I mean she is really pretty and fun and she has a boyfriend, but she cares too much about her job, don't you think? She drives all the way here; she works so hard. I don't think her boyfriend likes that very much. And I think when she decides to settle down, she'll have to get a job closer to her boyfriend and stop being so independent. American women get it both ways, they can be independent until they get married, then they have to be there. What do you think she'll do? I can't imagine her giving in.

Where did Sofia get these notions? Was it from how Ms. O'Malley talked about her life? Was it from the romance fiction she had been reading? Sofia's tone seemed as though she were really seeking clarifications or confirmation. It was one more example of the myriad ways these young women seek help in figuring out their future options as females in this new culture.

Four of the young female teachers (Stern, O'Malley, Garrison, and Meyer) became confidantes for their female immigrant students. Frequently, during lunch and after school, they would be engaged in conversations, confessions, and problem-solving sessions with their students over issues of boyfriends, birth control, parental control, and love. And every conversation became part of the journey maps developing in the immigrant girls' heads about expectations and possibilities as women in the United States.

"THE GIRLS IN MY RACE ARE TOO DARK. BACK IN INDIA THEY ARE OKAY, BUT HERE IN AMERICA, THEY ARE JUST TOO DARK."

The messages about female appropriateness also came in the discourse about beauty. Immigrant female students were well aware of the impact of dress and looks in establishing social capital. And part of the tug and pull of becoming American was determining to what extent one would accept American standards and give up one's own:

> They make fun of us for how we dress, like a girl wearing a sari and everyone laughed even though it was beautiful.

> American people are mean. You have to dress good or you will be laughed at. You either have to dress the way they do, join in with them, or talk like them.

> Do you think you can dress like them? No.

> We should say it is none of your business. I am Muslim, so I dress like Muslim. But that is hard, and many girls have forgotten who they are, so they try to dress American. But you never really can. Their skin is so light.

Although the discussion is about dress and beauty, it is also fundamentally about skin color and race. Again, to be American is to be white-skinned. And simultaneously, to be American is to cease wearing styles from other nations and cultures. This is an issue for the girls to a large extent, because it is also an issue for the boys. For immigrant and U.S.-born teens, issues of beauty are very present in the male equation of what constitutes a datable and desirable woman. One boy, an Indian Sikh, felt very torn because of parental pressure to date only other Indian girls. He told me: "I would like to date outside my race because most of the beautiful girls are found outside my race. The girls in my race are too dark. Back in India, they are okay, but here in America, they are just too dark."

The girls did not speak this way about the boys. Racial and cultural standards of beauty and attractiveness as issues in dating appeared very present for the immigrant boys and almost wholly absent for the immigrant girls. Boys made a distinction, however. Dating was one thing; marriage was another. Most of the immigrant boys appeared to believe that marriage is separate and apart from issues of attraction and beauty. Although they began to accept standards of beauty and attraction that were white-derived, they were slower to give up notions of what constitutes a good wife. Parvinder, an Indian Hindu, said:

> I would never marry outside my religion because my race would be wiped out, and this would mean destruction of the ancient scriptures. I might marry if the person would adopt the Indian ways of religion and morality, though. It's not who they were when they were born, but the ways they adopt.

Another Indian student wrote in an essay about interracial dating:

> Most Indian boys and girls are not allowed to date at all, as their religion does not approve of this. So they do not experience such an event as dating a person outside their race. However, Indian students are not the only victims of such restrictions. Afghanistanis, Pakistanis, strict Japanese, Chinese, and Cantonese students also suffer from such a restriction. Generally, Asians are forbidden to date. And most Asian parents discourage their kids to get married or have close relationships with people outside the race. This must not be mistaken as racial discrimination as this is not the nearest of the truth. The reason as to such a restriction is that the Asian parents do not want their kids to have their race destroyed by having their kids being only 50 percent of their race. We are already far from our shores and this destroys our race if we are not careful. So marrying in your race is being careful.

In the eyes of immigrants, one of the shameful aspects of "being American" is not caring about preserving your "race" or your religion. In their equation, race and religion and language were used interchangeably. In all of these arenas, they viewed Americanization as a state of nonattachment to roots. Those boys seeking partners to carry on family and cultural traditions said they prefer to find girls who are not Americanized. This made some of the immigrant girls angry. Rosa, a Mexican Catholic, many times spoke of the contrasts between her brother and herself. Here, she talks specifically about the dilemma of being caught between standards of marriageability and standards of datability.

> My brother runs around and does what he wants, and I'm not allowed. I'm the girl, so they are careful of me. I have to be home and I cannot go out like my brother. But he's all wild and he likes to go with American girls. Then when he talks about how he wants to get a girl from Mexico to be his wife, and maybe he'll go back and find one, I get all mad. It's like he wants someone who will be like my mother is for my dad, and he knows American girls have a mind of their own. And I think, they [parents] are trying to keep me Mexican so I'll be a better wife and mother, but I'm not really Mexican anymore. I'm not Mexican enough for guys like my brother to marry. And I'm not American enough for guys like my brother to want to go out with. So what am I? And how come they get to have it like they want it?

ROMANTIC LOVE: "IF YOU BOTH LOVE EACH OTHER, THAT'S ALL THAT SHOULD MATTER."

From the perspective of many of the immigrant girls at Madison High, American's do not believe in the importance of family culture or roots. Respect for one's religion and tradition is replaced by something else, they think. Instead, Americans choose a kind of giving in to pleasure and romance. Immigrants therefore measure their own level of Americanization on a scale with romance at one end and respecting the authority of one's parents and one's traditions at the other. In Stern's class, student discussions after the project in which they had interviewed other students about interracial or intercultural dating divulged an interesting pattern. Most were supportive of the concept, but very few immigrants thought they would marry across race.

> Interracial relationships don't bother me, as long as you never forget who you are and where you come from. Me? Give me a

someone of my own people anytime because we come from the same place.

If they both love each other, that's all that should matter.

Relationships should be based on love, and race should never be an obstacle. I wish more people would accept interracial relationships.

I think they are fine if that's what people want. But for me, I want to marry someone that fits my family.

Even though almost half believed there is nothing wrong with interracial dating, the fact that their parents would not approve was sufficient reason to decide to marry within their race. "My parents wouldn't like it. They just couldn't accept it." "I think my father would die first. I wouldn't go against him."

However, they appeared to believe deeply that romantic love can transcend gaps of language, culture and race. Of the eighty-five students interviewed, every one agreed with the statement, "If you love each other, race doesn't matter in a marriage." During discussions, this theme continuously arose. As long as you love each other, skin color should not matter. This appears to be, however, the ideology of romance and does not seem to bear out in behavior. There are mixed couples at Madison High but, as discussed earlier, most dating is within narrow confines of same-race relationships.

For immigrant females, the new land opens a realm of possibilities including possible shifts in religion, changes in clothing and style and shifting allegiances to notions of romantic love as opposed to marriage as mechanisms for continuing tradition and culture. Some have made these shifts. Others chose holding on to their language and culture with determination because of increased marriageability to a partner in the old land. But most tried to negotiate a middle ground. The choices were seldom theirs alone. Feeling little control over the big decisions about whether, when, and whom they will marry and where their future may occur, the girls feel enormous pressure to keep options open, to be "modern" and "American" enough to gain the independence and freedom they view will give them potential escape from abusive or unfriendly marriages, to be sufficiently "traditional" to maintain close family connection, and to remain "appropriate" within the homelands to which they may need to return. They do not expect their parents or families to help them with these dilemmas. Usually, they felt that their parents were a force in holding them to their home culture.

Many perceived parents and family as caring about them to the extent that they pressure their daughters to behave in line with their traditional culture. Despite, or perhaps because of, their own ambivalence and the attractive pull of American ways of being "women," many really value the strictness of parents that keeps them connected somewhat to the home culture. But they also by and large really enjoy being in high school as a time and place that suspends some of the pressures of adult womanhood. Staying in school can forestall marriage. And as long as they are in school, they have a freedom to explore the realms of American romantic love and of American female teen styles, at least vicariously. Because this study did not follow the girls beyond high school, we cannot know what happens in their development of female adult roles beyond the protected and (in their words) "free" atmosphere of the high school. However, while in high school, they were engaged in making very different choices about hedging gender roles in order to prepare for the uncertainty of life that might set them adrift in a wholly "American" context or send them back to traditional contexts.

The choices for immigrant girls are a range from remaining fairly traditional within the cultural expectations of their home, to becoming fully "Americanized" into the independence, freedom, "openness," and sexuality that immigrant teens believe characterize their American female peers. In between is a wide band of possibilities. Individual immigrants try to find a place on that scale between "tradition" and "being American," where they lose the least connection to their home culture and gain the most options for independence. Each young woman defines that place differently, watching anxiously as her friends define their place in the spectrum. The process is one of constantly trying to gauge a future that feels up for grabs; to have it shaped by the actions and preferences of parents, by the luck of the draw in who one meets or who one marries, and by the veiled world of work about which most are inadequately informed. And in this process, schools play a key role as sites for experimentation, sources of obscuring information, and profferers of credentials.

Families are far more active in making explicit what they expect for their daughters as they become women than they are in other aspects changes confronting them in this new land. For this reason, the immigrants in this study felt the greatest pulls back to the home culture with regards to gender identity, more than they did with any other aspects of finding their footing in a new land. But unlike the transition to a new language in which schools have an explicit role, schools are not explicit about their mission in helping female students make a transition to womanhood. The subtlety of the silence and lack of action around vocational preparation and sexuality information supports the hazy view girls have of their options for the future. School is more than just the context and setting of such a drama. School is an institution that is directly involved. And the nature and shape of a newcomer's schooling experience is enacted by adults who are themselves buffeted by some massive changes in their community and culture.

CHAPTER SEVEN

Creating a Supportive Place
for Immigrants

IT'S A hot afternoon in January on the track behind Madison High. Ms. Williams, the physical education teacher, is trying to get a class of tenth graders to get moving and do their laps around the field. It's the last period of the day, and the heat seems to make it even harder for her to get students to be active. Shafiqa sits on the bleachers with a friend whose arm is around her. When Ms. Williams approaches and yells, "C'mon, girls, get up and get moving," Shafiqa's friend hesitates for a moment, then joins the stream of girls chugging around the field. Shafiqa doesn't move, and again Ms. Williams yells, "Do it! I don't have any patience today, get up and run." "I can't, Ms. Williams, I feel so weak. I haven't eaten since yesterday." Ms. Williams pauses. "What's the matter with you that you don't eat? Go to the canteen and get yourself a candy bar or something for quick energy, and be sure you eat something healthy after school. It's stupid not to eat." Tears begin to drop down Shafiqa's cheeks, and she barely manages to reply: "I can't eat . . . it's my family . . . my whole family . . . we're not stupid. . . . I can't eat today . . . please don't make me run." And Ms. Williams, exasperated and needing to turn her attention back to the whole class, writes out a note and hands it to Shafiqa. "If you won't even take care of yourself, go to the office and give this note to Mr. Boyd."

In the office, Mr. Boyd asks Shafiqa to explain why she wouldn't participate in p.e. class. When she tries to explain that she hasn't eaten, he pulls out an apple and offers it to her. As he does so, he mutters about the schools having to take on more and more parental responsibilities. "I'm going to call your parents, Shafiqa. They have to be responsible for seeing to it that you get breakfast in the morning, and they have to know that you're not doing what your teachers tell you to do." Shafiqa looks at the apple in horror, and sobs: "Please, Mr. Boyd, please, don't call my parents. Call Ms. Ahmadzai at the Newcomer School, please, she can explain and she can talk to my parents. It's Ramadan, I can't eat. She knows. Call Ms. Ahmadzai."

Mr. Boyd, knowing he won't be able to communicate with Shafiqa's parents, who do not speak English, *does* call the Newcomer School. When he reaches Ms. Ahmadzai, she agrees to speak to the parents if necessary, but tells Mr. Boyd that perhaps the school should consider easing up on physical requirements for Muslim children during Ramadan. "It is, you know, a holy time of the year for Muslims, and it is important to them that they fast. It might be a good idea for your p.e. Teachers at least to understand this." When he hangs up the phone, Mr. Boyd excuses Shafiqa and suggests she spend the rest of the period restfully in the library. Then he says, "I didn't know. I didn't know. How could I have known?"

■ ■ ■

Immigrant students attend classes, interact with peers and teachers, but have little awareness of the forces that are shaping where they are placed in the school system or the kind of program that awaits them. Whether immigrant students are separated from English-fluent schoolmates and placed in separate classes, and whether those classes are taught by credentialed and prepared teachers, deeply shapes what kind of access they are being given to an education in their new land. Who gets needed information about college preparation or about changing a schedule affects who ends up with the appropriate program that will prepare them for where they want to go in life. And all of these decisions about the shape of the program, teacher preparation and assignment, resources and materials, access to information are enmeshed in a daily struggle over how teachers and administrators view their roles in serving immigrant students, in addressing culture and language, in ensuring access. These are all matters that are greatly contested at Madison High.

The world the students know at Madison is just a quick slice in time compared to the length of time most faculty and administrators have been with the school. They have felt "their" community change in swift and dramatic ways. In just twenty years, Bayview, California, has changed from a small homogeneous, white working-class community to a richly diverse city because of massive human migration, which has brought immigrants from literally every continent to settle in Bayview. Although the ethnic makeup of the school has changed markedly in the past decade—from a primarily white student body to a student enrollment where there is no single majority ethnic or racial group, where dozens of different home languages are spoken, and almost one-fourth are immigrants— the faculty of the school mirrors an older Bayview. Most are white-skinned, speak only English, and many were raised in Bayview. They mostly value the diversity of their school, and the majority feels strong connections to the city. But Bayview is their home, and many speak privately of feeling "invaded" by outsiders.

It is a community deep in the throes of demographic turmoil, and attempting to proceed with the business of schooling in the midst of that turmoil. In fact, the school and community officially and publicly take pride in their diversity. The city launched a "diversity is our strength" public relations campaign and became active and mobilized in a fight over accepting a state-adopted social studies textbook series. Bayview was one of only a handful of school districts in the state that rejected the state's choice of texts because they were not sufficiently multicultural. The school district also boasts one of the first newcomer high schools in the nation, placing it on the map as an innovator in serving immigrants.

Still, underlying the apparent articulated support for diversity, a struggle takes place among the adults at Madison High over the meaning of and responses to the increasing diversity of their community. It has been a source and subject of overt ideological and political struggle in Bayview. It is a struggle between those who view the answer to diversity as conformity to a single cultural model and to a single language, and those who view the survival of a multicultural community as relying on embracing the differences and rectifying inequities between groups.

The educational program in which immigrants struggle to learn English, skills students and college-prep students receive fundamentally different curriculum, and immigrants attempt to understand lessons taught in a language they cannot yet comprehend has been created by that larger context. Central to their experiences is the formal program designed as a direct and deliberate intervention to serve the needs of limited English proficient students. Whether or not courses are made available for LEP students is a product of decisions by individual teachers based on their interest and willingness to provide them. Where do the policies that shape these programs come from? How do the programs get designed? What do we need to understand about the district, the school, and the design of secondary programs in order to unravel the intent and struggle over the responses to immigration that are played out in the daily lives of the people immersed in these programs?

Formally, in the eyes of school, immigrant students are viewed as LEP, or informally as the ESL kids. Based on a legislative history designating the schools' responsibility to address the language barrier for students who do not speak

English, schools label and serve students expressly in terms of their English-language fluency and language group. Yet, the adolescent immigrant student population presents a complex array of academic and other needs which go far beyond language. It is the combination of these that present such a challenge.

By definition, LEP students are not fluent in English. But at every grade level in secondary schools, there is a wide range within the LEP population of English-language fluency as well as academic background. Secondary school courses are designed based on assumptions about basic literacy skill levels and prior academic background in a sequential kindergarten through twelfth grade curriculum that has remarkable consistency throughout much of the nation. There are some immigrant students with excellent previous schooling (within or outside the United States), others with some gaps in their schooling, and still others (an increasingly large group of students) with little prior schooling who lack basic skills as well as academic content.

Those with excellent continuous schooling prior to immigrating to the United States are well prepared in many respects, but face difficulties because of being educated in national schooling systems quite different from U.S. schools. The curriculum content and sequence, the teaching pedagogy, and the particular skills that are emphasized may differ radically from U.S. schools. Thus, even those who arrive as adolescents with strong academic backgrounds face what can be a difficult transition to our forms of schooling, and unexpected academic gaps, particularly in subjects such as social studies or history. However, these students (usually from industrialized urban centers of the world and from middle-class or professional families) are confident in their abilities as students, and arrive with strong academic skills to apply to new content.

At the other end of the spectrum is an increasingly and highly visible group of students with little or no prior schooling and little or no basic literacy in their native language. They tend to be from rural, impoverished, or war-devastated regions of the world. Addressing the needs of the these students requires approaches to developing basic literacy in an accelerated fashion, and mechanisms for filling years of gaps in academic content. Few schools have classes to meet these needs. Finding the appropriate materials for these classes, finding teachers with the necessary skills, and creating a pedagogy and accelerated program are deemed major problems for secondary schools.

In between the two extremes in prior schooling experiences is a large group of continuing LEP students who have some oral English fluency and academic skill. At Madison High, this is estimated at around almost half of the 500 LEP students. The average continuing LEP student has a fourth- to sixth-grade academic skill level when he or she enters high school, far below the academic level expected for the standard ninth-grade curriculum. They may be orally fluent in English but weak in English reading and writing. In the course of their secondary school experience, most of the students evidently complete the full sequence of ESL classes, achieve oral English fluency, but are unable to be reclassified as fluent English proficient (FEP) or to compete in challenging academic areas.[29] Many are placed in remedial classes. Continuing LEP students have been gloomily labeled "ESL Lifers" by staff. Many others are simply placed in regular classes with no support, because they have enough oral English fluency that teachers do not recognize they still have not developed academic fluency or literacy in English. Within this group are immigrant students who arrived in the United States with some gaps in their schooling, which they were unable to overcome, and continuing LEP students from elementary schools. Teachers and counselors suggest that many of these students have failed to make progress because of transiency and mobility, which have resulted in large blocks of missed schooling in earlier grades. There is also some indication that as they moved from school to school, or from grade to grade, they had been enrolled in very different (and sometimes conflicting) pedagogical approaches to LEP programs.

The effects of this overall diversity of academic preparation across the three groups is profound. If Madison High ever decided to try to address the academic range of needs, rather than using English-language fluency as the sole measure for academic placement, the implications for staffing and student grouping and course sections needed would be major. However, at this point, the academic range simply adds complication to the specially designed "sheltered" academic classes and difficulties for students who end up grappling not only with English-language difficulties in grasping content, but also with real gaps in skills and knowledge. A framework that persists in viewing the issue solely as one of English language fluency negates the many issues in the lives of immigrant teens that affect their involvement and participation in school.

Immigrant students face more than simply the academic challenges in their lives. Legal and economic pressures of immigration, and problems of adapting to a new culture all affect LEP student participation in school.

School attendance problems are common among LEP students because of legal concerns and the financial condition of many immigrant and language-minority families. Perhaps as many as 40 percent of the immigrants in California have been estimated to be undocumented, although there are no specific estimates for the Bayview community and no clear numbers available overall.[30]

For students, this means fear of divulging family information that may lead to detention or deportation by the immigration officials, and tremendous legal pressures on the family, which result in transiency and accompanying school changes as a result. These fears have become particularly acute in the past year as the woes of society have been increasingly blamed on immigrants in general and the undocumented in particular. Legally documented or not, most LEP teenagers feel tremendous economic pressure to work to support themselves or to contribute to their families. Others have to stay home to take care of younger siblings so parents or other adults can work.

Trying to make comprehensible a whole new culture, language, and way of life can be very difficult for teenagers who have spent their childhoods in other nations and cultures. Even the logistics of schooling can be problematic. Bells ring and everyone moves around, lockers need to be opened, and food bought in cafeterias. Moving from class to class in large schools, few students are able to develop close relationships with any one teacher. With thinking and learning processes shaped by other cultural and national backgrounds, they need to figure out how we teach and learn in U.S. schools. Speaking out in class, participating in discussions, the relative informality between teacher and students are all quite foreign to students who have been educated in other cultures and nations. And trying to bridge two cultures, particularly for a teenager, can be painful and difficult. Juggling culturally different expectations about what it means to be a mature and responsible person and handling culturally different sex-role expectations is hard. They often feel caught between two worlds.

From relatively homogeneous cultures, the immigrant adolescent has to learn to live in our heterogeneous and racially stratified society. In many communities, the new immigrant is at the bottom rung of the social ladder. Many experience the social world they enter as hostile and unwelcoming. A recent California attorney general's report documented an increase in anti-immigrant hostilities and racially motivated hate crimes in schools and among young people.

The immigrant teenager at Madison needs to face and negotiate all of this at once. And little in the legislative or state and federal programmatic framework provides acknowledgment or support beyond the one dimension of English language fluency.

However, there were a few visionary advocates in Bayview who early on began to recognize the complexity of needs among secondary school immigrant children. As a result, the district became actively involved in trying new approaches. It became one of the pioneers in immigrant education at the high school level. Most of this innovation occurred within the Newcomer School that serves students from Madison High School and is located just across the street from Madison. Little of the innovation there actually affected life at Madison High. Nonetheless, in the lives of the immigrant students who daily cross back and forth between the two campuses, and in the political interplay of the district, the two sites are closely intertwined.

It starts with the day a new immigrant arrives to enroll in school. In Bayview, enrollment follows a state-required procedure. Students and parents are given a "home language survey" to determine if further assessment is needed. If a student comes from a home where a language other than English is spoken, the student is referred to the Newcomer School, where she is tested to assess her English-speaking skills and English academic skills. The Newcomer School has developed both staff and testing instruments to test academic skills in the child's home language as well, and students and parents are interviewed in their native language to determine the amount of previous schooling a child has had. Based on this assessment, students are assigned an academic schedule and program.

Most high schools offer two types of classes to LEP students: English as a second language and selected electives in the mainstream taught in English, such as physical education or music. Beyond the two common elements, schools vary widely in the program they offer to LEP students. At the Newcomer School in Bayview, teachers use the home language of students to teach social studies and math classes for those who are non–English speakers. There is a strong commitment to primary language instruction for non- and LEP students at the Newcomer School. Not so at Madison or at the other comprehensive schools in the district, where instruction in any language other than English is largely resisted. Madison provides a limited number of "sheltered" classes, and where these are not available, it simply places LEP students in regular mainstream classes with no special support.

Ideally, between the Newcomer School and Madison's comprehensive campus, LEP students would be provided with full content coverage—that is, all subject areas would be taught in classes designed to address their needs and with offerings at all grade levels. LEP students in full-content programs would be enrolled in a complete menu of classes in ESL, math, science, social studies, and electives. They would have access to the same core curriculum that students who do not face a language barrier receive. That is the meaning of equal educational opportunity. This does not occur, however.

One common pattern is of a partial program: a few classes available, sprinkled throughout all the core subject areas. There are insufficient class slots to accommodate all LEP students who need all the core content classes. And so, some LEP students receive a short schedule of classes. The remainder of the school day is spent in study halls, additional elective courses, or classes that they cannot comprehend in which they, as the common expression is used, sink or swim. LEP students may, for example, have math but no science, or science but not math. They may have one class taught in a sheltered approach and two that are not.

In fact, throughout California, very few schools offer a full menu of academic content classes to LEP students. In Bayview, there has been an effort to attempt to provide better access to the full curriculum. It has involved district-wide efforts, but these efforts have been deeply affected by a roller coaster of changes in district leadership and policy on LEP students and immigrant education.

THE DOUBLE-EDGED SWORD AND THE FOUNDING OF THE NEWCOMER CENTER

The challenge facing Bayview in designing a program for the influx of immigrants they began to experience about ten years ago was mirrored throughout the state and nation. By the late 1970s, a landmark Supreme Court decision in the *Lau v. Nichols* case made clear that "there is no equality of treatment merely by providing the same facilities, textbooks, teachers and curriculum . . . for students who do not understand English are effectively foreclosed from any meaningful education." The Court further stated that schools were required to provide "affirmative steps to rectify" the language barrier. The federal bilingual education program provided some funding to support the development of bilingual education, and in California a bilingual education law was in place establishing the "Language Census" to count the numbers of students with limited English proficiency.

In Bayview, Maria Rodriguez, called by some the "conscience" of the superintendent's cabinet, was given the job of bilingual coordinator for the school district. She had been hired in 1977 to be the coordinator of reading and language development for the Bayview unified school district. She was hired because the district wanted someone who was Spanish bilingual and who could (as she reports) "deal with bilingual issues." A year and a half later, the job of bilingual coordinator was added to Maria's title. The district already had a core of people committed to bilingual education, primarily at the elementary level. There were federally funded, special exemplary bilingual education programs in a few elementary schools, and the district was beginning to secure state bilingual education funds. The bilingual program in the district was completely supported by outside funds. There simply wasn't enough local consensus about a bilingual program, or commitment to the program to fund it out of local school district funds. Resentment was beginning to be expressed by many people in the district who viewed it as "extra money" for "those kids."

Here, the contentious national history of the fight over access for language-minority students was being felt in Bayview. "Outside" funds from the state and from the federal government for LEP programs had been earmarked as such, specifically in recognition that if they were not so earmarked, the locales would simply elect to not create the programs to meet LEP student needs. The courts and federal government were well aware that this intervention was necessary if educational access was to be provided for language-minority students. But the earmarking and protection of the funds was felt locally by many teachers and administrators as a slap in the face, and they viewed it as evidence that LEP and immigrant students were getting something extra that their "regular" students were not. According to Maria,

> I decided that my goal had to be to bridge the gap that had become created between bilingual and nonbilingual staff. There was a great deal of animosity from mainstream staff who felt the bilingual department was getting preferential treatment and support and materials. Such a strange position to be in, because it felt to me that we were constantly having to beg and scrounge for the resources we needed to even provide for LEP students what other students were given as a matter of course—instruction they can understand!

The focus of the district's bilingual programs had been on Spanish and Portuguese speakers. Not until the 1979 state Language Census, the very first language census, did it become visible and tangible that there were thirty languages other than Spanish and Portuguese in the district, and that there needed to be some support and services directed to those students. Rodriguez decided that creating visibility for these students would be a necessary first step. She worked hard to disseminate the census. She says:

> For many people in the district, secure in the picture of Bayview as a happily diverse district, and with a picture of that diversity in terms of long-term Spanish and Portuguese communities, this came as a shock. It was the first formal wake-up call that something new was going on in our schools. People began to notice

that they had kids in their classes who didn't speak English and
weren't just Spanish speakers. The Language Census was a stroke
of political brilliance because it broke the invisibility barrier.

Teachers and administrators from throughout Bayview began calling
Rodriguez. ESL students were showing up at schools where the staff had no
history in working with culturally and linguistically diverse students.
Rodriguez recalls: "Teachers were panicked. They'd say, "Help, I have a child
who doesn't speak any English and I don't know what to do with him. Somebody has to come and do something."

The high schools were experiencing the sudden influx of Vietnamese
from the fall of Saigon and an influx of Afghan students as well. The principals
added their cry, "Do something!"[31]

Rodriguez was beginning to feel the mandate from the field to do something and was looking for an opening to propose something new when, in
1980, the superintendent directed her to come up with a plan to serve newcomers. In her recollection, this step was largely motivated by information the
superintendent received from his Filipino immigrant gardener warning him of
the increasing immigrant wave. The superintendent was not a supporter of
bilingual education, but felt that something had to be developed for the burgeoning immigrant population in the secondary schools of the district.
Rodriguez recalls:

> This was a man who hated bilingual education, and hated the
> people associated with bilingual education and hated the peo-
> ple who liked bilingual education and were advocates for it. But
> he developed a sense from his Filipino gardener that the Filipino
> were coming; he saw the language census and knew something
> had better be done, and fast.

Rodriguez was advised to find a way to "take care of the problem" and to
design "some kind of program for LEP students" in secondary schools. His
message to Rodriguez had the flavor, according to her, of saying "Fix those
immigrants! Do something with them so they are more like us."

The LEP students were dispersed throughout the districts' high schools.
The lack of faculty at the comprehensive high schools with training and
the will to teach LEP students, and the multilingual population of the immigrants in the schools made it difficult to provide courses within the three

comprehensive schools. Rodriguez worked with a small team to design a centralized and coordinated district-wide model. Thus, the Newcomer High School was born.

The bilingual education advocates in the district were highly skeptical about this plan. They wanted the new center to say bilingual education explicitly, and they worried about the possibly segregatory implications of a separate-site program. Rodriguez recalls:

> I had very mixed feelings and worries that maybe this was the wrong strategy I was using. The advocates I trusted were suspicious of the plan, and some of the people who were the most adamant supporters of the Newcomer School were people who were supportive for the wrong reasons. They liked the idea we were going to take the kids off the hands of the home-base high schools and we were going to teach them English. That was the beginning of the double-edged sword. They want the kids taken care of, somewhere other than in their own classroom or school.

As Rodriguez retells it, "visibility" and formal recognition of the existence of immigrant students was a key strategy to get support. She made huge maps of the district, posting them with information on where the students were who did not speak English, in what numbers and in what languages. Who is out there? Where are they? She and one other person holed up in a room, brainstorming everything they knew about regulations—how funding works, about the Language Census, and about what was pedagogically appropriate at that time. The few resource teachers and bilingual classroom teachers in the district were brought in to provide input and react to the proposal.

Rodriguez was called to make a presentation to the superintendent's cabinet, the major advisory body to the superintendent. The original plan had a price tag of $650,000 per year. This was unacceptable to the superintendent. Luckily, this coincided with the first allowance that state compensatory education funds could be converted and designated for LEP students. The availability of those funds "turned water into wine." Rodriguez's plan involved no new district or local funds, only the redirection of state funds to follow the students. Every school receives a set amount of funding per student. Rodriguez's plan was to have half of the money each comprehensive school receives to serve immigrant students go to the Newcomer School to pay for the half day at the Newcomer School; the other half of this state-granted fund would remain with the homebase school. The superintendent approved the plan. This was good news, but it did not presage clear sailing. Rodriguez, like many bilingual advocates in visible positions, was a target of attacks:

> It was probably the worst year of my life. Everyone was highly suspicious of me. The federally funded bilingual program in the elementary school was eroding and it no longer had the central-ized support from the district that had been possible when the federal funds were there. And I was trying to establish this new-comer school in the midst of devastating politics of resentment about the attention and money going to immigrant students.

There was an attempt to abolish Rodriguez's position, despite the fact that the district was proceeding with the Newcomer School plan. Finally, a fight resulted in Rodriguez being assigned coordinator of the Newcomer School. She assembled in that school a cadre of the trained teachers in bilingual methodologies, and it became, by design, a haven of support for the bilingual advocates in the district. A change in superintendents gave them breathing space. Three superintendents came and went. Not until only several years ago, in the wake of budget crises and the beginning of a backlash against immigra-tion, did murmurs begin about shutting down the Newcomer School.

Nonetheless, Rodriguez spent much of her time battling the district office and the school principals about incidents of lack of access for immigrant and language-minority students, politicking to keep the Newcomer School alive, and trying to keep the district focused on issues of immigrant student needs. People began to call immigrant education "Maria's project." The personaliza-tion, marginalization, and efforts to undermine her ideas were similar to expe-riences other advocates were having at Madison High as well as throughout the state.

Personal support and involvements in the program at a nearby university in multicultural education, as well as in the bilingual education movement statewide, kept Rodriguez going and became necessary perspective balancers and supports.

> I would have gone crazy if I didn't have some place to go where people were reading and listening to the research on bilingual ed, where people believed in bilingualism as a good thing, and understood what I was trying to do. . . . I would start feeling

> really crazy, then I'd go to a class at the university, or a meeting
> with other bilingual coordinators, and then say to myself, oh
> yeah, you're not crazy at all.

In the fall of 1981, the Newcomer School finally opened in Bayview to serve secondary-school LEP students (grades 7 through 12) who were in greatest need (lowest English proficiency). The design of the Newcomer School was deliberately to create a place where human resources could be centralized to better meet the range of needs of the new immigrant students, and where separation from the mainstream school campuses could provide protection for the kind of advocacy and multicultural model and philosophy that bilingual advocates in the district wished to implement. The intent was to shelter and nurture the advocates for immigrants within the district, as well as to provide a space and capacity for needed services.

It did all this, and also began to serve as a magnet attracting immigrant advocate teachers from throughout the region. Hannah Chang was teaching in Sacramento when she heard about the establishment of the Newcomer School.

> I wrote a letter and applied and spoke with Maria. And to me, this
> place seemed like nirvana. It was a place where teachers collabo-
> rated; where teachers were involved in building something
> together; where everyone was trained in bilingual education
> issues and believed in them, and small enough so we wouldn't
> have to worry about the headaches of operating in the midst of a
> big school where no one believed in bilingual education. And
> Maria's ability was a big plus. To know there was an administrator
> who actually talked about methodology and curriculum! Heaven!

The Newcomer School functions as a centralized intake and assessment facility for immigrants entering high school, and serves also as an instructional center, or extension campus, of the comprehensive secondary schools. It provides English-as-a-second-language instruction, as well as primary language instruction for half of each day as needed by non-English proficient immigrant students grades 7 through 12. Students from five intermediate schools, three high schools (including Madison High) and one continuation school are bused at district expense between the Newcomer School and their homebase school.

The Newcomer School staff has special experience and advance training in working with immigrants. Every one of them has lived, studied, and/or worked in a nation outside the United States, and usually speaks at least two languages. All are proficient in English and hold advanced graduate training in the teaching of English as a second language. These teachers provide instruction at the Newcomer School and also serve as itinerant resource teachers, tutors, student assessment personnel, trainers, and translators to teachers at the "regular" comprehensive secondary school sites. They also serve as advocates for immigrant students within the district. Thus, the Newcomer School provides a wholly different educational and social setting for immigrant students than their homebase comprehensive high school where they spend half of each school day.

In 1981, there were 425 secondary LEP students in the district. The Newcomer School was prepared to serve 112 (approximately 25 percent). It was not anticipated that the numbers and percentages of LEP students would continue to escalate at the rate they did for the next decade. Ten years later, the Newcomer School was still serving 25 percent of the LEP students, but the number was now at 550. There was no physical space for further expansion, and the emphasis shifted to trying to develop expertise and will for providing sheltered language arts and ESL level V (advanced ESL) classes back at the regular high school campuses. The high schools were not altogether happy about this shift. The expectation on their part had been that the Newcomer School would "take care" of the problem and that their program could continue unhampered.

In 1992, the Newcomer School again was unable to serve the increasing numbers of students needing services, and had to shift even more responsibility to the home-base high schools. The numbers were overwhelming. Students with higher levels of English fluency were assigned full day to the high school campuses. Although the high school capacity to serve LEP students has improved over the past decade, many obstacles hampered steady development of sufficient programs to keep pace with student need. One of the impacts has been that many people at the high schools believe the Newcomer School should be delivering all the services and is failing at its task. They are also unprepared and somewhat unwilling to take responsibility for the increased numbers of LEP students who must be served in the comprehensive high school. The fact that they are being pressured to take more responsibility for immigrant students needs is felt as a failure of the Newcomer School to do their job. The attitude tends to be: "These are your kids. They belong at the Newcomer School. Why should we have to serve them and do your job for you?"

Thirteen years after the founding of the Newcomer School, the district's secondary school LEP population has doubled to over 25 percent of the total students in the district's high schools. Forty-two percent of the secondary-school population is "language minority" (from a home in which a language other than English is spoken). There are 1,243 LEP students enrolled in Bayview's high schools. The growth in LEP population far exceeds that of the general student population. Furthermore, more and more of the new arrivals have little or no prior experience studying English and little prior schooling at all.

Currently, the Newcomer School serves 412 students. The major language groups are Spanish, Dari, Vietnamese and Chinese, although seventeen languages from twenty-nine other countries are currently represented in the student population.

The Newcomer School still assesses all immigrant students for the district and recommends placement either for half a day at the Newcomer School and the other half at a comprehensive high school, or for a full day at a comprehensive high school, depending on their English-language fluency and academic preparation. The Newcomer School provides orientation support for newcomer students and parents. The Newcomer School is explicitly focused now on serving students who are non–English speaking or very limited English speakers.

To guarantee the academic success of students at the school, as well as to ensure close adult-student contact, primary language support is provided. Newcomer School personnel fluent in nine of the major languages spoken by students provide help with the academic courses students take at their high schools as well. Currently, Spanish speakers are able to take U.S. And world history bilingually at the Newcomer School. Movement from level to level is made quarterly, and the master schedule and teacher assignments can be changed quarterly to accommodate the needs of students and provide maximum flexibility in movement through the system.

At the homebase high schools, the more advanced levels of ESL classes are provided, and there is an occasional "sheltered" content class in core subjects offered as teachers become available. None of the schools have ESL departments, and there is very little programmatic attention on immigrant education at the comprehensive high schools. Each school site does have a part-time resource teacher assigned to coordinate the program for LEP student who is paid for by the Newcomer School's special funding for immigrants. Beyond this there is little sense of responsibility or actual staff assigned to deal with their needs.

Over a thirteen-year period, Rodriguez has fought to keep the Newcomer School program alive through many changes in district leadership, massive budget problems, and shifting political climes. This has not been easy. The principals of the high schools are strong proponents for the Newcomer School, largely because it relieves them of the complexities of serving the students at their own schools. The principals in the three comprehensive high schools have autonomy and (in the void of district leadership) establish their independent leadership tones, making their own decisions about whether and how to advise or insist that LEP services be provided, whether or not to hire teachers with the skills needed to serve LEP students. There is largely a laissez faire attitude in the district.

THE DEVELOPMENT OF MADISON'S PROGRAM: LAISSEZ FAIRE AT THE TOP, ADVOCACY FROM THE BOTTOM

George Pereira has been the principal at Madison High for eighteen years. Though some of the faculty at the school predate Pereira, he has been responsible for bringing in the great majority of the teachers, cultivating his own administration and exercising great district-granted autonomy in developing the program at Madison. Pereira is a central figure at the school. He is friendly, and generally a supporter of whatever innovations teachers care to initiate. He is not particularly involved as a curricular leader, leaving that to the teacher leadership in the school.

Deeply concerned about providing a voice for "all students," Pereira is uncomfortable being a voice for any particular group of students. He feels that to do so is divisive, and that good education is good education across the board—the same treatment for all. Thus, he has not provided a leadership voice regarding meeting the needs of immigrant and LEP students. Availability of teachers trained to offer either primary language instruction or sheltered academic content instruction to LEP students, and availability of sections and courses for LEP students to take, is left to individual teacher choice and willingness to provide the courses, or to department chairs to decide that they want to speak out on behalf of adding sections of classes to serve these students. New courses, of course, require resources. The decision to add a course is not made lightly. There are few new courses or course sections added to meet the needs of LEP students.

The unwillingness of Madison teachers to participate in special training programs is an important limiting factor for the secondary LEP programs. Even among those few who have the training, willingness to provide the courses is a second limitation. Bayview, like most districts in California, has a state-approved plan to remedy the shortage of LEP staff. But because of both severe budget constraints and lack of strong leadership, it fails to offer the mandates or the range of incentives, paid training opportunities and special bonuses to teachers to take LEP program training, which some other districts provide. If individual teachers do not respond to the opportunities for such training, there is no mechanism and no pressure applied to compel or entice teachers to do it.

The departmentalization of Bayview (as is true with most secondary schools) also has major repercussions for the program for LEP students. Madison has a part-time ESL coordinator, who works with the Newcomer School to monitor the placement of LEP students in classes at Madison. But while she monitors placement, she is not formally in charge of a comprehensive approach to LEP student programming. She has no particular authority over the master schedule, the opening of needed course sections in academic content areas (such as math, social studies, etc.), the placement of teachers, or the budget. In fact, there has been strong resistance by the principal and others in the school to every suggestion that has been made by Newcomer School staff and the Madison ESL coordinator about according the ESL division departmental status necessary to grant resources or autonomy regarding developing new course sections. It is left up to each regular content area chairperson to respond to the academic course needs of the LEP student. Few have training or understanding of issues related to language and culture, and few feel it is a high priority to ensure that specially designed courses are provided for LEP students. Availability of content courses for LEP students, assignment of teachers, grouping and clustering of LEP students in content areas falls to these content area chairs. Almost none are assertive in developing a program for LEP students; most are resistant. The priorities and philosophies about whether and how to serve LEP students varies across the school's departments. The result is limited and uneven access to content courses.

Tension exists between the ESL and sheltered-course teachers and the mainstream teachers. Some faculty members feel that the ESL teachers are trying to "coddle" the LEP students and hence hold them back. The ESL and sheltered teachers feel that the majority of other faculty is refusing to deal with the academic needs of the LEP students. Lack of data or oversight about how LEP students are doing academically results in a lack of attention to the issue— and feeds the tension because no one has adequate data to back up his or her position. This tension is exacerbated because the principal does not articulate an overall philosophy or vision for the LEP program.

As a result of default leadership, decisions about programs are made by individual department heads or individual teachers based on their own preferences, levels of understanding or lack of understanding about the needs of immigrant/LEP students, and personal politics. One of the teachers in the Newcomer School who sought to raise the issue of availability of sections for LEP students at Madison High explained:

> The department heads don't believe in bilingual classes. They won't go searching for the textbooks; they don't try to figure out the proper levels for placing kids. I suggested they cluster the lowest ESL kids together in single sheltered classes so maybe a bilingual aide could work with them. But the department heads refused. They would rather scatter kids throughout the classes so it puts less burden on any one teacher. It's a constant struggle to make this an issue of kids' needs and not teachers' needs.

Within each department, teacher assignment to LEP classes is a highly political issue. The assignment is considered "voluntary." But overall, seniority and the ability to negotiate within the faculty hierarchy determines who can avoid and who gets assigned "undesirable" courses—who is pressured to volunteer and who can resist that pressure. LEP content classes are viewed by most teachers at Madison as an undesirable assignment. The difficulties of teaching students with whom one does not share a language, the lack of adequate training available and materials and resources for those courses, contribute to this resistance.[32] Furthermore, the teacher-student relationship is a fundamental aspect of the working conditions for the teacher and directly affects his or her commitment to his or her work and sense of efficacy. Skills courses are similarly assigned to teachers. The new hires in the school end up with disproportionate numbers of skills and sheltered classes.

The anticipated difficulties of establishing a relationship with students with whom teachers have trouble communicating, and of working with students they perceive to be at a relatively low level of academic skills, is sufficient to maintain a system in which those teachers with leverage use it to avoid working with LEP students. But the resistance goes beyond this. Teaching LEP students is considered low-status work at Madison High.

All of this is a major force shaping the LEP program at Madison. The frustration of trying to teach large classes of students across gaps in language and culture without appropriate materials and little or no training, has been exacerbated in recent years by the increase in the number of LEP students who do not have strong academic backgrounds in the content areas. The pressure from teachers to get LEP students *out* of their classes has been a major factor in the adoption of sheltered classes and a major element in why the Newcomer School is so popular as a district intervention. It removes lower-level ESL students from many other classrooms at Madison. But to create a sheltered class requires a teacher to teach it. Hence, Madison does not offer a full menu of academic content to LEP students.

Even in those courses offered, there are problems. Teachers offering sheltered sections often complain about problems in getting the materials needed for their LEP students, lack of time for curriculum development, and lack of support in accessing what might be available in the school or district. There are no native-language reference materials in the classrooms at Madison, although the Newcomer School does have them. Teachers also complain about the problem of a lack of materials written specifically for the purposes of sheltered-content instruction. They yearn for books that use simplified vocabulary but are written for the level of content and conceptual sophistication required for the academic content. Individual teachers do try to find their own solutions to this problem by buying their own books, seeking help on their own. But time and money are scarce for teachers in Bayview. Because most are young new teachers at Madison, the overload of creating their own units and trying to find their sea legs as teachers is overwhelming. This results overall in serious gaps in materials and ambiguity in what is taught.

English-as-a-second-language classes are generally taught by newer, young teachers with some certification or training in ESL techniques. Though it is clear that the quality of the instruction varied from teacher to teacher, there are very few complaints about issues of assignment or training from the ESL staff.

The result of the lack of sufficient sheltered courses, and the resistance to serving LEP students whose English skills are not strong in the advanced courses of the curriculum, is that large numbers of students who are designated LEP simply don't get the courses they need. Half of the LEP students are not in classes designed to address their language needs. These students are largely placed in mainstream regular classes. The situation worsened in the two years of research. Out of almost 500 LEP students, 333 were "not enrolled in any LEP instructional program" according to the annual language census at the school.

As teachers who have some training in second-language acquisition pedagogies and who were willing to teach LEP students have left the school because of the uncertainty of jobs in the district and demoralization over teaching conditions, the availability of sections has diminished. For those students who attend the Newcomer School in the morning, there are no math classes available at Madison High. Fewer sections are being offered, and teachers have not stepped forward who are willing to teach the courses. The leadership at the departmental level, and at the principal and administrative level, has not insisted they be offered. It has thus fallen to the advocates to try to pressure at all levels (individual teachers, the department chairs, and the administration) so that such classes are offered in the future.

Ironically, in creating special-educational programs to respond to civil rights mandates, Madison (and other schools in Bayview) increasingly appear to be creating a separate system for their LEP students. These separate classes are unsupported, without the needed texts and materials, and often staffed with new teachers and those without training in sheltered methods. And while there is some improvement in the access students are getting to education because they are in classes in which there is some effort to help them understand the instruction, it is still far from the level of access to education that their English-fluent schoolmates are receiving.

The formal curriculum separation has both academic and social prices. The lack of contact with English-speaking students may well reduce the motivation, let alone the opportunity actually to use English. In addition, social division between LEP and English speaking students is more difficult to overcome. As illustrated by the social maps of the newcomer and native-born students, and their discussions about relations with each other, the social price is high.

For those students who are not in a program designed for LEP students, their contact with English-speaking peers may be more frequent (though not necessarily more positive), but their access to the curriculum is severely hampered by placement in classes which are taught by untrained teachers and without provisions to address their language needs.

WILL THE TWAIN EVER MEET? MADISON HIGH AND THE NEWCOMER SCHOOL

At Madison, the immigrant students, at least those who are limited English proficient, participate in two different institutional worlds of school. They spend half their day taking classes across the street at the Newcomer School, and the other half day at Madison.

When Rodriguez designed the Newcomer School, the documented state and local shortage of human resources to serve the many immigrant language groups and the existence of very few trained teachers within the district made the concept of aggregating limited resources in one centralized location very attractive. The long-range plan had always been, however, to develop expertise and capacity within the comprehensive high schools over time to serve this new population of their students.

Among the teachers at the Newcomer School who serve as the major advocates for immigrant students within the district, the mood is one of frustration. As they grapple with trying to push the comprehensive high schools and the district leadership to provide access to core content courses for immigrant students despite cuts in faculty and support services, they have become increasingly aware of the double-edged sword that the separate Newcomer School program has created. At a meeting of some of these teachers, several concerns were identified.

The Newcomer School has become a somewhat isolated island of services for immigrant students. For immigrant students, their experiences at the Newcomer School and at their homebase high school have little connection. This is particularly true because budget cuts forced the abolishment of most counselors and the elimination of on-site and cross-site curriculum councils. Teachers of the same immigrant students at the two sites have little communication and cannot sufficiently monitor the progress of students or provide the articulation and counseling support needed. The existence of the Newcomer School, and the concentration of the districts' scarce supply of trained bilingual teachers and of those people who are focused on advocacy for immigrant students within the Newcomer School, have both relieved the comprehensive high schools of the pressure to respond to LEP student needs, and drained them of teachers who might be sharing expertise and serving LEP students within the homebase high schools.

An insufficiently prepared teaching force in Bayview secondary schools and a growing number of immigrant students have created the need to expand beyond the core of trained teachers at the Newcomer School to the creation of a mainstream teaching force within the comprehensive high schools that is prepared to work effectively with immigrant students. This is the rub. How to create an understanding of the need, develop a commitment to serve this group of students, deliver the training to teachers, and find the resources—all of which are necessary in order to offer appropriate classes. None of the high schools in the district has sufficient sheltered or bilingual teachers to serve the number of LEP students who need targeted instruction. The lack of this teaching force results in almost 60 percent unserved LEP students in the comprehensive high schools. Progress towards developing such a teaching force has been painfully slow. With specially funded federal support, fifty-six high school teachers have received training in second-language acquisition, sheltered

instructional approaches, and cross-cultural instruction through the Newcomer School. Of these, fifteen have left the district since their training, a loss
of over 25 percent. Madison has been much more heavily affected than other
schools in this regard.

Because many of those who are receiving training are the younger and
more newly hired faculty, layoffs and layoff notices have played a major role in
pushing these teachers to seek jobs outside of Bayview. The district is not able
to draw on a pool of new teachers with the training and preparation necessary
for working with immigrant students. There are, as yet, no nearby teacher education programs providing a pool of prepared new secondary teachers in this
field. Without this pipeline of trained new teachers, Bayview has had instead to
rely on enticements to get its current teachers into training programs that will
lead to the needed credentials and skills. And admidst the politics of Bayview,
this is an unlikely and resistant pool.

The anticipated capacity building at the comprehensive high school sites
has been severely hampered by the fiscal situation in the district:

> steady budget cuts of the general funds, which have affected
> all (including LEP) students;

> reductions in staffing formulas, which have adversely affected
> the total numbers of teachers and corresponding sections of
> courses that can be offered as part of the school program
> (including LEP student sections);

> a high turnover in nontenured and low-seniority teachers
> because of several consecutive years of "pink slip" layoff
> notices delivered by the district to teachers due to budget
> cuts—especially affecting the newer teachers who have more
> often received some preparation and training for working
> with LEP students;

> the abolishment of district-level teacher support positions
> for district wide curriculum and instruction issues.

None of this has anything to do directly with immigrant or LEP students,
but the severe budget crisis facing the district has deep implications for their
capacity to provide access. No immediate relief of these conditions is anticipated.

The "temporary" influx of new immigrants, which the district prepared to serve in the Newcomer Center thirteen years ago, has clearly lasted and there is no projected end to the immigration wave in the immediate future. What began as a temporary solution is no longer sufficient. There is no mechanism, however, for working out a more contemporary and permanent solution. Because of the major budget cuts in the district, there is no longer a bilingual coordinator position. Maria Rodriguez has now left the district and no replacement has been made. There have been three superintendents in two years and a complete turnover in the school board.

The "problem" of how to best serve LEP students is left then to the daily push and pull of negotiations between the staff of the Newcomer School and the staff of the comprehensive high schools, and to the interactions between those who view themselves as advocates for immigrant students and those who may be uninterested, unfocused, or unwilling to take on these concerns.

The issue of serving LEP students is furthered hampered by broader politics in the district. Teachers in the Bayview district were working without a contract for almost the entire period of time in which this research was conducted. Morale and trust in the system's ability and willingness to support the work of teachers are low; the sense of being overwhelmed is high. The negotiations over who is serving (and who should serve) LEP students are occurring within this context. It is a polarized and difficult dialogue, in which teachers at the Newcomer School band with the few young teachers of the sheltered and ESL courses at Madison High, to do battle with demoralized, veteran teachers and administrators at Madison. This dance over what will be offered for LEP students and how LEP students will be greeted institutionally at Madison is a key fact of life buffeting the immigrant students who arrive on the doorstep of the school to enroll. And it is a battle that embroils the adults in the school who are charged with implementing the academic program.

CHAPTER EIGHT

Adults in the Crossroads

MARIA RODRIGUEZ, coordinator of the Newcomer School and bilingual coordinator for Bayview Schools, had been my means of entry to Madison High School. It was her work as founder of the groundbreaking Newcomer School and as an advocate for immigrant student issues that first drew my attention to this community almost ten years ago. And it was Maria who arranged for my lunch meeting with George Pereira, principal of Madison High School, to discuss whether I might do a study of the school. She arranged the meeting as an off-campus lunch in a restaurant in downtown Bayview.

I approached the lunch nervously and was anxious to show that I had done my homework and that my reasons for wanting to study Madison were based on an understanding of the student population at the school. I arrived early with a file full of demographic statistics about the community. Pereira arrived a little late to the lunch, a big smile, a warm handshake, a hug for Maria. He and Maria began what I came later to understand was the ritual greeting of high school principals: a conversation about what happened at the last cabinet meeting, references to the latest political upheavals in the district, an anecdote about some frantic or crazy episode at the school site that morning that almost threatened to make him unable to get away from the school and was the cause of being slightly late. When Maria got up to go to the rest room, I used the opportunity of the break in their conversation to begin my explanation of why I wanted to study Madison High. In the first few minutes, I mentioned the swift and astounding growth of immigrant and limited-English-speaking students at the school to now being 24 percent—almost one in four. He seemed surprised. "You must be wrong—the numbers are off. We have a lot of diversity, but your numbers are wrong. We've had some growth, but it's nowhere near that high. It's more like maybe 12 or 15 percent."

I was embarrassed by the fact that my numbers were wrong, but the conversation continued. The lunch was pleasant. Pereira was thoroughly agreeable about my doing the research. He liked the idea that someone was interested in the school and might write a book about it. By the end of the lunch, we agreed that I would do research at the school over the next two years.

Later that day when I got home, I checked my files. Yes, I had recorded 24 percent LEP students in my notes. I called the Newcomer School to check the accuracy. They confirmed the 24 percent. I called Maria to debrief her about the lunch, and told her of the confusion over the percent of LEP students. "George should know that. For years I've been putting the language census numbers out there for all the principals in the district. I'm constantly passing along statistics to them, talking to them about the growth of LEP students. It just doesn't register."

I came to look back on that first lunch as an early warning and preview of the force with which the reality of population change is contested and resisted in this community, and the subtle efforts to maintain or reduce the invisibility of immigrant students as a point of struggle.

■ ■ ■

The program that serves immigrant students at Madison High is created by a complex interplay of formal policy, history and tradition, and the passions and intentions of the adults charged with implementation. In the struggle over whose needs and whose purposes Madison High School should serve, the lives of individuals intersect: those who view themselves as maintainers of a social order, and those who view themselves primarily as changers of that order, and those who think nothing of either of these positions and pursue other projects in life as teachers, workers, citizens. It is a drama, a struggle that is sculpted by and played out by people whose life histories, views of the world, fortunes and fates have placed them in the crossfire of demographic and social change. They try to make meaning out of the changes in their school and community, find their places in the politics of their time, and create a life, a stance, a place within the dynamics of Madison High School.

It is the faculty and administrators whose jobs are to teach, supervise, and "serve" the students at Madison High. The social and programmatic worlds they create are complex and busy. Beginning early in the morning, they teach their classes, and engage with others during the quick breaks between classes about subjects as riveting and diverse as committee work for school restructuring, union contract issues, planning assemblies, upcoming conferences, family problems, and rumors. The faculty of eighty split at various times into their own friendship groups, cliques, departments, and committees. There is one sharply vivid and salient division that permeates the faculty with strong implications for this story; the division between younger and older faculty, and between those who teach English-as-a-second-language and sheltered-academic classes on the one hand and those teachers who do not. It is a division that serves to contain the voices of those teachers (mostly young and working with the newcomer students) who believe the school needs to change to better serve and to embrace the immigrant newcomers. The world of the faculty reflects the programmatic structure that leaves immigrants at the margins of the school society.

All of the comprehensive high school principals in Bayview are white men in their mid- to late fifties, who have been high school principals in the district for many years. Their schools are, in some ways, fiefdoms. George Pereira has been the principal at Madison High for nearly twenty years. The vast majority of his faculty has been there for a long time as well. His style is friendly and relaxed. He is known by students and teachers alike for warmth, strong authority, and occasional and sudden (but short-lived) outbursts of anger. He is the kind of principal who is often seen around the campus shouting greetings to students or stopping and watching the lunchtime dancing in the Quad. He wears silly Halloween costumes and cheers loudly for school teams. Pereira seems sincerely to like the Madison community and takes deep pride in its accomplishments. He runs a smooth ship and is credited by the community for doing so.

Pereira's leadership style is to keep things generally running smoothly, to avoid intervening in the educational program of the school, leaving it instead to teachers to do what they do within the limits of what he considers acceptable. He likes to know what is going on around campus, but generally teachers feel free to pursue their ideas. Often the limits are discovered by teachers only when they do something Pereira regards as inappropriate and get called to his office to be told so.

The overall tone at the school for the teachers, largely set by Pereira but cocreated by the veteran faculty, is that Madison is a good, friendly, traditional comprehensive high school that offers students choices. In their view, there are students who work hard and students who choose not to do so. They believe their school is a good place for all kinds of kids, including those who are not academic and do not want to go to college. As one long-time teacher said:

> We've always been a good high school for the middle of the road
> kinds of kids who aren't too ambitious. They're good kids, and
> we're a good old high school. They're going to graduate from
> here and do the same kind of jobs their parents do—nothing
> fancy. Some will shine and go on to college, but most don't.

Teachers emphasize that the importance of school "for these kids" is "getting a basic education" and learning to "get along." During a number of indepth interviews with faculty, teachers explained that most Bayview kids "aren't going anywhere," "aren't going to be rocket scientists," "just want to find a satisfying way to make a living", and "don't have high expectations for themselves." And then, each assured me that at Madison, this is fine. "We're a really accepting place."

Although anger at the central school district administration is strong in the midst of this current fiscal crisis, and there is enormous frustration among faculty and the administration about the effects of budget cuts and perceived district mismanagement, when it comes to the internal functioning at Madison, the majority of teachers seem to feel things are generally okay as they are.

A majority of the staff at Madison has been at the school for fifteen years or more. Generally, the teachers who have been around for a while do not look to quitting, but rather to trying to maintain their jobs in as manageable and familiar ways as possible. They seek to be assigned the "best" classes, usually meant as the classes with the most motivated, hardest-working, and "college bound" students. They, in the words of the chair of one department, "wait out the trends and just keep doing what we're doing." They are rooted in Bayview and expect to retire from the district. To transfer to another district would mean a loss of earned salary tiers. Yet, the world they face by staying is a changing one. And the teachers at Madison generally speak about the changes in their job as a product of two factors: the worsening budget crisis facing the schools and the increasing "diversity" of the student population.

THE MEANING OF DIVERSITY: A STRUGGLE OVER IDEOLOGY

There is no question that Madison High is diverse. Most faculty remark on this when describing the school community, and say it with an air of pride. But the dimensions of that diversity remain unstated and in many cases unexplored.

Some of the veteran teachers lament the poor performance of their students today compared with students of the past, and link this to a complex interweave of declining values, increases in family problems, and the advent of increasing diversity on the campus. Comments such as the following are linked in these conversations: "Parents don't really care anymore," "Kids don't care anymore," "A lot of the cultures now don't value education," "We have more of the kids with family problems," "The groups that are moving in, the parents don't really discipline their kids." There is a also a sense that campus life is more precarious in general.

Their view of Madison High and Bayview is rooted in the past, where there was more unity and more focus. And concerns are expressed about "groups" who are unwilling to adopt a common culture, refuse to set aside differences, and are unwilling to adopt American values and languages. These are general comments. People seem reluctant to get more specific.

And yet, diversity is "celebrated." At Madison, the existence of people from other cultures and nations is acknowledged by almost everyone. Often, these acknowledgments are coupled with comments about how lucky the school is that everyone gets along. Emphasizing any differences among groups, calling attention to past injuries or struggles between groups in society, naming current inequities or exclusions are viewed as impolite, divisive, and dangerous. Lisa Stern's attempt to call attention to the division of students by class into "skills" and "college bound" levels, was an example of such behavior.

> I just don't see getting all worked up about all of these issues. It's the way schools are. It's the way our society is. We've got so many issues that you could get worked up about. I think you just have to focus on your teaching, not get sidetracked by all the things you could get worked up about. What's the point?

By reports of the principal, the school has been particularly well integrated in the past two years. When nearby Washington High School closed several years earlier, students from areas farther away from the school were assigned to Madison. Predominantly Latino, and many immigrants among them, this group did not become quickly or easily integrated into the life of Madison. The first year the schools were combined, there were many fights between Madison and Washington students. Pereira says all that is in the past, and his perspective is that the school is now fully integrated. Most teachers also report that the school is well integrated.

Students, however, report another reality. For the non-newcomers, the social life and structural life of the school is largely defined in terms of racial/ethnic separation. For the newcomers, it is largely defined in terms of nationality and language. But from both of these student perspectives, the social world is highly divided.

The social changes so evident in reviewing the student population in the past few decades at Madison are only partially apparent among the faculty, which is 82 percent white. Of eighty-one faculty members, fourteen have been at the school since it opened in 1960. Approximately 30 percent have been hired within the past five years, most of them young and relatively new to teaching. And most simply do not believe that the new population of students requires any changes in teaching approaches or programs.

Despite a state-mandated district plan written to remedy the shortage of available teachers to serve LEP students, few of the new hires at Madison have training or preparation to serve LEP students. Most teachers do not believe they need any additional training in order to serve the new diversity at Madison High, and most either bristle at suggestions that changes in what they do as teachers might be necessary, or simply go about their lives as teachers without giving it a thought.

Sandra Richards is a home economics teacher. Her view on diversity is reflective of many of the veteran teachers. She is passionate and outspoken about the need to end prejudice, and is proud of the diversity of her community. The key element about diversity, in her view, is that everyone is basically the same. Her job as a teacher is, she feels, to help students to break the way things have been done in their families. This conviction permeates her teaching:

> I believe very strongly in the fact that what happens in the family and what you do with your personal life is the primary determining factor in how successful you'll be in your life and career. It has nothing to do with your skin color or your language. Particularly for students here in Bayview, the important thing is that they learn essential living skills. It's not the academics that matter. It's not your skin color. Whether I teach home economics or an economics class, I teach the same thing. You'd better have some idea of what you can do with every single thing you learn relative to your future. Our kids more and more are coming from dysfunctional families, single parents, broken homes, and it all goes back to the kind of parenting they get. I want to help kids

break that cycle. And break that cycle of believing that life owes them something.

This perspective is related both to class factors and to racial/cultural and ethnic factors:

I believe in diversity and I believe that's the way people need to learn to live. Bayview is a special place, and Madison is probably even more special. People have chosen to live in Bayview because they don't value a snobby environment, because they want to raise their children in the real world, because they want their children to think of values that are more important than how fancy your house looks and what neighborhood it is in. People chose to live in Bayview because it is diverse. People that don't want that can move to Sun Valley or other suburbs over the hill. And we've had some stability. There's new immigrants of course, but we've always been diverse. I have the children of parents I had in the past as students. Most of Bayview has been around for a long time. It's always been diverse. This is the real world.

To Richards, the racial, national, and linguistic diversity now is basically equivalent to the diversity of Bayview in the past. Thus, what is occurring now is not remarkable and requires little notice. The word "diversity" is used broadly by Richards, as it is widely throughout the school, and is wholly ambiguous. Richards' second assertion, that diversity defines the "real" world, is also heard widely. With a badge of pride at being part of a tough real world, new teachers and old teachers, students and administrators alike talk about Madison as the "real world." This sometimes has negative, sometimes positive connotations.

This is the real thing at Madison. Kids who go to Madison learn to make it in the real world. If you can get along here with all our diversity, you can get along anywhere. It's preparation for the world.

This stance of "real world"-ness is also used as a defense when issues of poor student achievement are raised. For lower expectations, the excuses abound. One teacher explained:

> You know if you teach in one of the schools in the suburbs, of
> course your kids do great. When the test scores get published
> in the paper, and there's all the hoopla about which schools
> are good and which districts are good, you got to take it with a
> grain of salt. Yeah, if you've got a certain class of students,
> you're going to look good. But this is the real world here. We've
> got kids with lots of problems, kids of all cultures, kids who don't
> speak English. We're not going to look so good in comparison
> to other schools.

The pride in diversity is evident. Pereira once pulled me into the main office to watch the school television channel broadcast a portion of a student performance the night before. Three girls were lip synching a Supremes song. One of the girls was Chinese, one Filipina, and one black.

"See," he remarked, "we're such a melting pot! We've got something special here—the real world." He seemed to feel deep pride in the diversity and the mixing of students which was evidenced in the video.

When asked directly about the racial, ethnic, language, or national composition of the student body, most of the teachers will say that they do not notice skin color or who is what race, but that the school is mixed racially and ethnically. One teacher told me: "This is a great school—everyone just gets along. It's like a United Nations."

Another teacher said to me: "We have a lot of different kinds, but I don't see color. None of us really do, we just see all our students as the same. That's what is so wonderful about Madison, we're not all divided like some schools are."

Most of the veteran teachers seem to share this sense of Bayview as always having been diverse and a perspective that the multicultural student body gets along well. The attitude of "seeing all our students as the same" is part of the glue that makes it all work. This means that the formulas and approaches they have used all along should be sufficient and appropriate for students now. To this perspective, nothing is significantly different. If students are not doing well now, something must be wrong with the students' attitudes, values, or cultures.

Richards, for example, describes her approaches, explaining why nothing needs be to be done differently simply because of the influx of immigrants:

> We've always celebrated diversity in my child-development
> classes. We find out where somebody's from, and I think people
> meet and make friends and become close to people they didn't

know before they started taking the class. Just being in a class together is a wonderful way to bridge cultures. But then color and culture is just not a factor. We emphasize how we are really all alike. That's important for getting along. And I believe that once you are living here, there is really just one pattern I should teach about raising children. I feel a child needs to know their culture and value it, but they are living here, they have to make it work and raise the children the way they are raised here. If you help a child develop a positive self-concept, they will be able to do well and succeed, and that's what we are about—helping them do well. There is a real cultural attitude in some groups that if you don't knock your children around a little, they won't know who is boss. I have to in my classes let them know that that isn't going to make a child develop responsibility and succeed. Now if that's considered tearing down that cultural value, then it is, and that's okay. I don't think there are differences in the basic ways that you raise healthy and strong children to be responsible, productive, and successful. So I don't want my students to discuss child-rearing practices in Iran, for example. It wouldn't be helpful. I think it helps our students to determine that people can be different colors, they can come from different places, they can speak different languages, but that we all share in common an understanding of how to raise children to succeed in this country. We've got a good way to do it and that's what they need to learn. If they keep doing it the old way, they're doomed to have trouble because they are living here.

Because they believe that Bayview has always been diverse and is no different now, and that one form of diversity is the same as any other; because they do not see that issues of second-language acquisition and culture presented by the major influx of immigrants raises new pedagogical issues; because they believe that teaching in a diverse setting implies stressing commonality and a common single knowledge base, it is no wonder they do not see the need to make accommodations in their teaching as the population of students changes. It is this sense that nothing needs to be done differently that leads to the general resistance of many faculty to seeking training in sheltering techniques or second-language acquisition in order to teach LEP students. Suggestions that they might need new skills are generally met with hostility. The veteran teachers who have honed their skills and settled into ways that seem to work for them bristle at suggestions that there might be a need for new skills or new approaches, feeling it insults their years of experience. A few teachers, feeling that some of the same old ways are perhaps not working for the new students, have on their own begun to seek professional development related to second-language acquisition and teaching students who are limited in English. This is voluntary, and still involve a small number of the overall faculty. Teacher training focused on serving the new immigrant population is a hot issue. In the context of labor problems in the district, teachers already feel exploited and angry. The suggestion from the district office or from advocates that there is something they have to do in order to be better teachers is hardly welcome. Few know or understand what the content of the training is, and many have had dissatisfying experiences with professional development workshops in the past. Furthermore, taking the time to engage in professional development—on top of teaching a long day—is not attractive in the eyes of most teachers. But the major stickler is the suggestion that "we" have to change what we are doing for "those" students. It is not only the training that raises hackles, but also a status issue related to course assignments and which students a teacher teaches.

Immigrants are new to Bayview. They are the outsiders. The "extra," "additional" needs they present, and the mandates to serve them come from "outside" the school and community. They respond then by giving the job to the new and outsider teachers, the young, new hires. The young teachers, conveniently, also are more open to teaching the immigrant students, sometimes even requesting to teach them. Prepared by their credentialing programs to greet with relative openness the diversity of their students, these new teachers are unschooled yet in the status implications of teaching such courses at Madison. The head of one department outright refuses to get training in sheltering techniques or to be assigned a sheltered class. But her class list for a twelfth-grade class is in fact almost all LEP students. The class is not called "sheltered," there is no acknowledgment that it should be "sheltered," or that the students are LEP. The blindness is maintained as to the reality of immigration and of LEP students on campus. The status of the class, and of the teacher, is thereby preserved.

There are often references to maintaining the status quo in schools in the face of pressures to adapt teaching and curriculum to the needs of LEP students. The principal once said: "To tell you the truth, I'm not sure there ought to be any classes taught in any language besides English, because after all this is America and we ought to speak English."

He also resisted the idea that a college outreach program specifically for Latino students has any place on "our campus." His concern is for helping students to be English speakers and to learn the ways of the new land, and for avoiding any programs that encourage students to identify with anything other than a generic whole. In his view, efforts to address the needs of specific groups of students are catering to "special interests," and is divisive for the school as a whole. Pereira later said: "I'm against all that stuff that tells kids that if you're of one skin color or another you get to have some kind of special privilege or attention. Not at Madison High! We don't believe in it. We treat all our kids the same."

Pereira does not see that treating all the students the same, when their needs are different, produces inequitable access and outcomes. When LEP students are talked about in terms of requiring special efforts on the part of teachers, it gets twisted so that the implication is not that teaching needs to change to address those needs, but is instead a defense for maintaining things as they are. For example, one teacher feels she is upholding academic standards by refusing to allow LEP students into her class. She explains, "If they can't read English well enough, they can't make it. I don't feel the least bit guilty about that. I think it's important we set the standard and insist kids read well enough."

But this teacher, like others, does not view it as her job to help students learn to read well in English. She reflects the pervasive ignorance among many teachers about how to help students learn literacy in a second language.

There *are*, however, some accommodations to the changing student body in some classrooms. One English teacher, Lillian Edwards, loves teaching her subject and spoke in glowing terms about how wonderful it was to add *The Joy Luck Club* to the list of texts in her class, and how relevant the book is for her students as they are "becoming Americanized." She feels it is relevant because her immigrant students have to bridge two nations until they finally become American. *The Joy Luck Club* brings that theme into her classroom "so the immigrants can relate." To her, the "Americanization" of immigrants is synonymous with learning enough English and enough assumptions about American life that a student can participate in discussions. For example, she explained: "Once they know enough English, once they are far enough along in becoming American, there is so much we can discuss!"

Americanization is a process, in the view of Edwards and others, of leaving the old nation and language behind and accepting the new. The juxtaposition is striking. On the one hand, teachers make some changes in the curriculum in order to embrace issues of immigration. On the other hand, they are blind to the ways in which continuing to group students the way they do and to teach immigrant students the way they do result in excluding immigrants.

One teacher declared:

> I like getting immigrant students once they have finished ESL and the ones who can really speak English. But I just don't like having the ones who are still having trouble with English though, because they just can't participate. It bogs the whole class down, and it just doesn't work. Discussions are so important in my class. It's the cornerstone of my teaching, so if they can't participate in discussions, it just doesn't work. But I think it's great there are immigrants in our school. I have one short story about an immigrant that I like to use because they can talk about issues of assimilation and immigration and prejudice. Things that are really relevant to their lives.

The addition of *The Joy Luck Club* to the core literature list to be taught in the English program at Madison was not in response to a recognition of the immigrant community, but was instead a general move to diversify the curriculum in response to challenges from parents in prior years. In the wake of a controversial and long community battle over adoption of new state social studies textbooks,[33] Madison High's curriculum was cited by parents for not being culturally inclusive enough. In the eyes of one defensive white teacher, the matter boiled down to an African American parent who was upset that her son only got a C grade in an English literature class. The mother asserted that the reason he did not do well was because the class was geared toward dead white male British authors. It turned into what the teacher termed "a major investigation." The parent's concerns about the curriculum were, in the eyes of the teacher, personalized and invalidated. But the parents made their point, and the department was forced to review its curriculum. As a result, they *did* add some titles to the core list, and changed the honors class from British literature to American literature. The bitterness among some teachers was apparent. The issues again, for them, were being "forced" by an outside group to change what they were doing, not being respected as teachers, and having their judgment unjustly questioned about the appropriateness of the curriculum given the diversity of the community. One teacher said:

> It was like a witch-hunt. We were being told by people who aren't even teachers what we can and can't teach. We were told on the

spur of the moment to produce a list of all the things we teach that are culturally inclusive. It's a good thing our principal stood up for us and refused. I mean, we're totally willing to change what we teach, but we want it come from something positive, not something negative. This was all so divisive. The things we were teaching were good literature that has been taught for years, and we were treated like all of a sudden we have to make a change.

Not all teachers felt this way, however. Dorothy Meyer, a young English teacher and teacher of ESL, felt it was positive that they made changes, although she acknowledges that they ended up creating not a multicultural but a bicultural curriculum of white and black authors, "plus the *The Joy Luck Club* thrown to make it more diverse."The fact that one out of every four students at the school is Latino, and that no books by Latin authors were included, did not enter into the dialogue.

The major barrier is the belief that change is unnecessary. But there are other barriers as well. Once again, the issue of lack of time for teachers to find new literature and lack of budget to purchase new books dampened the efforts even of those within the department who chose to argue that a more inclusive curriculum was a positive direction. It is simply left to the individual teachers to find additional materials. This increased the resentment among some teachers. Even those with good intentions, and the recognition that the curriculum ought to be broadened, run into these barriers. Change is not supported and teachers are left on their own to do what they can. Nonetheless, the majority of teachers do not believe that *what* is taught makes a difference with regards to diversity issues.

Instead, the basic belief is that it is simply by *being* diverse that students learn about other cultures and places, and develop the skills of getting along. There is nothing that the school or the teacher needs to do to support diversity. And in fact, "doing something" to address the needs of one group or another is viewed as discriminatory and dangerous for the kind of resentment it might stir up. As one teacher described:

What's neat about our diversity is that it's totally accepted and a positive thing. It's not a problem or anything we need to overcome or address or anything. Some schools really get into bringing in workshops and speakers and having diversity trainings. It's all tense and self-conscious. We don't see it that way.

> It's neat. Nobody here bats an eye about how diverse we are, or
> who goes with whom relative to race. Everybody goes with
> everybody. It doesn't take doing anything to make that happen.
> This is just a very accepting place.

This theme returns again and again in Pereira's resistance to creating an ESL Department in the school (despite a Western Accreditation of Schools and Colleges accreditation report recommending that such a department be created) and his insistence that nothing he has control over will create "separation" or "labeling" of LEP students. Whether it is the creation of programs for LEP students, or bringing the voices of many communities into the curriculum, or bringing in speakers or training about diversity, the prevailing voices among the faculty and administration maintain that doing things that call attention to differences is divisive and dangerous. This is what Stern refers to as the "sweep it all under the rug program." But they seem to believe that this is what makes school life so smooth. Pereira recounts that there was a time in the "sixties" when things were not so easy; there was a Black Student Union that conducted a sit-in as a protest against something that significantly he does not remember.

> Everyone back then was really tense. And we were all aware all
> the time of being black or white and careful about what we say.
> But things are really much better now. No one even really
> notices skin color. We're just all part of this big mixed school.
> And I want to keep it that way.

The discourse of the school about issues of race, language, and iversity is largely based on these views. Diversity is a fact of life, but not something to be focused on, talked about, addressed. Color-blindness is viewed as a moral position, thought of righteously as linked to ending prejudice and racism. Underlying it is fear and a sense of the delicate balance in relations that would be disturbed through any kind of acknowledgment of differences. Meyer refers to the school as "an eggshell school. . . . [because] we walk on eggshells." Attention to differences and stirring up trouble about lack of access are viewed as highly divisive and explosive. And yet, it is precisely attention to the differences in need, the differences in opportunities and outcomes, that the program requires if it is to address the basic-access issue for LEP students. Without such attention, inequality of treatment persists and some students are foreclosed from their education.

It is not that teachers do not see a divided campus. The salient division they speak about is simply not a matter of race or culture. They do not "see" color or culture—or at least they elect not to speak of it. Rather, it is academic distinctions that take prominence in the social maps drawn by teachers. Teachers describe a world that divides students at Madison not by race or ethnicity, or even by language and nationality, but primarily by academic achievement level. A foreign-language teacher tried to describe the social system of the school to me during one of the first interviews of my research.

> This school isn't racially divided. It's really a pretty remarkably mixed place. Everywhere you look you see kids of different races. I think the fundamental division in our school, maybe even all high schools, at least the other one where I taught, is between the academic kids—you know, the college bound ones—and the skills kids, and the rest of the kids who are kind of in the middle. We probably have three different schools going—the college bound, the regular, the skills. Maybe you might have to throw in the ESL kids, too. I'm not sure they fit with the other categories. I'm not sure where they go. Eventually, they become part of one of the three.

These are the salient characteristics of the social maps described and used as a basis for categorizing students by teachers. At Madison, "skills" classes are the remedial classes for students who are not doing well academically. Most teachers, like students, also categorize students by the school activities they engage in:

> Like most schools, we have our jocks—you know, the kids who are really into sports.

> The student leadership kids, they really stand out as a certain type. It's not that they are the popular students really, but they are the ones that go out for student government.

> Our band students pretty much hang out together. We have a great band here—a great music department, actually. And the students who are involved in music do a lot of things together.

Overall, the maps developed by teachers reflect programmatic divisions; they view their school and the differences among students primarily in terms of academic relationships and abilities, and school activities. The academic distinction is the sharpest, and the realist institutional distinction, marking how and where students are placed in classes, the kinds of services and supports they get, and which teachers they will work with.

Teachers explain these distinctions as products of individual student abilities and motivation. The school offers choices to students, who then become responsible for their own selections and behaviors. Anyone who wanted to, anyone who was willing to work hard, the story goes, could end up in college-preparatory classes. The students who are in the skills classes, they say, are the ones who "don't care about school,""don't care about their future,""don't try." What does not get said or acknowledged is the reality that Lisa Stern's research uncovered—that the students in skills classes are the children of parents whose parents did not have access to continued education, and of parents who are not aware of the placement of their children in classes that foreclose opportunity. The students in the top classes are spoken of as "smart,""motivated," and "hard workers." The unspoken part is that the honors students are also the children of parents who have been to college. And unvoiced by all (Lisa Stern included) is the racial overlay. The teachers' maps are, fundamentally, maps that persist in viewing school as a meritocracy and all students as equally positioned to participate. Student failure is a result then of lack of effort.

In much of the literature on schooling, as in Lisa Stern's survey, it has been documented that these categories usually reflect class distinctions.[34] At Madison, as in many schools throughout the nation, these categories also reflect racial division. "Skills" courses are disproportionately Latino and black. "College prep" classes are disproportionately Asian and white. There is a racial reality, but it is not commented on, noticed, or acknowledged by most teachers. The major exception is that some teachers, such as Higgins, speak with pride of their Chinese students. Teachers sometimes mention issues of "culture" when describing students in the top or lower tracks of the school. Veiled references are made, such as "some cultures just don't value education," or the "new cultures" in the school serve as explanations for difficulties in getting students to do their work or conversely that certain cultures really value education. The implications of those statements, or the specifics behind the general references, do not get mentioned.

This paradigm of a diverse and mixed school in a color-blind system divided only by virtue of student choice and differential motivation into a hierarchy of academic achievement holds tremendous power, serves deeply vested interests, and obscures an entire realm of student experience and the actual exclusion occurring as well as the schools' class and racial sorting project. Yet, it is not uncontested. A stark reality defies it. The teachers may not see, speak, or use the categories of race, but the groups they label otherwise still have an obscured class, language, and racial reality. "Skills," "college bound" are not "race" neutral, and they are not class neutral.

"Crossing the stage," graduating, is thought of as the measure of having succeeded academically, both by the school and by most students at Madison High. Yet, many do not make it. Generally, the teachers at Madison view this also as a product of student choice. They believe that students who want to do well can and will do so. Students who do not care about their education won't do well. There is very little sense of school responsibility for graduation rates or drop-out rates. Generally, it is agreed that students "should" graduate from high school, because "education" is important and a high school diploma "essential" to get a good job. But there is also a sense of resignation that there is little that teachers can do about kids who "don't care about their future."

It takes amazing denial to not see all this. A look at who graduates and who drops out, and who leaves the school prepared to go on to four-year colleges tells a story of intense racial and class sorting at the school. The large numbers of LEP students who fail to accrue the credits needed to progress "on track" to graduation attest to the failure of the school to provide sufficient classes, trained teachers, and support systems to address the language barriers. The skin color and language background of the student is closely correlated with the chances of being among those who do cross the stage. At Madison, Latinos and African American students have the slimmest chances of making it through high school.

The school does not seem to keep or look at student achievement or participation data by race or ethnicity, thus they are not confronted with statistics about who is in which academic track. Without that data, people rely on their own opinions and experience to come to conclusions about the fairness of the system—and their conclusions conflict. Some picture is provided by the data the state requires for the California Basic Education Data System (CBEDS), in which schools report selected measures of participation and achievement by race and ethnicity.

In a nonracialized society, where no barriers or discrimination exists based on skin color, one would expect random distribution of each racial group in all categories of achievement. We would expect "proportionality." That is, if

Asians comprise 25 percent of the people in a school, they would be 25 percent of those in ninth grade, 25 percent of those who graduate, 25 percent of those who go on to college, and 25 percent of those who drop out. Racial matters would not be a factor affecting achievement. In fact, on most measures of achievement, at Madison High as well as statewide in California, we see evidence of racial sorting. For example, in a four-year period, of the 181 Latinos who entered Madison as freshmen, only half (94) "crossed the stage" four years later in the graduating class. Although Latinos comprised 39 percent of the freshmen class at Madison, they were only 23 percent of the graduates, and 10 percent of those who completed the course requirements for the University of California admission. They become increasingly underrepresented.

On almost all measures of success at making it through the educational system and into higher education, African American and Latino students fare far worse than their peers in other racialized categories. This is not a Madison High School problem alone. Statewide, only 58 percent of those Latinos who enroll in kindergarten actually graduate from twelfth grade. And only 12 percent graduate having completed requirements for public four-year colleges.[35]

The rare times the teachers at Madison are pushed to contemplate these figures, they tend to hold on to their explanation in terms of student choice, aspirations and cultural values. The students, they explain, come to Madison already with a shortfall in academic preparation and with very different goals. This is to some degree true, as the product of eight previous years in an educational system that provides differential treatment. The ideology of individual choice and the persistent belief that the salient divisions of the school into academic track is a race-neutral system, leads to ignoring the kinds of data that abound about the racial project of the school.

And yet, Madison plays a continuing role in the narrowing of chances. It is the faculty at Madison who actually sign students into their academic tracks—making determinations about which students can handle which levels of curriculum. And it is the faculty and administration at Madison who make the choices to get the training needed to serve students who are not fluent in English, to offer the courses needed for those students to have access to the curriculum. Madison receives students already with differential preparation, but it plays its role in exacerbating and perpetuating a system of sorting.

A small group of faculty see this. They draw a somewhat different map from their colleagues and draw different conclusions about the diversity at the school. They, too, remark on and dwell on a view of their school as remarkably diverse, but also unfairly divided. The meaning they draw acknowledges racism and exclusion, and attempts to honor, respect, and make visible the cultural perspectives and different national backgrounds newcomer students bring. They call for attention to the needs of students related to language and culture and race that must be addressed by the school in ways that acknowledge and nourish the diversity they represent. This perspective is a distinctly minority perspective. It is experienced by most of the others on the faculty as divisive, naive, and by some as just plain dead wrong. The minority voices tend to come from faculty who entered Madison High with the closure of Washington High School and from new teachers. They are clearly felt by many of the rest of the faculty as disruptive.

CHAPTER NINE

A Different Voice,
A Daily Struggle

AT MADISON High, it is the responsibility of ninth-grade English teachers to determine what academic level students should be placed in for tenth-grade English and social studies. Their tenth-grade level is most often the level at which they continue throughout high school. Students placed in "skills" classes (remedial classes) stay there. Students placed in "honors" classes end up with the courses needed for admission to four-year universities. Students in the "regular" track have some opportunity for sliding downward into "skills" classes or climbing "upward" into college-preparatory classes. Most, however, appear to stay in the regular track. There is no formal policy or criteria determining how these decisions should be made.

When Lisa Stern first began teaching social studies at Madison High, as a brand-new teacher, she was assigned to teach three tenth-grade "skills" classes. It was the tradition that first-year teachers would be assigned these courses, reputed to be the toughest in the school. A faculty member consoled her: "I'm sorry you're stuck with the garbage kids. You'll be able to teach other students after a few years."

Fresh out of graduate school, Stern had read research about the way in which the division of students into academic tracks is detrimental to students in the bottom levels, and the fact that such tracking often relegates students of color and poor students to an inferior education. She decided to conduct some research of her own with the students at Madison High. Stern surveyed six classes: two skills classes, two "regular" classes, and two honors classes. The survey asked, "What level do you think this class is? (high, medium, or low)" "How far did your mother go in school?" "How far did your father go in school?" and "Has your family ever been consulted about the level of history class you are taking?"

The results were stark. Students knew clearly what level they were placed in. All of the skills class students' parents did not finish high school or graduated from high school but did not go to college. Almost all of the students in honors classes had at least one parent who completed college. Most of the honor's-class students' parents seemed to be aware they were taking honors classes. Only one skills-class student thought his parents were aware that he was in a "lower"-level history class. To Stern, this was clear evidence that the school was just perpetuating a class system: the children of people who have had access to higher education also get prepared for higher education, and the children of people who have not had higher education don't get prepared for higher education.

Determined to do something about the tracking of students in social studies, Stern put together the survey results and some of the research on tracking. She recounts bringing it first to her department with a proposal to detrack the tenth-grade social studies classes. She received a lukewarm reaction, and the suggestion that she take it to the next level—the district-wide Social Studies Curriculum Council. She was deferred from there to the next level of decision making, the districts' Curriculum Council. An associate superintendent told her, "there is no evidence that would support detracking social studies." He brought in a parent of an honors student to speak on behalf of gifted and talented students and their need for honors classes. The Curriculum Council told her, "we don't know enough to make a decision." A vote was taken, and nineteen people abstained.

The next day at school, Stern was met in the hall by the principal. He told her that what she was doing was misguided: "You're going to hurt our kids who want to get into college. We need honors classes here. You're just hurting our kids. I'm going to fight you on this all the way."

Stern was so upset that she dropped the subject. No one ever mentioned it to her again—not the principal, not the department faculty who had passed her along to the Curriculum Council, not the members of the Curriculum Council who abstained on her proposal. Yet, the memory of that experience continued to affect Stern deeply throughout her years of teaching at the school.

"I was a political rookie! I was an idiot! I didn't understand that you can't change schools, at least schools like Madison, by opening your mouth and speaking out about what's happening to our students, and expecting people to listen. They've been doing it their way for years and years, and here I was, this young new teacher trying to make them look at what they've been doing critically. I should have waited for a few years until I'd proved myself first as a teacher. I had no influence, no base of support. To them I was a new kid on the block, a kid from an elite school in a community that distrusts elite universities. And I was raising an issue they didn't want to hear. At least Pereira told me what he thought. No one else was willing to engage with me. They passed me along to someone else. They abstained. They never talked with me. The worst part was the silence. I was just met by silence."

■ ■ ■

On the first day I spent at the school, Pereira gave me a list of the faculty to help in contacting people I might want to interview. He took three colored markers and proceeded to code the entire list. One was for teachers who had been at the school for more than five years, one was for "new" teachers, and one was for those teachers who had switched from Washington High School to Madison when Washington was closed down. At the time, I assumed he made the distinction to give me a sense of who I might go to as sources for particular periods in Madison history. I did not fully realize the meaning of these distinctions or the depth of the chasms and tensions they represented, but came to appreciate them as deeply rooted in the functioning and life of the school. Forty-seven of the seventy-nine teachers had been at Madison for fifteen years or more.

Four young teachers at Madison High are the primary and sometimes the only advocates who attempt to name the exclusion, voice the need for more active inclusion, address the specific needs for access of immigrant students in order to build stronger programs. At times, on particular issues, there are others as well. But these four represent a distinctly minority view among the faculty and play a role in shaping whatever dialogue occurs about language and immigrant education issues at the school. The four are identified by other teachers as a distinct group, called by several "The Rookies," and referred to by others simply as "those Young Teachers." They teach the sheltered classes.

The growth in student population in Bayview meant a growth in the teaching force as well. For about a four-year period, Madison experienced an increase in new hires of mostly young teachers, hireable at the bottom of the salary structure. Joining a cohesive faculty of veteran and older teachers, the newly hired quickly became a distinct social group among the faculty. The split between "older" and "younger" teachers in this school is one of the most salient ways to understand faculty politics and power relations. From the principal to the teachers and students, the school talks about these two groups. Framed sometimes as a matter of "style" or as a matter of "values," the younger teacher/older teacher issue has fundamentally shaped how the teachers of "sheltered" and ESL courses relate to the rest of the school. Their youth is a factor in how those who do not agree with their analysis treat them, how their ideas are accepted, and how their students view them. None of the young teachers seemed to feel that Madison was a welcoming or easy social system to enter.

One of the "young" teachers marked by the green pen on Pereira's list was Linda O'Malley. O'Malley views her role as having been instrumental in pulling together the young teachers into a closer social and support circle in response to the cold reception they felt at Madison. O'Malley begins the story of her life at Madison by telling about how they built a cohort of young teachers.

> My first year, it was just Dan and me. I was really in my own little world. I spent one year without real contact with any colleagues and decided that it wasn't for me! I wasn't going to sit there and listen to people complain all the time. With all these new teachers coming on board, I thought we had to make it a network, even it if was *us against them*. I didn't care. The next year, everybody came! We had four new teachers, and we wanted the new teachers to get together and find out stuff about the school that we weren't getting from the administration. So we used to get together. And when these guys came the next year, it was sort of built up already. It felt like a massive group of people and it was neat—it really worked. We had written down everything we came across that no one had told us, and so Tracy and I did an orientation for the next batch of new teachers. We were all new and in this together. How were we going to make it work?

After a three-year cycle of new hires, few new teachers were hired. Budget problems were paramount in the district. Layoff notices every year to the younger teachers caused a state of real insecurity. Some laughed it off and hung in at Madison High, receiving layoff notices in the spring, but getting rehired before school started again in the fall; others left. Fourteen new teachers were on the layoff list one spring. Says O'Malley: "How many times can you be laid off and feel that you're so dispensable to them?" She received layoff notices three years in a row. Lisa Stern got layoff notices for two years. O'Malley describes the effect of this:

> People are tired of being jerked around, and if they're in any position to leave, they're looking to leave. And that generally tends to be the younger teachers, because we don't have as much investment in staying and we don't have the protections

to know there will be a job down the road. If there is still a chance to get on at a better district at a higher salary, they're going to do it. And so will I.

Despite these hardships and insecurity, there still remained a cohort of new young teachers. Within that social group, a group of four developed structured ways through which they have become friends and stronger colleagues. Rebecca Garrison and Lisa Stern commuted everyday together, using their drive to talk about their classes and their work and their students. Many of these younger teachers had come from credential programs that encouraged working together. Now they found themselves plopped into a school where the long-time traditions and practices were quite the opposite, and so they sought each other out. Stern recalls being told by her department chair on the first day of her job, "We don't meet. We meet as infrequently as possible, and here are your textbooks." She says she knew then and there that her survival would depend on finding at least one other person who wanted to work more closely. This became even more important as Stern, in her fervor, inadvertently created enemies.

Forever marked afterwards, Stern committed a social error among the faculty by doing her research project on "academic tracking" in social studies at Madison. She identifies that incident as the first time she heard the principal use the category of "young teachers," and it was not favorable. In her memory, he said, "If the young teachers would stop doing this kind of thing . . ." Another young teacher looked back on that incident, sharing Stern's perception of the faculty reaction:

> Lisa's proposal on detracking just focused the way other teachers were feeling about us. I mean, here's this topic being put out there by one of the young teachers, and . . . The faculty never really talk about this stuff. If someone brings something up, it isn't examined or dealt with. They run from it—nothing happens. People don't want to touch it with a ten-foot pole. A small group of us acknowledges it and wants to talk about it. But most don't. They just turn off the conversation. They act like the survival of the school depends on letting issues like that alone. And they were annoyed by the whole thing, maybe scared by the whole thing . . . but the messenger was "one of the young teachers."

The young teachers say that the strength of their connection to each other grew in opposition to how they felt they were being treated and viewed by others and by their isolation.

The friendship and alliance between the four teachers began off campus, largely as a result of a suggestion by Maria Rodriguez. O'Malley had been isolated and frustrated as the designated resource teacher coordinator for LEP students. Rodriguez wanted to provide some support to O'Malley and thought that involvement in one of the conferences bringing together teachers from throughout the state who are concerned about immigrant issues might do the trick. She suggested that O'Malley attend a conference that was being held on Latino immigrants and that she invite a few other teachers who might become interested in the issues. O'Malley invited Dorothy Meyer, Rebecca Garrison, and Lisa Stern. Garrison recounts:

> I mark the Latino Newcomer Conference as the first time I heard the radical edge of education. It [involved] things I believe [in]. Education should be about helping kids feel strong and good about their language and their culture. Everything important, moving forward, radical that was happening in education seemed to be rolled up in the bilingual movement—whole language, student-centeredness, community pedagogy. This is where it was happening. It was so exciting to me. And here were three other teachers, excited, committed to their students, interested in new ideas. It was the start for me of wanting to work with immigrant students, and of wanting to work with Linda, Lisa, and Dorothy.

The foursome articulate a very strong position about the diversity at Madison High. As Stern describes:

> When I first walked in and saw my classroom filled with kids here, I felt so moved . . . And a kind of excitement that has never worn off—just staring at the incredible diversity and realizing what a historical thing this is. How can I put my finger on why it's so amazing to look at a class full of kids from so many cultures? For some reason it makes me happy. It makes me happy thinking they're all sitting in the same room together thinking it's normal! I mean, there is nowhere in the world that's as integrated as my classroom! And they don't understand how amazing that is.

This is the same kind of recognition and valuing of diversity one hears throughout the faculty. As much as Stern believes that the diversity is amazing, she also believes that the school does not serve this diversity well. The ongoing analyses shared and developed by these teachers are about racism, exclusion, refusals of the school to see and meet the needs of the students. In many ways, this small group of teachers stands alone on a campus in which the vast majority of teachers and the administration deny both the racial sorting and the denial of access to an education for LEP students.

What was not so evident at the point the young teachers began to coalesce as a group is that the closing of Washington High School was also reshaping the faculty. The "old family" faculty at Madison was invaded not only by what some of them experienced as the group of new "smart aleck" young teachers, as one veteran faculty member referred to them, but also by a group of outspoken teachers from Washington (many of them from the strong bilingual program at Washington) who were unhappy with the closure of their school. The only Latino faculty/staff at Madison had come from Washington. The images of the increase in Latino students from Washington, the increase in immigrant students because of the immigration explosion, the new young outspoken teachers (many of whom were being assigned sheltered and ESL classes), and older outspoken bilingual teachers from another school became mixed in the minds and reactions of veteran teachers.

The integration of teachers from Washington High into Madison was difficult. As one of them explained:

> Most of us had been really involved in the fight to keep Washington open. We were a tight-knit community, with parents and teachers trying to hold on to our school. Then we lost critical mass when we were all divided up among the other schools. The closing of that school tore a hole in the fabric of our community. It was the only active Spanish bilingual program in a high school in this district. We had a good group of Latino teachers and counselors. We had gotten good grants to set up programs. And then it was all destroyed. I feel displaced here at Madison. I think we all do.

Although the district maintained that the decision to close Washington was made solely on the basis of attendance estimates, murmurs throughout some segments of the Latino community and the bilingual education advocates were that the strong bilingual program and Latino community involvement at Washington may have made it somewhat of a target. The year of the closure was not an easy year for any of the teachers at Madison. Stern describes:

> My first year was the worst ever. It was when Washington teachers came in. Faculty morale was at an all-time low. Washington teachers were really upset because they felt Pereira and other faculty at Madison were partially responsible for the Washington closure. Politically, Pereira had a lot to do with it. So Washington teachers were feeling angry. Then Madison teachers got mad because some Washington teachers got department chairships and there was all this tension. So there was the Washington faculty, the old-time Madison faculty, and the new teachers.

Although one split among the faculty is an age divide, another is by the students they teach. Teachers in the school know their corner of the school. Because students are tracked and faculty assigned their classes often by the types of students and levels of tracks, they know different student groups as well. Over the years, the four young teachers who were working with sheltered/ESL students became particularly tight. Some friendships developed with other young faculty at the school, but the foursome were to a large degree set off from the other teachers because of the student population they taught. They supported and encouraged each other to become schoolwide advocates for immigrant students.

O'Malley explains the divisions among faculty in terms of the students they serve:

> We have teachers who only see one kind of kid. The type of kid that also doesn't know other types of kids in the school. The high-academic subject teachers and the low-academic subject teachers—that's an immediate split right there. Then old and young teachers are a contrast—the burned out and the energetic. And most of the time these are all connected. You know, it's the young teachers who are the energetic ones who are also the ones with the ESL or the skills kids. And it's the old teachers who get the higher academic tracks. The old teachers who don't get to have all the higher tracks are burned out.

The college-preparatory classes are largely taught by teachers who have been around a long time. They socialize together and generally comprise the leadership of the school. The ESL and sheltered classes are considered to be lower-status classes: less academic, less rigorous, and more difficult to teach because of the students who do not understand English. The teachers who teach these classes take on the stigma that the students have in the eyes of the rest of the teachers. Recently, Rebecca Garrison ceased teaching sheltered classes after being offered a "move up" to mainstream classes and one college-preparatory class. She looked forward to the change and the opportunity to teach a new course, was pleased that it had been offered to her as a mark of being more "accepted" by the older teachers, and perhaps could not resist the lure of a more prestigious teaching load.

The split between the older and younger teachers, the sheltered/ESL teachers and the "mainstream" teachers, is also a division over idealism and new pedagogies. The young teachers came to Madison fresh from credentialed programs pushing new educational reform ideas. Their training included explicit coursework on the theories and methods related to second-language acquisition and culture. They were prepared to teach heterogeneous, "detracked" classes, and were convinced by the research that this was the way things should be. They had little preparation, however, for handling the power dynamics of school change. The older teachers felt it was arrogance that led the inexperienced teachers to assume they knew better about what constitutes effective teaching. The young teachers indeed did not view the older teachers as having worthwhile expertise and were anxious to push aside the old approaches and bring in new ones.

As O'Malley explained: "Young teachers try to make things interesting and active. Our training has been different. The emphasis has been hands-on. It's not that old traditional stick-to-the-text-and-answer-question approach anymore. It is a new era for teaching and learning."

But a more experienced teacher spoke with equal passion:

> I have been here for twenty years. I've seen educational fads come and go. These new teachers come in full of all kinds of ideas that I heard about years ago and then they were discredited and now they are back. Eventually, you learn what works for you and your students and what doesn't, and you stop jumping up and down with excitement at every new idea. You just stop listening, it goes in one ear and out the other. Good teaching is good teaching. I may seem traditional to some of the young

teachers, but I don't care. Some kids don't like it, it may not be fun and games, but they've got to learn some discipline and my way works as good as any.

Pedagogy, idealism, and the ability to relate to the students become mixed together whenever the young teachers talk about what they feel they bring to the job, and what they feel the older teachers lack. As one example of this continuing theme, Stern explained:

I guess students have changed a lot, and that the ability to relate to students today is very hard for older teachers—you know, to look at the kids today without judging them as being less—you know, "kids today don't do this" or "they don't respect us," etc. There is a litany of complaints against kids today.... And then there is suspicion of the younger teachers, too. They don't want to be our friends, they don't want to hang out with us, they don't want to discuss curriculum, they don't want to listen to our ideas. And they really don't want to hear what we say because it has implications for what they're doing.

The teachers that stay in the job too long are miserable and the anger turns to hatred of the kids and of people who still like teaching. There are too many teachers who hate the kids. And the older teachers stereotype the younger teachers in this way that's kind of judgmental. It's like we're closer to the kids in age and we do things with them, so they are down on us, too. You know, these kids are trash, and the younger teachers relate to trash so the younger teachers are trash.

In many ways, Madison is a hard school and Bayview is a hard district (and these are hard times) in which to be a teacher. The teachers (young and old alike) talk a lot about the enormous emotional drain of teaching and the sheer exhaustion. It is a drain they attribute to working in a district that is in financial disarray, to the pull of 150 kids a day with needs for their attention, to being depleted by their work, and to the drain of feeling physically vulnerable in schools that feel unsafe. The pay scale in Bayview is well below that in neighboring districts. The unsettled contract situation, the fallout from past fiscal mismanagement in the district, and the shifting leadership contribute to an ongoing faculty conversation about how much more teachers can and will be willing to take. Garrison explained:

> When your material life is easier, you are less stressed out. From district to district, you have teachers living really different emotional lives. About 35 percent of my mental energy is worrying about money in some way. Worrying about bounced checks. Worrying whether I'm going to make it this month. If you didn't have that, you might have more teachers with emotional energy to give to kids. But every teachers has to give to thirty different kids each hour for five hours every day.

And O'Malley embellished:

> When you get home, you don't have anything to give to anybody else. It negatively impacts your emotional relationships—especially new relationships. At the end of the day, you have nothing to give to anybody. By the end of a day or a week of teaching, I have nothing left.

The fiscal drain has its price. Quite a few of the veteran teachers in the school have second jobs—as realtors, as accountants, etc. One of the young teachers sped away from work every Tuesday and Thursday to her job in a cafeteria. But the emotional drain is more complicated to manage. Several of the more experienced teachers explained that they had learned not to get so involved with their students. But for the young teachers, such withdrawal seemed impossible and even unethical. On one of the regular after-work get-togethers, Stern explained how this impacts her as a young single woman:

> I have had more guys who I start to go out with and they tell me it feels like I'm not there enough for them, and I feel like screaming, I can't take care of you. I'm one hundred people's mom every day. I can't, I can't, I can't. All day, it's "Ms. Stern! Ms. Stern! Can you—will you—please help. It's not specific. They need help with their work. They need to talk to me about some problem. Or they just need some attention. There is no way I can turn my back on my students, but by the end of the day I just have nothing left.

Meyer picked up on the theme:

> Especially these kids—the sheltered kids. They need help with
> everything. They need so much more. For everything you do in a
> class that you could give to a normal English-speaking class-
> room and they would just understand, you have five kids need-
> ing help understanding what you're saying, asking questions. In
> a sheltered classroom, you have to give the directions and then
> go to each student and be sure they understand. In a fifty-
> minute class, I must hear my name one hundred times. And it's
> always asking for help. Then between classes, I have clusters of
> kids around me asking for help.

Garrison echoes:

> You say hi to everybody in the hall because that's the only way the
> community becomes safer. You're going down the hall and you
> just want to think. You need a little time for your own thoughts.
> But you don't get it. In most jobs there is some privacy for people
> at some point, a time when they're not public. But for us as teach-
> ers, you're "on" all the time. You don't have time to think. I never
> have time to think about my own life when I get to school.

O'Malley tries to give some feel for what it is her students seem to need:

> Sometimes you have a student who just needs so much, it's bot-
> tomless—like Trang-Anh. You have to tell her to go away sometimes.
> She just needs. She needs a family. She's here without her parents
> and living with her uncle, who is a jerk to her. She has found in the
> four of us people who really care about her. I used to think of her as
> the backpack girl. She never puts her backpack down, she never
> takes it off. She's a turtle, carrying her home with her. It's a sense of,
> something belongs to me. This backpack belongs to me and I have
> nothing else that is mine. She can drive me crazy. She gets mad at
> me when I can't give to her. She goes through stages of being really
> angry because I can't give her enough. But Trang-Anh reminds me,
> sometimes I think it doesn't matter so much what we teach them;
> it's that we're there every day and we listen.

These four women are inspired by a vision of what they want to do as teachers, but exhausted and (outside of the support they give each other) feeling generally unacknowledged and unsupported by the school. They complain about the lack of feedback they get about their teaching and are surprised when they anger Pereira and find they have overstepped some line of what is considered appropriate at the school. They generally feel not respected by other faculty. One of their functions for each other is to provide feedback and support. They also turn to their students for feedback. All four regularly have students evaluate units and assignments, as well as evaluate their own work. Garrison explains:

> I know from the kids whether I'm doing a good job. I hand out evaluations all the time or have discussions with them about a unit I've done, or I have them write in their notebooks, reflecting about the activities and the readings I've given them. I constantly ask them, "What about this activity, did it work for you? Should I do it again next year? What should I do differently?" Constantly. They are the only ones with any real information to give me about what works. And I want them to be in the habit of thinking about their experiences anyway. Did they learn anything? What? And so that's the main feedback I get. And it sustains me, it gives me ideas, it gives me new ideas.

Another difficult aspect of teaching for these young teachers is learning to cope with fear about their safety. As young women, they feel they have less "natural" authority with students and are more dependent on the kind of relationship students have with teachers they know and respect. This is a familiar topic of conversation between the four. O'Malley talked about issues of safety:

> Who you work with—who you know makes a big difference in how safe we feel. In my skills classes, it's a different world. It's the underworld of the school. For people living in one world of the school, it is very safe. And then for people in the underworld, it's completely treacherous, as treacherous as the street because that's where it comes from. Once a personal connection's been made between me and a student, I feel very safe and I feel very good about the students. But if I don't have a personal connection with students and they don't know who I am and what I'm about, then it's scary. It's just plain scary. Just

yesterday I walked up to a group of guys—something was going on. I actually know one of the guys and have a good relationship with him. I just stood there and didn't say anything. I just stood there. I was so scared. The guys were huge compared to me. I looked like one of their little sisters. Finally, I just had to rely on my personal connection with this guy. I said, "You need to tell your friends not to do whatever it is they are doing, or I'll have to send somebody from the office down here." He said, "Okay, you guys, knock it off."

Similarly, Garrison described an incident:

We were all sitting around the teacher's lounge one day and a student came running in saying there was a fight going on in back. I noticed that the young teachers (all women) got up, but the others just sat there. They weren't going to get into the middle of a fight. They said they had learned from experience. But I couldn't just sit there, even though I was so afraid. So we went out there and one person yelled [that] she was running for the office to get help, and I walked into the middle of it. Someone said, "Lets fuck up the teacher." I was devastated for two weeks. Even though nothing happened, it broke through some sense of being safe and having authority because I'm a teacher. At that moment, I felt how vulnerable I am—how young, how female, how weak I am. I walked around for weeks feeling "This is an awful school." It really hurt me. When I turned around and saw kids I knew in the crowd who weren't saying "shut up" to their friends—it scares you. All of a sudden I had to stop and think "what if they decide to do something to me?"

Meyer added:

I'm at the point when I walk through the school I say hi to every single kid. I make eye contact. Every single solitary kid. I must say hi fifty times between my room and the office. "Hi, hi, hi. It's really important. It's the only strategy I have for coping with the school. Be nice to everybody. Maintain positive contacts with

> kids that are in gangs. Build connections so they know you as
> a person.

For teachers as well as students, friendliness and getting along become survival strategies, and they live their lives daily in school with an overlay of tension. It is a subtle fear. The day is much too full of other riveting matters to notice the fear unless some incident breaks through.

In trying to describe a day in her life, O'Malley came up with the metaphor of a soap opera or television series:

> Do you know the television show *Cops*? There ought to be
> one called "Teachers." My day is so intense and incredible.
> There are so many dramas and traumas and little stories and
> lives that crisscross. One day can have me going through the
> craziness of trying to administer the REACH test [minimum
> proficiency] to immigrant students who can't even fathom
> what it's about. Being yelled at by the principal. Interrupting
> fights. Drying the tears of a Vietnamese girl who lives with an
> abusive uncle. Cheerleading when a Guatemalan immigrant
> boy speaks out in class voluntarily for the first time. Racing to
> meetings about whether we have enough people of color repre-
> sented in the literature program. It's intense. One hundred kids
> a day needing you, needing to be acknowledged, to be seen, to
> be personally greeted. I get home, I can't talk on the phone.
> I don't have an ounce left for anything. And then I come back
> the next day.

On top of their teaching and the relations to their students, these teachers have taken on trying to get their new ideas about education and their perspectives on the needs of students across to the faculty and administrators. There are times when the ideas, the projects, the curriculum developed by the "rookies" have some influence, but most often they fizzle school-wide, either caught in the hostility toward the four or simply lost among the thousands of other issues the busy school is dealing with. Stern put it succinctly:

> Simply, these are not issues people have any interest in dealing
> with. Immigrant students? Not much interest. Racial tracking?
> No time to deal with it, and it's divisive to bring it up.

Embittered by these experiences, O'Malley and Stern stopped after that point trying to involve the principal in their ideas about what might be new approaches for the school. They still worked with him, however, on ongoing school activities and projects. O'Malley in particular still maintained a friendly and open relationship with him. But she turned her attention away from whole school possibilities and toward her students, immersed herself in teaching and individual student advocacy, and shared her ideas primarily with the foursome. She and the others thrived on the bond. Says Stern:

> I consider it the greatest thing in the world that I can go to school and have friends there. I think that's the primary perk of my job. And we have structured it so we've gotten to know each other by talking about school issues, by going to conferences and workshops together. We talk about teaching and education a lot ... And we work, and we have fun doing it. It's great feeling we are facing this challenge of figuring out how to work with all these different language groups and cultures, and we are figuring it out together.

The split in the faculty was obvious to everyone. Pereira at one point tried to mediate, concerned primarily about low teacher morale because of district contract problems and with the tensions after the Washington High faculty joined the school. Pereira, for a while, convened regular faculty forums to build a more cohesive group out of the demoralized and fragmented faculty. The forums are spoken of by all the teachers as a positive beginning step toward sharing ideas and knowing each other. It helped some. The forums were, however, a weak solution for improving faculty morale, the resentments in the folding in of Washington High faculty, and the growth of hostilities between the growing cohort of new teachers and the administrators and teachers who viewed them as naive and rebellious. At any rate, the forums ended the next summer as a result of the Bayview "budget nightmare." Everything in the district was impacted. Hundreds of thousands of dollars had to be cut from academic programs and positions in the district, teachers were pressured not only to defer cost-of-living increases but also to absorb pay cuts and larger class sizes. The district in three years was forced to eliminate almost $19 million in services and programs. During the summer of 1992, an additional shortfall of $6 million was "discovered," leading to drastic cuts at the beginning of the fall semester. By the time the faculty came back to school the following fall, morale was ata its lowest. No further attempts were made to address splits among the faculty. Then there were fall layoffs. All departmental chairperson positions were eliminated. At the end of October, counseling services were drastically reduced, leaving less than a full-time counselor at Madison for the entire school of 1,800 students. From five counselors in June, the school opened in fall with a .7 position. The librarian was laid off and library classified services were cut.

In an attempt to vitalize the school, Pereira announced a restructuring plan. The faculty voted it down. They were definitely not in the mood to entertain thoughts of any reform. That year the school was up for a Western Association of Schools and Colleges (WASC) accreditation review, the first one in twelve years. Preparing for a WASC accreditation involves a self-study process and a great deal of extra effort on the part of school personnel in preparation. The WASC process had to take center stage. Most of the dialogue in the school was by department, reflecting the nature of a WASC review. It was exhausting for a staff already feeling pushed to the brink. But it also provided a sense of unified effort, an ethos of "pulling together" to portray the school in the best possible light, and more time for faculty dialogue than had occurred in years. The exhaustion and fissures still existed but they took a back seat for nine months. The commendation section of the WASC report by the visiting reviewers dwells largely on the survival of the school in the midst of crisis:

> We . . . commend the entire staff on completion of a thorough, frank self-study report in spite of tremendous pressures caused by severe cutbacks . . . commend the staff on the dedication, collegiality and good humor they bring to their work in spite of the many potentially overwhelming negative events that have occured this year . . . commend the administration who have shown extraordinary leadership, sensitivity and support to help staff and students cope with major budget shocks in this year of crises . . .

The four "rookies" worked hard on crafting a special section in the WASC report about meeting the needs of LEP students. Although there is no ESL or sheltered department in the school, they were able to do an analysis and report to the committee. It is written, as are all sections of the self-study, in somewhat veiled terms, emphasizing the positive. Thus, for example, they handled the lack of trained teachers in sheltered instruction in the following manner:

> Although one science teacher does have sheltered training, she does not currently hold a physical science credential and therefore teaches sheltered biology only every other year. Our current sheltered physical science teacher is credentialed in physical science and has many years of teaching experience, therefore, even without formal or authorized sheltered training, he is doing a good job.

In other words, the teachers of sheltered science courses do have the full and required training. Under the section on "Organizational Structures" for the program for LEP students, they wrote:

> Some of the sheltered teachers meet regularly on and off campus to establish goals, evaluate progress of the curriculum and students, and to revise previous plans when necessary.

In other words, four teachers voluntarily get together after hours in their homes, and that is the only faculty dialogue that occurs about the program for LEP students.

Though they were tempted to "tell it like it is," in the end the description in the formal report never explicitly stated the fact that they do not have departmental status, that they do not have a budget, that there is a severe shortage of trained teachers resulting in an insufficient list of courses available for LEP students, and that they meet voluntarily on Saturdays at one of their houses with no organizational support or formal recognition. There *is* no organizational structure to support them. Under "Areas for Improvement," they begin to hint at some of the problems.

> Madison's LEP population is growing. The need for more teachers who are trained in sheltered instruction is urgent. The ESL/Sheltered Program MUST be recognized as a unique department with all the rights that are granted to other departments ...

Later they wrote: "Typically, sheltered students need extra time at home with a book in order to fully understand a concept." Yet there exists at Madison no sheltered texts or materials that deal specifically with the California frameworks.

At the end of the section they write:

> While Madison's staff is enthusiastic about adopting a multi-cultural focus, we feel that more schoolwide multicultural awareness is needed as well as more training of nonsheltered teachers in sheltered techniques. All present sheltered and ESL teachers (all five) will encourage other teachers to become trained in sheltered techniques. Having more teachers to teach sheltered/ESL will help decrease class size within these classes.

Later, Stern mused about why they had so carefully worked to protect the school:

> Were we scared? Were we being loyal? I don't know. Looking back on it, it seems like here was this opportunity to really put it out there, to talk about the student needs that weren't being met, to talk about the resistance of the faculty and administration to really creating a program for LEP kids. But instead we played the game. We were the good team players who protected the school. We just got caught up in it. But I think fear was the real thing. It was just so clear that it wasn't okay to do anything but paint the school in the best possible way.

Nonetheless, the WASC visiting committee sufficiently picked up on the situation to recommend in its report to the school the establishment of an ESL/sheltered department. The principal's response later in a meeting was "over my dead body." In his view, it would contribute toward fragmentation of the school, begin a series of "special interest" groupings, and contribute toward segregation. Even the voices of the four young teachers (the few teachers with training in this issue), combined with the weight of the WASC accreditation committee, could not override this ideology.

The following fall, Pereira again announced that he had a restructuring plan that would be good for teachers because it would reduce the number of student contacts they have in a day by adopting a block schedule (double periods). Only four courses would be taught per day. The big push for a restructuring plan at the school was not motivated by instructional or curricular reasons, nor was it particularly based on an analysis of student need. It was directly designed to cut class sizes and student contacts and to ease the stress and pressure on teachers of the conditions imposed by budget cuts.

While the rest of the school wrestled primarily with these schedule restructuring plans, the four "rookies" instead concentrated on supporting each other's work in the sheltered and ESL classrooms. Experiencing their voices and concerns as isolates within the department discussions for the WASC review, they increasingly turned to each other for "reality checks" and support. But their own reform energies could not totally discount the restructuring promise. Garrison was more enticed than the others. O'Malley and Stern had been too hurt in previous efforts to bring reform ideas into implementation in the school. Meyer simply did not believe any structural change would affect the attitudes that she felt underlie most of the problems of the schools. Only Garrison became involved in the restructuring planning effort at the school.

The perspectives of the four teachers derive not only from their youth. The ideas they bring to the faculty are also rooted in a body of knowledge and information that most of the faculty at the school do not have. Their training in sheltered techniques and English as a second language, the intensive involvement in conferences and workshops on these issues has made them aware of severe problems in lack of access and inappropriate teaching in the school for language-minority and immigrant students. What becomes problematic for them is how to act on this expertise and perspective within a system that does not acknowledge or welcome their expertise. Stern says:

> We chose to see these issues, to seek out training, to try to learn about language and culture. I think other teachers choose not to see it. It's not even a matter of caring or not caring. It's choosing to let that be a focus. It's a heavy mental stretch. If you're going to open up that whole discussion in your mind, you're going to have to make a major paradigm shift. You're going to have to change everything you think about how you teach. There are teachers in our school who don't want to let it in because it's just too big. So they have to work hard to tune us out because we talk about those issues—to tune the LEP kids out because that would make it obvious there are needs there to be met.

The four feel like outsiders. They speak often about the differences between themselves and the other teachers, the differences between the worlds they live in and Bayview, and the differences in their own upbringing and their students. Stern, a Jewish woman from the East Coast, living twenty-five miles away from Bayview, explains:

We came here from someplace else. And in some ways, there is a weird thing about getting up at the end of the day and leaving Bayview and going back to the little haven of your own little life, and it's outside of Bayview. We leave Bayview every single day! And the kids know that. And other teachers know that. And I wonder what that means. But one thing it means, is that we know and are constantly reminded that what is going on in Bayview doesn't have to be what goes on. It amazes me that this keeps going. Kids keep coming to school, even though they aren't getting what they need. Teachers keep coming to work, with less and less support to do the job. We should just refuse to do it anymore. But maybe it's only us who know it could be better. And maybe that's because we come from someplace else, where we know it was and is better, where you have supplies, where the school is clean, where there are counselors, where LEP students are welcomed, where kids of all classes achieve high, where teachers work together. And I think it might only come from the teachers like us saying, nobody in this community knows it, but you're getting ripped! But I'm not real sure of myself. One of the teachers in my department says to me, "Relax, Lisa, they're not all going to be rocket scientists. Let 'em alone with your high expectations of college." I was criticized as being a snob and an elitist because I was trying to argue for preparing all of our kids for college. And I don't know what to make of that. Is he right? Am I imposing my expectations? Or is he dead wrong? Are my outside eyes on Bayview something that gets in my way, or is it something that is useful?

Garrison also agonizes about this issue.

The biggest conflict for me is not living in the same community in which I teach, not being part of—I don't know—the culture of Bayview. I go home every day to a whole different world. I don't live in the kids homes; I don't even know what their homes are like. I don't even share with the white kids. I mean, I believe in getting the community involved and reaching out to the community, but I can't do that because bottom line I won't be part of the community. I don't want to live here. I don't know if the kids

pick up on that. I mean, they know I don't live here and that I
dress differently from adults in Bayview. And they perceive me
as different somehow. But I don't know what they make of that.

As a foursome, the women are able to explore these dilemmas and support
each other's perceptions and understandings of the needs of their students.
Attending conferences together on issues of language and culture, sitting and
spending hours talking about individual students and discovering the holes in
the system (courses needed and not assigned, prejudices of other teachers
expressed in put-downs of students, etc.), they embolden each other to be
advocacy forces within the school. Who should go talk to the principal about
the lack of math classes for LEP students? What strategies should they use?
Would it be better to go to the chair of the math department first?

For two years, this group continuously raised issues at faculty meetings and
departmental meetings, and attempted to push the school toward more
responsiveness to the needs of their immigrant students. After school over
beer, on weekends sitting on a deck of one of their houses, on long car rides to
work, and over the phone, the four engaged intently in trying to figure out
what might move the school forward. They often felt very alone, but could and
did turn at times to a larger structure of advocacy in the district that includes
some of the teachers at the Newcomer School and Maria Rodriguez.

THE STRUCTURE OF ADVOCACY

The dimension of the struggle to get the needs of LEP students recognized
in the school is clearly broader than four young individual teachers. The
challenge of how to develop a sustained and sustainable advocacy presence is
ongoing. It is the challenge that Maria Rodriguez faced from day one in the
Bayview school district. She knew then that a system of advocacy would need
to be built. The Newcomer School was to be the heart of that advocacy, bringing together teachers with training, expertise, and passion about addressing
language and cultural needs in the schools.

But within the Newcomer School, teachers who have great depths of
training in immigrant education cluster together, far away from being able to
see or touch what is occurring for immigrant students in the homebase high
schools. As a result, the Newcomer School teachers often feel isolated in their
separate site, frustrated with knowledge about lack of access for their students
in the mainstream comprehensive high schools, but without the relationships
or means to advocate for them. They are limited in impact.

Formally, the Newcomer School is charged with providing the first levels of ESL and bilingual social studies courses for LEP students in Bayview high schools. It is Madison's responsibility to provide advanced ESL, math and science courses, and the necessary social studies courses that are not offered at the New-comer Center. The fact that these courses are not often provided at Madison is understood by the folks at the Newcomer School as an illegal act resulting in denial of education through a lack of access to core academic subjects.

The dialogue about these patterns has been a long and contentious one in the district. With the removal of a bilingual coordinator position in the district and the lack of leadership setting direction, this struggle becomes a one-to-one dialogue between teachers and between the Newcomer School staff and Madison High staff. Newcomer School staff who feel angry about what they view as lack of responsiveness to LEP student needs end up confronting Madi-son High School staff who feel overburdened, undersupported, and over-whelmed, and often unknowledgable and uninterested in the issues of LEP students. This occurs in myriad forms, but one illustration provides some sense of the dimensions and depth of the struggle.

In a class discussion in an ESL class at the Newcomer School in November of 1993, it became clear that tenth-grader Gilberto Perez was unable to do some basic math pertinent to the discussion. His teacher admonished him about needing to study his math more, when Gilberto looked at him with sur-prise and said that he had no math class at Madison. The teacher went directly to the principal at Madison and reportedly threatened a lawsuit if Gilberto was not given a math class. The principal assured him it would be dealt with. But two months later, Gilberto still did not have a math class.

Once alerted to the issue, faculty at the Newcomer School checked out the programs of all Newcomer School students currently attending Madison and found four other students who had no math class. The students were being sent home early because they had short schedules. In talking to the staff and an administrator at Madison, it became clear that these students had not been put in a math class because there was no sheltered math class at the lower level. The lowest sheltered math class offered was a pre-algebra class with a placement test that starts with the addition and subtraction of fractions. Three of the four LEP students who took the test were unable to answer even one question. There was nothing that could be done, a representative from Madison explained, because it was mid-semester and the courses were set. The person from Madison felt that the Newcomer School staff were being unreasonable, and that they just did not understand the complexity of a master schedule in a large comprehensive school. But the Newcomer School faculty members were angry. Having the students miss eight more weeks of math would put them even further behind.

Pointing out that students only need two years of math to graduate, a Madison administrator insisted that it was too complicated to change a master schedule of an entire school to address this need. The students would have an opportunity in other semesters to take math. When the Newcomer School staff raised the concern that most four-year colleges require more than two years of math, the response was simply that these students did not strike the administrator as "college material" anyway. A Madison math teacher pointed out that too much attention was being given to students "at the bottom" (like LEP students). In her perspective, it was students "in the middle" who were getting completely left out. If another math section were possible, she would prefer it be aimed at that middle group and not for low-level ESL students. Finally, the administrator asserted that it would be hard to find math teachers that would be interested or willing to teach students with both low math skills and low English language skills.

By mid-November, the struggle had heated up. An administrator from Madison was called in, who argued strongly against trying to create a math placement for the students. The argument was framed pragmatically.

> We have much bigger problems here. Ideally, we'd have math for everyone, but that's just not reality. The classes in the school are too full as it is. We have regular students needing math, too. It would be too divisive to create something special for these kids, when it's a problem for a lot of people.

Here, the resentments of many teachers seeded years before became evident. The mythology that LEP students receive special extra resources that "regular" students suffer without, and that teachers of LEP students have it easy, resurfaced. In the context of a district in which fiscal crises created larger class sizes, the issue of which teachers get smaller classes is a hot one. A Newcomer School staff reported that the adminstrator then said:

> We are doing more than enough for LEP students, as evidenced by the fact that we are offering a sheltered social studies class with only twenty-four students, even though other students get placed in social studies classes with far more students. Giving you this math class would just add fuel to the fire.

The math class was seen as a concession to an advocate rather than as an educational response to an educational need of students. Referring to the mission of the Newcomer School, she suggested they offer the class there.

The specter of a lawsuit was again raised, and a meeting in late January brought together administrators of Madison, the chair of the math department at Madison, and a Newcomer School teacher with math teachers at Madison. The atmosphere was reportedly contentious. If the students could be added to an existing math class, the Newcomer School said it would provide a bilingual instructional assistant to assist in the classroom and to do an assessment for math placement, sending the result with each new student so that math teachers could be relieved of that burden. The conversation focused on the difficulty of the large class sizes in math at Madison, and how hard it was for teachers without training to take on students who had both low language abilities and low-level math skills. One teacher talked about his frustration with some recent immigrant Afghan students. The consensus of the math teachers was that they really should not have to take in "these kinds" of students at mid-semester, if at all.

The administrator, caught between a faculty unwilling to take on the students and the pressure from the Newcomer School backed by civil rights law, reminded the group that information about Madison not offering math classes to language-minority students could be very damaging if it leaked out to a reporter. Finally, one teacher offered to give up her fifth-period prep to supervise a bilingual assistant in teaching the five students in question. The administrator insisted, however, that the Newcomer School would need to pay a stipend to any teacher offering the math section. As one of the Newcomer School teachers remarked later in anger, "the word stipend was mentioned no less than ten times in the next fifteen minutes." The meeting closed when the administrator stated that this arrangement was a one-time-only solution and the Newcomer School could not expect it to happen year after year. She profusely thanked the teacher who finally agreed to do the class.

The Newcomer School coordinator said that she called the principal the next day to make it clear that the Newcomer School would not pay a stipend and that giving the students a math class was Madison's responsibility.

> You offer math classes to your other students, it is your responsibility to offer math to these students as well. The fact that they have special needs is not an excuse from your basic responsibility. You don't get to pick and choose which students you're going to teach math on the basis of who is easy to teach.

Madison then apparently refused to offer the special class, and instead placed each of the five students in "regular" basic math classes. The math teachers were reportedly furious, especially after having raised their concerns about how hard it is to take students in who do not have English or math skills. They felt set up for failure and angry that their needs were being ignored. Their fury was directed toward the administration, the Newcomer School, and the students.

Only four weeks later, it was clear that four of the five students were failing the classes. The Newcomer School teachers took this as yet another message about their own lack of power in the district and the hopelessness of trying to move the comprehensive schools from the outside. All of this demonstrates the difficulty of creating a program within a system without adequate resources, leadership, or political consensus—and the levels of frustration that layer each confrontation over serving the needs of LEP students.

Yet, the Newcomer School is still important as an advocacy support. Within Madison High, as one of the district homebase high schools, the four young teachers depended on being able to call Rodriguez to their defense when necessary. It functioned, they said, like bringing in the big guns. Many times policy could be enforced that might otherwise be evaded. But in the daily workings of Madison High, the staff of the Newcomer School remains remote. Although the Newcomer School may have managed to nurture some measure of advocacy within the district, it has also functioned to keep that advocacy marginalized and separate from the daily lives of the high schools. The problem was not only how the advocates within the Newcomer School could have more impact on the comprehensive schools, but also how to move beyond that, to providing support to the individual teachers who are isolated in the mainstream high school campuses like Stern, Garrison, Meyer, and O'Malley.

For example, in O'Malley's first year of teaching, she taught a class called ESL skills. Two of her students seemed to know English well, and she considered them brilliant. She was also teaching a tenth-grade accelerated class and thinking these two students could easily do the work of an accelerated tenth-grade class. O'Malley went to the English department chair and said, "I have a student and her brother who are very intelligent, write very well, and need to be in an accelerated class." But she was faced with a policy that defined the progression out of ESL into skills-level classes first and then to regular level and then into accelerated. O'Malley argued, "They could die in the system before they make it to accelerated." Eduardo, the brother, was already a twelfth grader, so she decided there was little hope for him. But O'Malley was angry. The department chair had not been willing to look at any of Luciana's writing samples as proof of the girl's abilities. She had simply insisted it was a matter of cut–and–dried policy. O'Malley realized she could get nowhere working only within Madison High. As she tells the story:

> I went to Maria, got her to look at this girl's writing, and told her the situation. She instructed me carefully to go back to the department chair, force her to look at the writing. I did that, but she still didn't budge. I offered to put Luciana in my own tenth-grade accelerated class. The answer was to go to the principal. So I went back to Maria and she called the principal. She had to threaten to take away all of his Title VII funding for LEP students if he didn't do this. That's what it came down to. She said, "Listen, George, I pay for these students at your school with our EIA LEP funds and Title VII funds, and if you don't serve them, the money is gone." Two days later, my department chair found me and said, "I've reconsidered and I think you're right. You can go ahead and put both kids into your tenth-grade accelerated class." I was mad. It wasn't right for Eduardo as a twelfth grader to be put in a tenth-grade class, but it was at least better than staying in a tenth-grade skills class. Maria suggested we let it rest. She advised we needed to take it a little battle at a time and not create a war we wouldn't win.

The language they use to describe this constant dance over meeting students' needs is the language of battles and wars. The young teachers and Newcomer School teachers speak of feeling "attacked" and "besieged," of going to "battle" for a student's rights, etc. They are concerned with increasing the number in their ranks. The structures of advocacy depend on educating, teaching, organizing, and bringing in others one by one to teach sheltered classes and to advocate for immigrant students. When O'Malley was hired as ESL coordinator, Maria began to counsel her about finding other teachers. When conferences were being held on issues of language and culture, she would suggest that O'Malley try to find other teachers who might be interested in attending with her. Rodriguez pursued a strategy of active recruitment and mentoring to try to build the numbers of teachers in Bayview supportive of bilingual education. Bilingual instructional assistants were encouraged and helped to pursue teaching credentials. Teachers at the Newcomer School were encouraged to get administrative credentials and then apply for jobs as school administrators in the district.

Another example of the crucial role that an "outside" person with some district authority played in supporting the program within Madison again involves the young teachers calling on Rodriguez. This story was also told by O'Malley:

> In the spring, a counselor came to me, angry because I had submitted to her a list of students who signed up for Spanish bilingual United States history at the Newcomer School. The sign-ups called for four full classes of thirty-three students each. The counselor insisted it wasn't possible that all of those students could really need bilingual history. It would be a scheduling nightmare, she explained, and she suspected that the English-as-a-second-language teachers were just trying to coddle the students. "There can't be this many kids on our campus that don't understand what's going on in history classes!" I told her, "Easily, and more." The counselor felt that bilingual history should only be for ESL levels I, II, or III. I had to tell her that it was my belief and the Newcomer Center's belief that the point of teaching history is to get content across to kids, and you need a strong fluency and literacy in English to get that content in an English-taught class. The counselor didn't want to schedule the students for bilingual history. So I had to invoke the "Maria" threat. It was great to be able to say to her: "You're not going to get your way, because Maria will come unglued if you tell me you won't schedule them into bilingual history!"

Later, O'Malley worried. The student sign-ups for bilingual history had all been on her recommendation. She basically felt that it would be more interesting for them and they would get a lot more out of learning history in Spanish than in English when they were not that proficient yet in reading and writing or understanding abstract social studies concepts in English. But then she began to worry. Was that recommendation sound? Had she made a mistake? Was she wrong? She checked again on their English levels, and then went to Maria to get validation that her assessments were correct.

In story after story, the four young teachers at Madison spoke of the importance of having a bottom line. The bottom line was that they had behind them a structure of advocacy. There was Maria. And Maria had behind her the law. Those were useful tools for trying to push the system forward. But it was not sufficient. Their work, they perceived, was not only to push the system to be responsive, but also to be the agents of responsiveness in the midst of a system that resists. At times, helping individual teachers, counselors, and administrators understand the student needs and educational issues worked to get a student placed more appropriately into classes, to get needed materials, or to create some small change. But on a policy level, whether it was trying to affect the course offerings or the practice of other faculty, most battles were lost. On some large issues, invoking the law and calling on Maria could work. Increasingly, however, the four teachers gave up on those levels and concentrated instead on one-to-one work with students. This task required advocacy as well, and propelled them into areas of tremendous confusion about what it means to provide guidance at the intersection of cultures. It brought the four into regular confrontations with the understandings, standard practices, and unwritten codes of Madison High.

THE PERSONAL RISK AND GRAY AREAS OF ADVOCACY

It's a Wednesday in June, and the school year is winding down. Linda O'Malley has lessened the pace of activities in her ESL IV class, and has given students five to ten minutes at the end of the period simply to sit and talk with friends. It is in that context that a student told O'Malley of her suddenly arranged marriage, and that the next day (Thursday) she would not be in school because she was going to be engaged. She would meet her husband-to-be and his family and they would exchange rings and wedding clothing. Several other girls overheard the conversation. "Aren't you scared?" "What happens on your wedding night?"

Padma was extremely scared and nervous. She told them that if she does not bleed on her wedding night, he can divorce her and she would be shamed. O'Malley decided the time for sex information was now, and said outright, "Do you know that there are other ways that hymens break? Has anyone talked to you about sex or about getting pregnant?" The look on Padma's face was enough for O'Malley. She called Lisa Stern on the phone, whose class Padma would be going to next, and arranged to excuse her. Second, O'Malley canceled a meeting she was supposed to have during her prep period. "Stay next period," she suggested to Padma, "and we'll talk." Padma said, "yes, please." Her good friend, who O'Malley had suspected from previous conversations might be sleeping with her boyfriend, said "me, too." And a third said, "I get married next year," which O'Malley took to mean that she wanted to stay also.

Padma and the two friends stayed. "I'm afraid that if I get pregnant I won't get to go to college because we have to rent an apartment and support him and his father. I don't want to have children yet. Please help me." So O'Malley first asked them what they knew. One knew about condoms, another said her boyfriend had reassured her that pulling out keeps you from getting pregnant. O'Malley decided to "tell them everything." She explained about condoms, how they work, what they look like in a package, where you buy them, and what you do with them. She explained birth control pills and how hormones work. And having been raised herself as a Catholic, O'Malley also explained the rhythm method. The girls liked the thought of the rhythm method because they agreed that it would not be right for Padma to trick her husband with pills, and did not think she could ask him to use a condom. But then the idea of sewing a little pocket into her jacket was developed so she could hide pills in there and simply take one every morning in the bathroom. She was worried that she could not keep them in her purse in case he needs something and looks there. O'Malley left the issue of ethics regarding honesty with a husband alone and tried to focus back on the issue of birth control. She explained that to get birth control pills, Padma would need to see a doctor. O'Malley offered to make an appointment for Padma at Planned Parenthood and to take her there, even though she knew that she could get into trouble if Padma's parents or the school found out. She felt her presence might be important to help with English and to provide moral support. Her friend then piped up. "Ms. O'Malley, I've already slept with my boyfriend and we are not using a condom. " As O'Malley said later:

> I tried to sympathize with her, to say I know that it's hard when you're in the back of his car and your emotions are going wild and you want to be loved, but you either need to make the decision before you get into the position or find a boyfriend who will be more supportive of you and help you use birth control. At that point, I realized my mission was not just about giving information, but giving advice. I didn't want the girls to just happen to get pregnant.

In the end, O'Malley took the girls to Planned Parenthood. On the drive, Padma started to cry. "I don't want to have children." O'Malley asked if she knew whether her husband wanted children soon, and Padma reminded her that they had never met before, much less discussed this kind of intimate issue. "Perhaps he will be very modern, and we can decide it together. But it isn't my place to bring it up."

It was at the end of this day that O'Malley talked to me, exhausted and worried.

Am I crazy? All this was such a risk! I could be fired if the principal found out, or if the parents found out and complained. In a
way I don't care. It's worth the risk. It's sad I have to take this risk.
But Padma is so bright and intelligent and she deserves to go
places and she wants to go places, and so much is out of her control. She deserves to be able to make a choice about having a
baby. And so I just kept thinking that and thinking that, and
knowing I had to do it. I had to help her have that choice. And for
me, I'm not sure what I'm doing. Was it right to help her when
clearly birth control is not something her parents were about to
help her with. Was I mucking with her culture?

And yet from O'Malley's cultural perspective, to get pregnant while young
had dire consequences. And her belief that early pregnancy would limit Padma
was so strong, she overrode her worries.

Teaching is secondary to this kind of dilemma for me. There
is no real sex education in the school. Here is this young woman
who is going to marry and is culturally expected to have children soon, and she personally wants to have a life before
she has kids. I need to help her have that opportunity to control
that. Nowhere in my teacher training did anyone tell me how to
deal with things like this. And if it means taking risks, well, if
I can help her make her own choices and not get pregnant,
it's worth it to me. But I feel such overwhelming sorrow and pain
that this has to be so secretive—that she can't go to her family,
that she can't come to any one at the school openly, and that
I have to take a risk to help her. It's so sad, and I'm so drained. I
don't want to lose her. I want to see her dreams come true, and I
would risk anything to make that happen. And it feels crazy that
out in the world, we all know about teenagers having sex with
boyfriends and teenage pregnancy and going to Planned Parenthood and buying condoms. But inside school, it's not a
talked-about part of life. And do I participate in the big secret?
Or do I just refuse to give in to it and go ahead and help kids
when they need it?

O'Malley kept saying, "maybe this isn't my line of work!"

Several days later, the principal called O'Malley to his office and warned her against putting the school in a difficult position. "It's not your place to be giving every girl advice about sleeping with their boyfriends and having sex." O'Malley had no idea whether or how word had gotten to him, or if this was simply a general warning out of the blue. She thought of calling Maria Rodriguez, but issues like these were not exactly protected by legal matters of access to education. It falls in a different kind of category that O'Malley felt put her on her own, standing alone.

The next day, Rosalyn, struggling with wanting to and trying to be an "American" girl, knocked on O'Malley's office door. Hearing about Padma's trip to Planned Parenthood, she too came to talk to O'Malley about sex. She had lied to her parents and told them that Easter vacation was canceled by the school because they decided it was not right to give students a vacation for a Christian holiday when so many other religions were now in the school. She spent her days that week with her American boyfriend. Since then, he kept pressuring her to find ways to have sex with him or else he would break up with her. She was not pregnant, and she did not want to be. And she was tired of lying to her parents. O'Malley asked her to sit down and quietly shut the door.

I never heard a report from O'Malley about what happened after that incident. In fact, we didn't really talk in depth at all after this. The next day was the end-of-school barbeque that O'Malley and Stern were throwing for their ESL students, and there was no private time to talk. During the summer, I got a note from O'Malley that she had gotten a job in another city and would not be returning to Madison.

THE VULNERABILITY AND TRANSITORY NATURE OF THE ADVOCACY STRUCTURE

The foursome of young advocate teachers at Madison were often able to forge a strong advocacy voice andto support each other's work where little other support existed. They made an enormous impact on their students individually, but their work did little to affect the regular patterns of practice and policy at the school. And their alliance did not last. As young women, other factors in their lives were affecting their career and life choices. Without protection of jobs in Bayview given the layoffs, given the low salary structure of the district, and in the context of how hard it was to continue to be marginalized and in battle with an older faculty that was not interested in their ideas, some of them began to look for work elsewhere. Theirs had been a close friendship forged by a particular institutional context. Outside of that context, back in their lives in other cities and in other realms, the close connection no longer held. Linda O'Malley left Madison to take a job closer to her home in the Valley. That same summer, Lisa Stern left Madison to enter a doctoral program in education, pursuing her dream of having a greater impact on the field of education.

The day Stern made public her intention to leave the school, she made a public announcement to the students at Madison High through the school's in-house television studio. Her message was broadcast along with the bulletin of the day, announcements, and various other snippets of interest to the Madison community. The going-away speech was passionate. In Lisa Stern style, she chose the opportunity to say things that are not usually voiced in official channels at the school. She spoke to her students about the importance of "hanging in at school and believing in yourself even when so much in the school and the system is trying to tell you that you aren't worth much." She talked about the hurt she knows students suffered from the teachers' strikes and the low teacher morale. She spoke of how the budget cuts and loss of counselors meant they were not getting what they needed and deserved at the school. Stern told them it was not a fair deck they have been dealt. But she urged them to keep trying and to insist on getting whatever they can in an education. She urged them to speak up when their teachers are unfair, to speak out when their courses are not challenging. And then she said goodbye, she would miss them, and offered to give her address to anyone who wanted to correspond with her.

At the end of the broadcast, Stern had tears in her eyes. The students watching in Garrison's class where I sat were uncharacteristically silent. Later that day, the speech was a topic of conversation for students and teachers alike. One teacher said in the teachers lounge, "I guess Lisa Stern is done trying to fix us and now she is going on to fix the rest of the world." Another teacher answered, "And wouldn't you know it would have to be an elite school for Lisa." Later, a teacher commented to me: "Isn't that just like Lisa? Telling the kids their lives are awful and then saying good-bye. What good does she think that will do?"

A crowd of about twenty students were hanging out around Lisa Stern's bungalow classroom as school let out. Students asked for her address, asking if it was really true that she was going to leave them. Jani hugged her and said "Don't leave us, Ms. Stern! Take us with you." Evangelista added:

> The whole school is becoming so bad. Ms. Stern and then Ms. O'Malley may not come back. Who will we tell our problems to? Who will care about us? Soon it will be only me here. Who will take care of us? What will happen to us?

Janet refused to go home because she was afraid she would not see Stern again. Mike, a teacher in the auto shop who was on an emergency credential, came over. He had just received a layoff notice about his job and had heard that auto shop might be canceled altogether because of budget cuts. He and Stern were commiserating and Huan (a student) overheard them, and said: "They cut everything. Nineteen hundred eighty-nine was the best year, they had it all then. Now every year it gets worse."

She is only sixteen and was not in the school in 1989. But popular mythology is strong. The school is believed to be going downhill. A math teacher who had come from Washington High came up to Stern and congratulated her. Then she said, "I wish I was leaving, too."

Later, Rebecca remarked, "We're all feeling left behind in the muck. Abandoned, and wishing we had ways to get out." Dorothy Meyer was pregnant, looking forward to cutting back her hours to be with her new child. In looking ahead, Rebecca was devastated:

> I don't know what I'm going to do next year. If these guys are all going to be gone, I don't know what I'm going to do! I'm glad I'll be in the Master's program because otherwise I'd be on my way out the door. And there are reasons for me to stay, personally. But I don't think I want to work in a place where this kind of team effort isn't there—I don't think I can make it alone. I don't think you can remain a good teacher for long if you're isolated. You go crazy.

And thus, the forces and structures of advocacy in Bayview are maintained as marginal, limited in their impact, and highly vulnerable. The institutional history at Madison High has resulted in a veteran faculty power structure that holds to a particular perspective on diversity that does not tolerate what they view as divisive catering to "special needs" or efforts to (in their eyes) separate and segregate students in the name of targeted instruction or special supports. Their map of the world is one of a meritocracy, where divisions by academic level have been constituted through student choice and aspirations. Intently blind to the racial and classist sorting process of the school and to the out-and-out denial of access to education for language-minority students, this perspective holds that once immigrant newcomers to the school learn English, their success will simply be a matter of individual effort.

The new young teachers who enter the school with training in second-language acquisition issues and a different map of the world and its divisions have strikes against them from the start as they attempt to espouse a different perspective on the needs of immigrant students and the role of schools in addressing issues of diversity. In addition, the budget crisis in the district sets the stage for resentment among faculty about the use of resources, and makes the positions of the new young teachers highly vulnerable to layoffs. The combination of isolation and battle fatigue as advocates, the job insecurity in their positions, and their own youth eventually scatters the advocates to other places, other districts, other occupations. Meanwhile, the Newcomer School continues to serve as a support and shelter harboring teachers in the district who share an alternative perspective on diversity. Most staff at the Newcomer School focus on language and culture as the major components of diversity. In this way, they, too, collude in a color-blindness as to the racial project of the schools. Nonetheless, the Newcomer School provides a place where those who seek to advocate for more inclusion can openly act on their knowledge and ideology about supporting the cultures and home languages of their students, and where they can offer their students an environment of some support for multiculturalism. But the separation that shelters them and their efforts, limits their impact on the comprehensive schools in the district and serves to constrain them at the margins.

The law remains—clear in its articulation of basic civil rights and the right of access to an education—but it requires advocates on all levels to breathe life into it and see it implemented. As the advocates attempt to make the promise of access real and try to build and implement strong programs that support the inclusion of all students, they win some and lose some ground. And the resultant program is a hybrid compromise.

The formal school programmatic world that has been constructed for immigrant students at Madison High provides some arenas of shelter and education, but it also institutionalizes fragmentation and separation of realms and provides only a weak structure of support for them in negotiating the process of becoming "American." And the overall structures of the comprehensive high school with the task of creating monolingual English-speaking Americans, and maintaining silence on the racial sorting, is basically preserved.

CHAPTER TEN

Madison High, The State, and the Nation

I WALK into the Newcomer School just before lunch for an appointment with Maria Rodriguez. The front office is buzzing as a teacher speaks in Spanish to a new student and mother. The phone is ringing while two students are trying to explain to the school secretary why they need to go home for lunch but don't have a note from their parents. This is a normal day. I stick my head into Maria's office and she looks uncharacteristically still. "Maria, are you okay?" She looks up, visibly upset, and hands me the newspaper, pointing to a story about a new California state ballot initiative for which signatures are beginning to be collected. It calls for ending public benefits, including schooling, for undocumented immigrants. "Do you believe this?" she asks softly. "It's terrifying! The backlash is really heating up in this state. Where is this going to lead?" Then almost immediately she refocused on her job there in Bayview. "We should get a notice out to parents right away from the Newcomer School assuring them their kids are welcome here and no one is being asked or turned away because of immigration status."

And in that moment I felt again the weight of the world beyond Bayview—the larger political struggles over immigration and diversity and the rights of children to have access to schooling that shape what we do in any one local context. I think about a little litany my young son likes to recite: "There is a boy in a school in a town in a state in a country in a hemisphere on the Earth in the universe . . ."

■ ■ ■

Sandra, Juanita, Jani, Corinne, Padma, and the other immigrant students described in this book arrived in Bayview as part of a massive human migration in which people from all over the world have immigrated to California.

They have been greeted there by Vivien, Jessica, Tony, Jeff, and other students, born in the United States, in communities being changed by the impact of that human migration. They all meet on the playing field of a school, interacting across and through the divisions in classrooms, academic tracks, and program separation that have been created by educators. The teachers and administrators at Madison High—Pereira, Stern, O'Malley, Richards, Garrison, and others—do their best with their own philosophical and political perspectives to forge a response to the new diversity, but struggle with each other over what that response should be. The program they have created at Madison High is neither designed nor delivered in a vacuum. State and federal mandates require a program that will address the language barrier facing LEP students and ensure educational access for these students. But a national politicized and polarized struggle over language and culture, race relations, and diversity shapes the attitudes of educators charged with interpreting and implementing these mandates.

Bayview is not alone in its struggles. It is not untouched by the political battles in other parts of the nation. And it is not atypical of communities through this nation being reshaped by immigration. The formal educational program, as well as the relationships between individuals, is shaped heavily by a political and ideological struggle over diversity in general, and the specific mandates and programs emanating from court and legislative battles over access, civil rights, and education.

There is a history of civil rights battles and racial, cultural, and language relations that deeply shapes the laws and policies governing programs at Madison High and elsewhere. Today's immigrants journey to the United States to become part of a diversity in which ethnic, racial, and language-minority groups have been battling for economic, political, and educational access for years. The voices and demands for access to an education, for equity and representation from these communities are a major component of the pressure on schools to respond adequately to the needs of newly arrived immigrants. In some cases, the pressure is direct—as parents, community members confront the schools in their town to provide full access and respect for their children who face barriers to access because of skin color, lack of English fluency, or immigration status. In other communities, it is people like Rodriguez, Stern, Garrison, and others, who as professional educators attempt to push schools to be more inclusive. In a few states, for periods of time, the legislatures have provided some leadership and guidance regarding the creation of programs for access. But fundamentally, bottom line, it has fallen to the courts of this nation to provide the legal framework and teeth to insist on the rights of children to equal access to schooling regardless of skin color, national background, or home language.

The lawsuits have resulted from years of advocacy, organizing and sheer persistence on the parts of communities frozen outside of the educational system. Understanding some of this history, and the directions the courts and legislatures have taken, is a necessary context for understanding what is occurring at Madison High and other high schools throughout our nation.

Leading the movement for educational access for immigrants, immigrant rights, and language rights are advocacy organizations from long-standing racial and ethnic "minority" communities. They include, for example, the Mexican American Legal Defense and Education Fund, the National Council of La Raza, the mutual assistance associations of resettled refugees, the National Coalition for Immigrant Rights, ASPIRA, and others. These groups have for decades documented the denial of access for language-minority and immigrant students in schools, monitored the resources allocated to education in the schools most impacted by immigrant children, and lobbied the federal government for attention to the needs of immigrant students. These advocates have been responsible for bringing numerous lawsuits against schools and hence have built a body of case law and precedent to define and protect the rights of immigrant children in school. They build on a tradition of using the law to gain educational rights, which was established early in the history of the nation.

Although the law has upheld the rights of access, popular sentiment has not followed. The past decades have been full of deep political struggles over interpretation of the laws, over bilingual education, social studies textbook selection, the inclusion of immigrants in schools, affirmative action, and cultural diversity in the curriculum.

The Bayview schools, similar to schools in diverse communities throughout this nation, have been directly embroiled in these political fights, and also deeply imprinted by the national ideological dialogues about diversity and the mandates and programs stemming from civil rights law, legislative battles, and administrative policies.

The right of equal access to an education for immigrant students is based on the Equal Protection Clause of the Fourteenth Amendment to the U.S. Constitution, which states that public schools are barred from denying access to schooling on the basis of race, national origin, or alienage. It is a fairness argument, not an educational one. The argument is not that every child has a right to an education, but basically that if schooling is being provided as a public service, then a group of people cannot be barred from access to that public service solely on the basis of race, national origin, or alienage.

The clearest court action shaping this era was the Supreme Court decision in *Brown v. Topeka, Kansas Board of Education*. After more than a hundred years of struggle over racial segregation, the courts determined that denial of equal protection exists where separate provisions are made for groups who are similarly situated without adequate justification. The famous ruling states: "In the field of public education, the doctrine of separate but equal has no place. Separate educational facilities are inherently unequal."

Separate is not equal. Equal is interpreted as the same treatment for all. This was a race-based legal paradigm. And with it, integration, same facilities, same treatment became the law of the land—if not the practice of the nation.

In the 1960s, this nation was alive with the struggle over civil rights. The federal government became very actively involved in funding school programs considered in the national interest (anti-poverty, building up math and science instruction to "compete" with the Soviets in the space race, racial integration, etc.). And along with this federal involvement were a host of programs designed to improve the educational performance of racial minority and poor students (for example, Head Start, school lunch programs, etc.) The major paradigm was compensatory. Students from poor families and students of color were viewed as being at a disadvantage, requiring help to gain the background, skills, nutrition, or language necessary for success in school. The 1964 Civil Rights Act stated that there could be no discrimination in any federally funded programs on the basis of race, color, or national origin. Because schools throughout the nation were receiving federal funding, this applied to all public schools.

On a federal level, the bilingual education movement is rooted in Title VI of the Civil Rights Act of 1964, which states: "no person shall be subjected to discrimination on the basis of race, color or national origin."

Following the passage of that act, the Office of Civil Rights issued a memorandum specifically addressing the situation of language-minority students with limited English skills. They determined that the implementation of Title VI demanded that schools must take "affirmative steps" to rectify the language barriers in order to open up access to schooling. This was the beginning of the analysis of national-origin discrimination as a matter of language access, and it was an early statement of a view of equity that clarified that equal access depended on specific supports and assistance to address specific educational barriers. It is a subtle but essential development of the understanding of educational equity from the "treating students the same is equity" paradigm.

In 1965, Congress enacted the Elementary and Secondary Education Act (ESEA), and several years later, bilingual education was added to this act as Title VII. It became effective January 1, 1968.

The Title VII bilingual education program was structured to provide funding for three years to schools and districts and after that time, the federal government expected districts to assume financial responsiblity for the programs. This was problematic for many districts and provided an impetus for state action on bilingual education. Schools may have wanted the federal funds, but were largely unwilling to spend their own dollars. When the federal funds disappeared, they would turn to their states to replace those funds or dismantle the programs. The struggle was thus passed along to the states and to locales where the efforts to implement were taking place.

Almost a decade later, a lawsuit filed by Chinese parents against the San Francisco school district reached the Supreme Court. The parents had sued the schools because they believed their children were being denied access to an education because there were no special English classes to help them learn English. The Supreme Court ruled in *Lau v. Nichols* that

> there is no equality of treatment merely by providing students with the same facilities, books, teachers and curriculum, for students who do not understand English are effectively foreclosed from any meaningful education.

The difference became ever clearer between the popular operating definition of equality, which viewed any kind of different or separate treatment as inherently unequal, and the increasing understanding that there is no equality of access or opportunity if people are treated the same in situations where one group is facing barriers resulting from that same treatment. This distinction reverberated throughout the bilingual-education wars that followed, and is evident every day in the struggles of educators in schools such as Madison.

Although the courts mandated affirmative steps to overcome language barriers, exactly what was meant by "affirmative steps" was up for grabs. To implement the *Lau* decision, the Office of Civil Rights established broad remedies for instructional programs and for the integration of children belonging to ethnic and language-minority groups. In the final months of the Carter presidency, the federal Department of Health, Education, and Welfare issued (known as the Lau Remedies) guidelines as regulations binding on all school districts in the United States. These regulations prescribed transitional bilingual, bilingual and bicultural or bilingual and multicultural programs for the elementary schools.[36] English as a second language was deemed appropriate for the secondary level. These remedies were subjects of great political controversy, and there was widespread heated opposition to the draft federal regulations as overly rigid and prescriptive and too supportive of primary language instruction. There was also building support from within the bilingual-education movement, which was beginning to amass a body of research and some program experience. Rhetoric about "the threat to the English language and to national unity" had mobilized opposition to primary-language instruction.

In the midst of this controversy, the *Lau* Remedies were never accorded the weight of law and were withdrawn by the Reagan administration in early 1981. And despite subsequent court mandates to develop official regulations, none have been issued since.

The failure of leadership on the federal level shifted the fight back to the state level, but the heat of the national political debate worked to further polarize what was occurring in California. Pressure built for the state legislature in California to interpret *Lau* for school districts and to help them pay for programs. The central points of disagreement then, as now, focused on the use of a child's home language in instruction, the amount of prescriptiveness the state ought to employ in defining programs, the requirements for teacher training, and concerns over segregation.

BILINGUAL EDUCATION: YEA OR NAY?

In the two decades since, the struggle over responses to diversity and over what we mean by equity and fairness was fought on the language rights front in the battle over bilingual-education policy. Bilingual education, like most movements for educational access, has primarily relied on a top-down intervention of the federal government and the courts, seeking to ensure access to the curriculum for language-minority students and responding to the mandates of the 1964 federal Civil Rights Act. The involvement of the courts and of the federal government was crucial in framing the Bayview story, both in their support for a language rights movement within education and also in setting the stage for a contentious resistance to "top down" and "outside" programs. With pressure from the courts and from civil rights advocacy communities, the California state legislature became a site of highly political scrambles to try to contain and resist provisions for primary-language instruction. In Bayview, California, immigrant advocates were bolstered by the laws and compliance apparatus that supported their concerns, but caught in the crossfire of a tense and polarized statewide and local fight.

California provides a case study of what such statewide struggles looked like. California received a large portion of federal bilingual education Title VII funds when the federal bilingual program was started, beginning with $3.5 million in the 1969–70 fiscal year, reaching $21.4 million by 1975–76.

Title VII raised the public visiblity of bilingual education and required that the state superintendent of instruction enforce the Civil Rights Act in districts receiving ESEA funds, including Title VII. At the time, Wilson Riles was an activist state superintendent of instruction and the legislature was confronted with the likelihood that Superintendent Riles would set his own agenda for bilingual education if they did not enact a state statute themselves.

Out in the field, Title VII programs became the first arena within which people who were concerned with language rights and bilingual education could come together. The early Title VII projects knit a community with shared values and the fire and will to push the state on developing supportive policy. They were a largely grassroots movement for bilingual education emanating partially from the organization of farmworkers, migrant educators, and the Latino community was forming. Their organizational efforts laid the groundwork for the establishment of the California Association for Bilingual Education, the state's major bilingual advocacy organization.[37]

By 1972, California had enacted its first bilingual education law. It promoted bilingual education, called for an annual census of non-English-speakers, and appropriated $5 million for a new state program for bilingual education. The fight against it at that time was framed around concerns for local autonomy for school districts who did not want the state prescribing programs and resistance to state government prescriptiveness. The compromise was that local school boards would have authority to design the bilingual program. The legislation stated only that limited or non-English-speaking students "shall receive special assistance in any manner approved by local boards." No requirements were specified regarding the qualification of teachers, again in deference to the opposition. For those concerned about integration, the bill required programs to include both English-only students and non- or limited-English-speaking students.

The Chacon-Moscone Bilingual Bicultural Education Act (AB 1329) was a compromise between those who wished minimal prescriptiveness about the use of children's primary-language for instruction and those who argued for primary language literacy as a goal in addition to English literacy.[38] It attempted to mediate concerns over integration with the need for targeted instruction to students with limited English proficiency. It acknowledged the need for training for teachers, but softened requirements by offering substantial numbers of waivers. Importantly, it also established a language census, an initial language assessment for all language-minority students, and formal exit criteria governing when LEP students would be done with bilingual programs. It was this language census that was to become such an essential tool in the hands of advocates such as Maria Rodriguez in Bayview. Almost immediately, the pressure of resistance to bilingual education began to mount for amendments to the law. There was explicit resistance to the idea of using children's home languages in the schools and to the implication that more Spanish speaking and Latino teachers would need to be hired.

When the *Lau* decision settled the issue that something proactive had to be provided children whose first language is other than English, advocates had a new tool to push for implementation of bilingual programs.

In the 1980 legislative session, there were three major bills on bilingual education introduced as revisions of AB 1329. All sought relaxation of some of the mandates and introduced new "ways out." Some of the sentiment was coming from people confused by the contradictory messages from the research community, and convinced that the field was so new and so inconclusive that more experimentation and research on alternatives should be encouraged before "buying into" a single model. Others were outright opposed to the use of state dollars and public institutions to promote primary-language use. Arguing for a stronger state role in explicitly outlining primary-language instruction and bilingual-program models were the growing numbers of educators convinced by both research and their own program experiences. Whether the state should prescribe or allow primary instruction; whether a single model and approach was appropriate; the discretion of local sites; and the length of time that primary language should be allowed were the hot topics surrounding the legislative debate. Furthermore, although early on in the bilingual legislation process the issue of teacher qualification was not even on the table, it now became a key piece. As the pool of LEP students grew and the numbers of teachers fell short of the numbers needed for Chacon's preferred bilingual model, he was forced to author bill after bill extending waivers to let existing teachers remain in the teaching force and teach LEP students without bilingual training or authorization. The resistance on the parts of teacher unions against any requirements of additional training mirrored those of the voices we heard in Bayview.[39]

Another key issue was requiring non–LEP students to be in bilingual classes. Superintendent Riles was a major proponent of desegregation and feared that bilingual education might become segregation. He felt strongly that all bilingual classes must also have English-only students in them. But districts did not want to require unwilling English-only parents to keep their students in bilingual classes. Especially in districts in which the number of LEP students was growing rapidly and disproportionately to the English-only students, the pressure to release schools from the requirement was intense. Meanwhile, while the legislature was embroiled in the political fight over bilingual education, federal Title VII implementation funds supported several bilingual staff positions within the California State Department of Education. A proactive group of bilingual staff and consultants put together a research-based theoretical framework for bilingual education, which became the blueprint for practice in the field. It was an attempt to speak into an atmosphere of political contentiousness with a plea and a tool for educators to attend to research-based educational practices. They also set up a bilingual county coordinators network, understanding that advocates out in the field desperately needed support from each other and to be kept in constant notice of what was occurring in Sacramento. This network was, as one coordinator said: "The lifeline for all of us, the main political support, the place we could go when we were reeling from all the resistance in the field, and the way we could mobilize the forces when we had to to go to Sacramento."

Bilingual education had grown as a public and political issue in California, representing concerns far broader than effective educational pedagogy. In the fall of 1986, opposition to bilingualism in schools, voting pamphlets, and official documents was framed in a public ballot initiative called simply "Proposition 63," which declared English as the official language of California. The initiative, a dry-run for similar campaigns to be run in other locales and states around the nation, passed by a 2 to 1 margin. It fed on fears that language diversity was contributing to a dissolution of a common culture.

Despite numerous attempts to reinstate a bilingual law beyond the sunset date, then Governor George Deukmejian vetoed any extensions, allowing the bill to expire. When a categorical aid program sunsets, such as the bilingual education program, the state funds for the program continue to be allocated to school districts for the general purpose of the program but districts gain flexibility in program approaches in the use of the funds.

With the expiration of state law governing language assistance programs, the federal mandate emanating from *Lau*, with all its vagueness because of the lack of federally prescribed remedies or guidelines, remained as the legal underpinning of current California efforts to educate language minority students.

In 1987, the legislature and the governor were deeply involved in school reform legislation, much of it shaped by the free-market theories of the corporate sector and the Business Roundtable. In that atmosphere, the mandate language of the bilingual law seemed dated and out of step with the new push for reform (allowing more site-specific innovation, releasing sites from the shackles of intervention from above). Superintendent Honig's position on reinstatement of the bilingual mandate was ambiguous. His focus was instead on state-developed curriculum frameworks as a vehicle of reform. These frameworks were guidelines about what should be taught at which levels of schooling, and relied on voluntary adoption by individual teachers. He did make some statements supportive of bilingual education, but did not bring his political capital to bear on extending it in law. When the law expired, the California Department of Education's legal office issued an advisory to districts which laid out continuing post-sunset requirements as a response to federal law and the *Lau* mandate. Opponents of bilingual education continue to oppose the department of education's enforcement of bilingual mandates and to assume a local right to figure out what program they desire for their LEP students, if any. Bilingual advocates continue to act on the regulations issued by the legal office at that time. It is the resultant struggle between these that we witnessed at Madison High. The product is almost always partial programs.

The bilingual-education fight is a specific version of a much broader societal struggle. The underlying struggle that has continued to be waged is between two fundamentally different perspectives. On the one hand a concern over the civil rights and educational access for language-minority children, and on the other an insistence that an overiding priority is that of cultural cohesion (understood as language cohesion) in the face of increasing cultural diversity and threats to the dominance of the English language. And while these cultural and social battles are being fought, the application and implementation of the laws protecting educational access are up for grabs—and a deeper concern emerges.

In looking into the lives of the immigrant students at Madison High, it is clear that the legal frameworks are far from adequate in addressing the complexities of barriers to access to schooling that they face. As young people who cannot yet adequately speak or learn in English to adequately to gain access to social studies and math and science taught only in English, the language barrier has yet to be addressed because of ambivalence and lack of leadership and accountability in the implementation of our laws. However, the problem is deeper. The "language access" paradigm addresses only the language issue. The young people we met at Madison High are not only language-minority students grappling with a new language in their new land. As young people learning their places in a racial order that consigns too easily young people of darker skins to places in less rigorous curriculum and forecloses opportunities for preparation for higher education, the legal frameworks around language access are simply insufficient. Without programmatic regulations or mandates, guidelines, or accountablity "teeth" offering specificity and meaning to the *Brown v. Board of Education* decision recognizing that separate education is not equal, students will continue to sit in classes sorted by skin color within schools that may be integrated overall, and in classes with less rigorous curriculum and fewer resources. And as newcomers to our nation, immigrating across national borders, it is becoming increasingly in question whether they will even be able to exercise a right to participation in school. There are increasingly serious proposals to exclude undocumented immigrant children from schools. Without guarantees of the right to an education in this country, young people who are immigrants will likely continue to face threats to access to the schoolhouse building at all.

The battle has heated up for us throughout this nation, as it has for the individuals at Madison High in Bayview. Will we choose to guarantee schooling for all children? Will we stand up for equal access and equal opportunity? Will we finally grapple with the ways in which our schools sort or exclude children based on their skin color, class, national origin, or home language?

CHAPTER ELEVEN

Conclusions: What Future Will We Choose as a Multicultural Society?

TAKING A break from writing this last chapter, I met with Frida Camacho, one of the leaders of the Latino student movement at Madison High. The articulate, excited young woman described a rally she had just helped organize in opposition to Proposition 187, the California state ballot initiative that had recently been passed by the voters excluding undocumented immigrants from schools. The leaders of the rally had done broad outreach among all Latino students in the city, but also included other students as well. She was excited, feeling that perhaps the student movement was really beginning to grow and move, and that despite the snowballing of a backlash against immigrants, perhaps there was hope in the younger generation—a generation raised amidst a degree of multiculturalism unknown to their parents. Frida had told me:

> We have to live with all kinds of people now. Young people are
> more used to it. And if there is a solution to all the discrimina-
> tion and hatred and racism, we're the ones who can do it. We
> can. Maybe our time has come.

After meeting Frida, I stopped at the Newcomer School to say hello, and met Rebecca Garrison there. She introduced me to a new teacher at Madison High, Loretta Cleveland, an ESL teacher full of energy and commitment to immigrant education. The two were deep in conversation about creating a student lounge for the immigrant students, a place where the students can hang out, where information about colleges and school credits and gatekeeping courses could be made available in many different languages. The new teacher was new energy, a newcomer to the ranks filling in the void created by those advocates who had left the school. We walked together to a meeting of all teachers of sheltered and bilingual classes in the high schools in the district—

a meeting set up to begin to articulate a clearer vision and agenda for strengthening access for immigrant students. I felt excited. Perhaps the efforts to push toward more inclusion will continue with even greater strength. But I also wondered how long it would take to create schools that really embrace multiculturalism. Perhaps the intensity of the backlash will continue to erode much that had been fought for over the past twenty years of the bilingual movement.

Stories do not start and end where the researcher enters and exits. This story is only another chapter in the long struggle. There can be no neat and tidy ending—only the shivers of fear in indications of increasing exclusion during this era of backlash and the glimmers of hope in the possibilities of continued resistance. These are scary times. But I left the school still believing that a multicultural and inclusive solution can be ours. And Frida's words were singing in my head:

> . . . if there is a solution to all the discrimination and hatred and racism, we're the ones who can do it. We can. Maybe our time has come.

■ ■ ■

Madison High, one multicultural high school campus in one of many communities being changed by immigration, demonstrates how a community can both "celebrate its diversity," yet continue to reproduce a stratified and inequitable racial and language hierarchy and a narrow version of what it means to be "American." It illustrates the efforts and heartbreaks of those engaged in activity to provide more educational opportunity and equal access to schooling for immigrants, as well as the confusions, blindnesses, and concerns of those who resist changing their ways "for them." In the lives of the students—immigrant and U.S. born—we have witnessed a social life among the young people on the campus in which their very desires to affirm who they are meet headlong with American racial systems, and where students abandon the fullness of their human identities as part of the process of becoming and being American. Madison High has offered a hard look at the ways in which our schools still sort and consign students to very different futures based on their skin colors, class, and language. The students and adults who spend their days at Madison see the world through what at first glance seem to be three very different lenses.

Newcomer immigrant students spend their days either in classes taught wholly in English, which they cannot understand, or in separate "sheltered" and ESL classes. From this vantage point, they believe and hope that the key to becoming American is simply to learn the language. They do not yet see the prices they will be expected to pay or that becoming American involves a racializing process. Most teachers "see" that students divide into academic levels, but they view this as a product of choice and effort (or perhaps ability) and not as a responsibility or result of what the school does in sorting students into very different futures by skin color, class, and language. Differential achievement of groups appears rational and reasonable to them. As one teacher explained: "Of course most of our Asian kids are in college prep, I guess that's like most schools. They work harder and care more. It's a smart bunch. Anyone who worked as hard as they do can be in college prep." The map the "American" Madison High School students inhabit is divided by color and barely acknowledges the newcomers, but is closest to acknowledging the racializing process of the school and begins to challenge the ideology of meritocracy that teachers hold so dear. For the point is not simply to understand one school, however.

Despite its unique personalities and particular demographic mix, Madison High School is an illustration of the daily negotiations that go on within the structure and tradition of high schools in this nation to enact a contemporary version of Americanization and the latest chapter in the long struggle in the United States over responses to immigration and diversity.

This is not simply a story of three separate realms of experience or ways of viewing the world. Newcomers, Americans, and teachers contest each other's experiences at Madison High, and the discourse among these versions of "reality" provide a very powerful illustration of the silencing and neutralization of what might be a potential multicultural alternative to a narrow monocultural model of what it means to be American. In the end, the three seemingly contradictory maps work together in a powerful racializing process of Americanization. The highly racialized world of the "American" student is not a product of the way students group during their free time on campus, but is produced, to some degree, through placement of students in academic tracks of the school which looks alarmingly like racial sorting.

THE AMERICANIZATION PROJECT OF SCHOOLS

There are three pieces to the process of Americanization that newcomers to these United States undergo in our high schools: academic marginalization and separation; the requirements to become English-speaking (despite many odds) and to drop one's native language in order to participate in the academic and social life of the high school; and insistent pressures to find and take one's place in the racial hierarchy of the United States.

Exclusion and Separation of Immigrant Students Academically

As we saw at Madison High, because of a lack of capacity and will to serve new-comers, immigrant students are either placed in inadequately supported classes where they do not have access to English-speaking peers or friends or placed in "mainstream" classes taught by unprepared teachers who do not address their needs and they cannot fully comprehend, hence dooming them to academic failure and loss of access to the academic program. With insufficient English language development and insufficient access to the curriculum in a language they can understand, most immigrant students are (through the forces of schooling) denied equal access to an education. Some manage to achieve, but many drop out of school or become stuck in the category of "ESL lifers."

Pressure to Give up One's National Identity and Language

Immigrants learn that to become English speaking is not sufficient for membership in this new society. They must cease using their mother tongue in public places and must give up their national identities as a condition of being accepted as "American." Immigrants face what feels to them to be polar choices between being accepted by becoming as American as possible (which includes becoming racialized into the lower echelons of an American hierarchy and giving up their own national and language identities) and remaining marginalized and holding on to their traditional cultural forms (national identity, home language, and home culture). The middle ground of multicultural identities is intensely uncomfortable, for they find little support either in their home or school worlds for simultaneously embracing both. Their experiences examining and then determining their relationship to nationality and mother tongue occupies center stage during the early years of the immigrant experience.

Taking One's Place in the Racial Hierarchy of the United States

Newcomers group together with others of their same religion and language in what becomes social shelter from the exclusion and hostility of U.S.-born peers who laugh at their accents and foreign ways. The journey immigrants understand they must make as a condition of acceptance in this new land is to become English speakers. They assume at first that the language is synonymous with becoming American. But they discover a different reality. As they become more English speaking, they participate more and more in the social world of the high school and discover that they have to learn and find a place in the racialized structures of the school. What they do not yet understand is that these racialized places also have implications for the paths that are open to them academically. As students become Americanized, they begin to group more like their American peers, racially.

In all three of these elements of the Americanization process, the slots waiting for newcomers are positions of only partial acceptance. As they adopt the English language as their sole language, they are not given sufficient tools or access to develop the levels of English really required for full academic participation and inclusion. They become English speakers, but seldom proficient readers and writers of the language, grappling with academic content in English. And as they learn English, they also learn to abandon their mother tongue. Giving up one's native language for the sake of learning English and being accepted has a high price in loss of strong family connection and access to one's history. Furthermore, giving up one's national identity to become American is a one-way journey. The places they are to take in the racial hierarchy are largely at the bottom. There is no going back for immigrant youth, although their new nation makes the message clear that it is not at all sure it wants them here. This is the racialized Americanization of the 1990s.

The world of Madison High is an enormously complex social system. Newcomer immigrants, living at the margins of the school, are focused on negotiating that journey from foreign nationality to "American," viewing that journey primarily in terms of learning English. They learn, however, that the conditions for acceptance and participation in American life include not only dropping their native language and adopting English but also dropping their national identities to become American, and leaving behind the immigrant dream that school success is the path to economic mobility and the product of individual effort.

All of these transitions are painful, for they involve giving up a significant aspect of one's identity and accepting a place in a system that not only will not acknowledge or prize the cultures and languages of the newcomer, but which offers them only marginalized and subordinated places in the hierarchy of their new land. Whether a result of policies and leadership that do not recognize or respond to the academic needs of immigrant students, or the result of prejudices and exclusionary attitudes of their teachers and fellow American students, the impact is the same. The process for immigrants of participation in American high schools is one of loss.

And the teachers? As we saw, they too are immersed in an effort to make sense of the new realities of diversity. But they remain largely oblivious to the day-today intense maneuvering of their students over issues of racial identity. Their world is one defined by academic program and tracks. "American" students and teachers collude in establishing the criteria of English fluency for participation in their school world. And so English becomes the measure of denationalization and the explicitly acknowledged path to citizenship and participation. To the degree people hold on to this notion, it denies the reality that American students see so clearly, that taking one's place in the racial order is the measure of arrival on the American map. But the racializing process of the school becomes obscured behind an ideology of pride in diversity, an insistent color-blindness, and a belief that learning English is the only barrier to participation.

It is a seamless web of Americanization and racialization. While immigrants are engaged in trying to understand the racialization and Americanization processes, they also become instructed in practices of getting along. They learn silence and denial. Students learn a way of moving through their social world, where what they experience and what they are safe in articulating are quite different. This mirrors the experience of the adults, who learn a similar silence. To name inequality in an "eggshell" atmosphere is dangerous, viewed as divisive, and leads to marginalization for teachers.

Students and teachers alike become schooled in denying the existence of exclusion and racism, and in becoming numb to the pain of culture and language loss. It is a silence fed by fear that to notice and acknowledge the tracking and separation and enforced losses would be to open doors to the wells of grief and anger, which are potentially explosive. The school and community in one breath, then, speaks in celebration of its diversity, believes intensity in fairness, but is involved in an intense racial and Americanization process the few dare to try to expose.

RESISTANCE EXISTS BUT IT IS MARGINALIZED AND CONTAINED

These painful patterns do not occur wholly uncontested. There is active resistance on many levels. The small number of young advocate teachers at Madison High together with advocates from the Newcomer School attempt to raise the visibility of immigrant students and bring attention to the patterns of loss, exclusion, and denial of participation that occur at the school. They work hard to provide what support and access they can for their newcomer students, often locking in battle with formal policies, informal practices, and persistent attitudes of many others at the school. Meanwhile, individually, immigrant girls engage in deep soul-searching about how much they will and how much they must give up in each of their worlds, and develop complex trade-offs in trying to define the most feasible and comfortable place between cultures. A new Latino student movement calls for recognition and respect for their culture and language, and provides students a way to voice their anger and loss and to collectively seek to mold an alternative world. Political movements for language rights, immigrant rights, bilingual education, and racial justice continue to use the courts and engage in an active public discourse to try to win the conditions for full inclusion and acceptance of immigrants.

Through the story of Madison High School, we have witnessed the process by which these various impulses of resistance and the voices of advocacy for a multicultural model of society, and the forces which would craft new educational and social approaches affirming the languages, cultures, and inclusion of immigrant students, are pushed off to the side, neutralized, or contained.

The grim reality is that newcomer students who do not speak English are tracked, separated, provided with inadequate materials and poorly trained teachers, and denied access to core content areas. As they become more Americanized, they continue to be tracked and ill served in patterns relating to their race and home language. Despite the existence of the Newcomer School as an explicit force in the district that provides an empowering, additive multicultural force for immigrants, and despite a program of sheltered instruction offered by committed advocate teachers, these benefits are neutralized.

The administrators at Madison and in the school district did not recognize or take responsibility for the need to make accommodations to serve immigrant students, leaving the problem of how best to serve LEP students to the daily push and pull between the staff of the Newcomer School and the staff of the comprehensive high school, and to the daily interactions between those young and marginalized teachers who view themselves as advocate for immigrant students and those who may be uninterested, unfocused, or unwilling to take on these concerns.

Because the advocates at Madison tend to be the young and more recently hired teachers, their concerns are ignored or undermined and personalized. The young teachers who struggle to hold together a program and serve as immigrant advocates cannot gain the clout needed to hold the rest of the school accountable for meeting the needs of their students. The vision of schools as places that support a multiculture that they represent is thus never viewed as a serious alternative.

The end result is a program for immigrant students that is far from sufficient for addressing the barriers to access they face. The other result is the maintenance of a high school structure and program that remains unchanged even as the faces and needs of the students pose new challenges. This protects them both from the hassles of making changes, but more significantly it silences a multicultural alternative.

Yet, the movement continues.

IMPLICATIONS

Madison High School in California is not an aberration. The patterns of exclusion, and silence about exclusion, that were evident in Bayview were not created out of whole cloth by the individuals in that community. An historical and political context shaped much of what they had to work with. The ideology of color-blindness and the ways of thinking that support not serving immigrants well are reflected even in the cutting-edge discourse of school reform. The people in Bayview schools who resist addressing the specific needs of immigrant students, and who so energetically deny the racializing process of the school, echo and are bolstered by voices in the professional leadership of education as well as by the political and social discourse surrounding schools.

As long as the larger discourse continues to provide legitimation and to obscure the project of Americanization, exclusion, and racialization, the Madison High Schools of this nation will continue to act out those patterns. Therefore, it becomes essential to both break the silences in the larger framework and develop a critique that identifies where and how that framework serves as an instrument of exclusion.

Looking beyond Bayview, California, the reader who has become acquainted with Madison High will see mirror images in the broader dialogue over the role of schools and will hear echoes in the many discussions about education. The rhetoric of school reform speaks to the deep desires for intergroup harmony and the need to pretend that separation is not being produced. It affirms that schools exist to teach all students and often calls for multicultural tolerance or respect. But it also assiduously avoids attention to the deep divisiveness of the school endeavor that persists in dividing students from one another and denying access to some.

This has been a decade of unprecedented focus on educational reform. Many hundreds of reports have been issued, more than a thousand reform initiatives have been launched in the professions and in state legislatures. No state has been untouched by the movement for educational reform. This movement is generally silent about addressing exclusion and does little to address the intense Americanization and racializing processes in schools.

A commitment to serving "all" students is reiterated over and over. The "all" is intended as a sufficient term to imply inclusion. But beyond the insertion of "all" in statements about serving students, there has been little leadership or explicit reform dialogue addressing exclusion, equity, and the needs of students related to language and culture. This stems from a pervasive and determined color-blindness, posited as a moral position signaling an end to prejudice and racism. In this scheme, all students are seen as the same. Therefore, there is no need to examine the specifics of language and cultures or how race and ethnicity affect children's experiences in school and society. In fact, attention to such differences is viewed as here, as it was in Bayview, as divisive, as "special interests" speaking, or as "off the subject."

The people whose color-blindness and refusal to examine issues of different needs, and their emphasis on serving "all" children as the "same," have managed to claim the moral high ground. Their position is based on a language and framework that uses the paradigms and words of civil rights to argue for a status quo that actually prevents full inclusion and access. The new way to do things in school reform are contrasted to what is defined as the "old paradigm" ways of doing things. The lineup looks something like this:

TRADITIONAL CIVIL RIGHTS APPROACHES
Schools on their own are not and will not provide access to language-minority students. The courts or federal government need to specify responsibility for providing access and set up monitoring and compliance apparatus.

Special targeted programs are needed to address special needs. Equality and integration require addressing the specific barriers students face.

NEW SCHOOL REFORM DISCOURSE
We need freedom from mandates so we are free to innovate. Mandates and compliance apparatus are insulting to us as professionals and prevent our responsiveness to students.

Special targeted programs are a form of segregation; we need integration.

In the popular school reform discourse, specific educational approaches that have been about equity are thus stood on their heads, taken out of their educational and political contexts, and discredited. Thus, compliance and monitoring, which were put in place by the courts and federal government to ensure enforcement of educational access and protection of civil rights, are viewed as "old paradigms" and a kind of prescriptiveness that prevents teachers from serving students. In other words, mandates get in the way of schools engaging in the kind of innovation necessary to serve "all" children. The efforts of advocates to promote the capacity of schools to deliver programs fulfilling educational rights and access, or to push for teachers to get the training to deliver "sheltered instruction," are felt as denying teachers the freedom to make their own decisions—it becomes anti-rights instead of pro-rights. Identifying children in order to ensure that additional resources flow to them to address their additional needs becomes interpreted as racist labeling. It is framed as racist rather than antiracist. Providing primary-language instruction in order to ensure access to an education is framed as a special-interest approach that encourages segregation and prevents the development of a common language. It becomes thought of as anti-unity rather than the basis of inclusion. The values being asserted are felt passionately as coming from a place of desire for integration and unity, but their effect is to prevent or dismantle the very programs that are the instruments of inclusion.

The "old paradigm," which consists of much of the educational pedagogy and set of policies flowing from civil rights concerns, is now associated with such negative references as "segregation," "divisiveness," or "special treatment." When voices for inclusion and equal opportunity are raised, they are characterized in the larger reform dialogue as inappropriate, unwarranted, unpleasant, and unproductive diversions from the "real" issues facing schools. The responses that greeted Stern and other advocates at Madison High are played out manifold in educational circles throughout the nation. And in this lineup, the voices for bilingual education and immigrant education and the calls for supports that provide access for children facing barriers of culture and language are interpreted and twisted to be understood as the "old paradigm," as racist, as divisive, as constricting.

Many educators in the school reform movement in California and elsewhere have generally believed that generic overall school reform would work equally well for all students. "Good education is good education, period!" If one believes this, that good teaching for one child is the same as good teaching for another, then efforts to focus on the specific needs of special groups of students are really unnecessary. But they seldom look at the different outcomes of their efforts, and there is little accountability for inclusion. In schools where reform is proceeding without voices at the table who can provide expertise on issues of language and culture, new, more complex, and more devastating layers of exclusion and denial of access are being enacted.[40] This era is threatening to be a generation of reform that bypasses the needs of language, cultural, and racial-minority children, and leaves exclusion intact.

The discourse is vigilantly silent about forces of exclusion and racism. Responsibility for poor educational outcomes, for lack of full participation and involvement, and even for weakening the school and the community is often placed squarely on the students (and their parents, their cultures, and their advocates). The educational outcomes of the school are viewed as products of choices students and/or their families have made.

Thus, rather than opening up a discussion of the Americanization role of schools or of the racialization process in our schools, school reform in this era simply sidesteps and obscures these roles. Perhaps none of this should be so surprising, however. Why should we expect schools or school reform to be otherwise? The patterns at Madison High in this current school reform era reflect deep trends in American ideology that stem back hundreds of years and serve dominant power relations in this country.

DEEP TRENDS IN AMERICAN THOUGHT

Each historical era produces its own version of the struggle between inclusion and exclusion in public schools. Yet, there is consistency in the larger dimensions of that struggle, a reflection of something deep in our society, in the basic tenets of a persistent ideology in the United States.

The argument posits the fragility of our form of government and the fragility of our common culture, asserting the role of public schools is to protect that fragile bond by teaching a narrow and restricted set of beliefs as "national culture," to protect a single language (English) from erosion by other languages (specifically, Spanish), to project an individualistic perspective that success is a result of merit, and to maintain an emphasis on a Western and American dominance.[42] It thus involves public schools in mediating, monitoring, evaluating, and transmitting one version of public life and culture, while sidestepping other aspects such as equality of opportunity and exclusion.

It is, furthermore, an ideology that defines "belonging" in terms of conformity and that relies on public schools to achieve that conformity. It is fundamentally threatened by diversity of culture, race, language, and perspective. It couples a concern with conformity with an emphasis on tradition.

Finally, it is an ideology of individualism that defines outcomes as a function of merit and seeks to resolve social problems through the emphasis on individual effort. We individually and collectively get what we deserve. The emphasis and insistence on the individual as the essential unit of society come at the expense of recognition or allowance for group experiences and collective affiliation—and denies the degree to which circumstances and institutional sorting plays a role in the kind of access, opportunities, and resources an individual has available to them.

Together, these elements create an ideological system that justifies current power relations. The dirty business of exclusion, of systemic oppression, lies outside the realm of this articulated ideological debate unless it is forced on to the table.

Back when the common schools were being shaped, Benjamin Rush and Horace Mann, who spoke passionately for common schools for "all," did not speak out on the exclusion of blacks from the schools in Boston. During the humanist and Progressive era of school reform, Charles Eliot and John Dewey, although speaking eloquently of the needs of the whole child and the power of reasoning, elected to *avoid* the subject of the forced assimilation of Native Americans in boarding schools and the inferior and segregated schooling to which African American children were being relegated. And in this, our era of American history, Diane Ravitch and E. D. Hirsch established basic dimensions of arguments for school reform by rhapsodizing about an education for all and cultural literacy for all, but chose not to bring notice to the problem of inequality of resources or access. In California, past Superintendent of Instruction Bill Honig and then Governor Pete Wilson (despite viewing each other as political enemies) collaborated in shaping an era of educational reform that cited pride in the diversity of California, but equally ignored issues of language, culture, and equity. Wilson went on to stake his political future on a public policy stance calling for the exclusion of some immigrant groups from schools. Their silence on these issues within school reform, coupled with the overt and conscious attack on immigrants in other aspects of public policy, leaves the structures of inequality intact in schools—and in so doing, deflects attention from systemic injustice and allows inequities to be viewed as failures of individuals or of minority-group cultures. The silence thus reasserts the privileged position and dominance of their race, class, and language group.

The staff at Madison High would be surprised to read this analysis and view the effects of all their hard work for children and their staunch belief in diversity as being aligned with the forces in this society that serve to exclude immigrants and children of color. Most teachers and administrators there view

themselves as believers and enforcers of civil rights and fighters against prejudice. But as the incidents I observed throughout this book illustrate, their
actions perpetuate an opposite effect. The continuing blindness to the needs of
immigrant students, the fear of seeing or confronting the enormous losses that
are extracted from newcomers as a price of admission to our society, the denial
of the racializing and tracking by race that occurs within the academic program,
and the silence and efforts to put down or neutralize the voices of those who
attempt to create more access—all these actions speak in loud contradiction to
words and beliefs. And those who struggle to pose an alternative view and be
the creators of a more open and more fully multicultural society are still too few
in numbers to provide a viable alternative vision and direction for the schools.

What occurs at Madison High and the discourse within the school reform
movement also reflect broader social relations and power relationships in both
the social and economic systems in our country. There are segments of our
society which resent the use of scarce resources in a recessionary economy to
meet the special needs of language-minority children. Our labor market benefits from an immigrant class that is not fully literate and only partially assimilat-
ed. Immigrants (and particularly the undocumented) fill a particular niche in
the lowest paid and least protected rungs of our labor market. They are convenient targets for exclusionary public policy and political rhetoric. Our high
school programs reproduce and reinforce these larger societal patterns of
power and place, and they are key institutions for determining who will get
what in this society. The program and dynamics at Madison High, which mar-
ginalize immigrants and leave them neither prepared to join a mainstream
English-speaking America nor allow them to maintain and hold on to their
native tongues and traditions, reinforce stereotypes about immigrants and
socially legitimize limited access to job mobility.

WHERE WILL ALL THIS LEAD US?

As is evident, the general attitude and dominant philosophy of the schools are
shaped by the deeply conservative bent of the times. The silence of educators
and refusal to acknowledge the social, political, and economic implications
of their role in marginalizing immigrants and racializing children are a continuation and perpetuation of myths that inequities are the result of individual
capabilities and efforts. Beneath this denial is fear and anger, and (sometimes)
outright racism. An overtly exclusionary backlash against immigrants
emerged in the midst of this research. But its seeds were evident on the local

level in the years of my research at the school. At Madison High, the seeds of the anti-immigrant backlash were there in the confusion and anger of the non-newcomer students aimed at newcomers, in the efforts of the immigrants who arrived in years past to distance themselves from the newcomers who are the brunt of the backlash, in the expressions of those long-term teachers in the district who resented the pressure and expectation that they should change what they do in order to better serve immigrant students.

In this era of swift demographic change and economic recession, many educators express a sense of loss of control, a sense of eroding and eroded economic and personal security, and frustration over the uncertainty about what their role is and should be as educators. Spinning together the loss of control due to strikes, budget cuts, and recession, with the loss of control facing students who are of languages, skin colors, and communities different from the teachers, an intricate web was woven. The unsettled anger became associated with a binary opposition of we/they. "We" were the culturally homogeneous, hard-working, decent, white, long-time community members who have not been given their due. "They" (racial and language minorities, immigrants, and the new young teachers who serve as advocates) are diverse, pushy, angry, ungrateful outsiders trying to get something for nothing and not caring about the basic values of the community they have invaded. In this view, discrimination appears to be against the "real Americans" who are being invaded, pressured to bend over backwards to make room for newcomers when their own children are not well served and receiving none of the supports and breaks that they perceive newcomers are getting.

In the past few years, as anti-immigration forces grew in California and began to spread nationwide, less and less consensus and support exist within school districts for programs to address the language barrier. State and federal law continues to require that a program for LEP students be delivered, but the support, leadership, and resources devoted to implementing such a program is insecure at best, eroded in many cases.

In a three-year period, we have witnessed a shift in the debates. There has been a decrease in the intensity of the multicultural education debate and cultural literacy debates which had raged so strongly in the early 1990s. Now, attacks on affirmative action and on immigrants have taken the forefront. The ballot initiative called Proposition 187 passed in California by a 2 to 1 margin and seeks to exclude undocumented immigrants from public health care and public education services. It rode to victory in a frenzy of frustration captured by Governor Pete Wilson's analysis that an invasion of immigrants was the cause of the state's economic, social, and cultural woes. And within a year, the U.S. Senate and Congress were debating legislation that not only excluded undocumented immigrants, but also broadened proposals to exclude legal immigrants from a wide range of public services. A widespread mobilization by people concerned with access to education resulted in political compromises and the removal of the proposals to exclude children from schools—but the exclusions of legal immigrants from many necessary public services was signed into federal law. And so the battle continues.

The protection of a cultural and language status quo turned from having sown the seeds and ground through cultural debate and the re-establishment of a conservative ideology, to having a more explicit political means of exclusion. And the school reform movement continues, still largely untouched by explicit concern about equity and exclusion. Without knowing what these shifts will mean for the students, teachers at Madison High, for the community of Bayview, it is difficult to end the book conclusively.

What would a multicultural and inclusive alternative be? It would certainly require seeing and changing the institutional sorting and tracking of students into different futures. Furthermore, it would necessitate full support for the language development (in English and in the home language) of our newcomers. But it involves something beyond that. The newcomer students at Madison, entering school and bringing with them the world's cultures and languages (literally) have much to offer each other. Instead, they learn to play a role in perpetuating separation and narrowness. They do so out of protection for themselves, but they get little help in doing otherwise. They need help in affirming their broad identities, in claiming the multiple human dimensions of their heritages, languages, and cultures. Instead, like Sandra, who wished to claim and share her Brazilian heritage, they are pressured to fit themselves into the few narrow boxes allowed in our racial system, and rid themselves of their languages and national identities as a price for becoming American. They need help in hearing and listening to each other, and in beginning to access the human understanding that could be theirs through real dialogue and connection. Instead, they are separated from each other and offered little in their curriculum or school life that might prompt the connection. Who might offer that help? Who might restructure the curriculum, provide programs and school climates that rejoice in and affirm the richness of human experience? This responsibility falls on the adults and the educators who have the task of remaking schools into institutions of equal opportunity, places of support for diversity. As long as the time and resources to identify and buy new materials in order to make the curriculum more responsive to the needs of a diverse population falls on individual teachers, as long as the job of naming and trying to call attention to inequities is left to the newest hired and youngest and most vulnerable teachers, as long as school districts neither collect nor examine data about school achievement that might indicate where damaging sorting is occurring, it becomes obvious that we will not have a school system in this country adequate at delivering on the dream and vision of equal opportunity and inclusion. That dream must be reaffirmed, and the public voice to actualize it must be heard.

There can be no simple conclusions about the direction our state and nation will take. It is still undetermined whether this will be an era in which the United States will turn toward increased disparities between groups and increased exclusion, or whether we will pull together those forces for inclusion and write a proud new chapter in the history of the struggle of *e pluribus unum*.

The story of Madison High and Bayview, California, is not only about "them over there." It is about us and the dynamics of our time, our state, our nation. And you and I stand in the web as surely as the students and educators whose voices and experiences fill the pages of this book. You are not only readers of this story, we are all its writers. The conclusion will not be read in a book, but will be read in our daily lives as each of us make choices about relationships to those whose languages and cultures are different from ours, as we each play a role in adding to the silencing and denial or the visibility and legitimation of the rich multicultural diversity we are privileged to participate in. The conclusion will be written as people join in resisting efforts to track us to different futures based on our skin colors; as we together break the silence about the damage being done by excluding and ill-serving students whose home language is not English and whose national backgrounds are from beyond our own borders. And in our collective action and voice is the hope for a new more democratic, just, and inclusive multicultural America.

INTRODUCTION

1. The concept of racialization is central to this book. The term rests on an understanding that "race" has neither a biological nor a natural basis, but is a social construct that is constantly being taught, learned, recreated, and renegotiated. The process of the social construction of race is termed "racialization." As people learn the expectations and beliefs that others have for them because of their skin color, they are becoming "racialized." As our society decides on new categories of "race," and determines the importance and implications of those categories, we are engaged in "racializing."

2. According to the U.S. Census, by 1990 there were nearly twenty million foreign-born residents in the United States, the most in the country's history. An average of 600,000 immigrants and refugees have been legally admitted into the country during the past decade and a sizeable if uncertain number of others enter and remain without legal status. During the 1970s, more than 6.6 million immigrants were admitted to the United States in one of the largest migrations in our nation's history. The total foreign-born population of the United States was estimated at more than fifteen million after the 1990 U.S. Census. Three out of five live in Southern and Western states. And almost 40 percent live in only two metropolitan areas: Los Angeles, California, and New York, New York. More than a third of the nation's immigrants are concentrated in California, by far the most impacted of all states in the union. [Portes and Rumbaut 1990; National Coalition of Advocates for Students 1990; McDonnell and Hill 1991] California has grown more than twice as fast as the rest of the nation. As the port of entry for Pacific Rim and Central and South American immigration, close to 88 percent of this growth has been among the foreign born. The 1990 census counted six million foreign-born residents in California, the result of a major immigration wave in which newcomers from every continent and dozens of different cultural and language groups have joined an already diverse California population to create an unprecedented diversity. Almost two-thirds of those arriving in California in 1990 were immigrants.

3. It is not only the struggle over language, race, and cultural relations that has shaped the public schools in this nation, however. Radical educational historians of the schooling system in the United States (such as Michael Katz, Ira Katznelson and Margaret Weir, William Reese, and others) have tended to focus on the process by which conflicting class interests have shaped the structure of American education. Although their focus is on class conflict and not

on race, language relations, or immigration, nonetheless their works strongly support a view of the role of schools as contested and struggled over regarding their function in reproduction, and focus on similar key eras in U.S. history that framed the current structure of schools. Furthermore, it has often been widescale immigration that precipitated the class struggles focused on by these historians.

4. Most notably, Paul Willis's study of Hammertown, England, working-class "lads" described how the students reacted to the structural barriers of class and to the institution of school by producing a culture that celebrated their class position and rejected school, thus ending up in working-class jobs. His work added immeasurably to the concept of reproduction by offering the critical perspective of "production"—that people are not simply acted on by forces of reproduction but are engaged in shaping their own cultural responses to their conditions, which have within them seeds of resistance. His work also offered a depth of understanding of these processes that was previously unavailable—one that comes from looking at the daily interactions, reactions, and productions of students in relation to school.

Beyond seeking to explain how it is that young people learn, accept, and play out their roles at the bottom of the class hierarchy, Willis's *Learning to Labor: How Working Class Kids Get Working Class Jobs* is a complex and rich theoretical argument. Willis agrees that schools legitimate and reproduce the economic class structure. Willis, however, sees this occurring through contestation and resistance to class dominance as well as through direct reproduction.

> I view the cultural, not simply as a set of transferred internal structures (as in usual notions of socialization) nor as the passive result of the dominant ideology downwards (as in certain kinds of Marxism), but at least in part as the product of collective human praxis (4).

Schools are a context, a lived world in which reproduction is continually reproduced and contested. For Willis, human praxis is the basic process of cultural production for all classes of people. In this cultural production process, the contradictions of a class society are expressed, resisted, and mediated. For Willis, it is the dialectic between penetrations (understandings of the real underlying mechanisms of a class society from the perspective of the working class) and limitations or blindness related to privilege, which lead to reproduction of the class structure. These penetrations are possible because the Lads are at the bottom of the class hierarchy and are not invested in maintaining it. Therefore, they are able to see through, to "penetrate," the ideological subterfuge that masks the reproductive functions of schooling. The dialectic dynamic for Willis is between penetration and limitations, and it is within this dialectical relationship that the potential for political action resides. This has been an essential theoretical construct in my research, directing my attention to the tension at this intersection.

CHAPTER ONE

5. Alan Peshkin, "Introduction" to *God's Choice* (University of Chicago Press, 1986).

6. The 1960 U.S. Census only provided two racial categories: "white" and "other." Hispanics were counted as white. African Americans, Asians, and Native Americans were classified as "other."

7. The "Bracero" program was a federal program that brought agricultural workers from Mexico to the United States for limited periods of time to provide seasonal labor for the fields. It was a temporary seasonal workers program.

8. The city was also undergoing change in its housing and commuter patterns, with impact on the student population. Early in the 1970s, the City Community Improvement Office issued a strategic plan for Bayview. One of the chief recommendations was the need for an accelerated building program to create a more open housing market. The advent of a region-wide subway system in 1972 held promise that Bayview could increasingly become a commuter community, as access to the major urban centers of the region became easier and more convenient. Workers from those major employment centers could move to Bayview to more affordable and less urban center communities if the housing were made available. Bayview responded with a growth of multiple family-rental units and the city then saw a decrease in overall average household size, a higher percentage of single-adult households and childless couples. Most of the new housing was clustered around the downtown area near the station of the regional rapid transit system. These patterns represented a shift from the single-family, owner-occupant houses of the 1960s, as well as a shift from small town to an urban community.

9. The lure of the suburbs resulted in a large out-migration in the 1970s, particularly among families. It still has not been overcome by growth, and the high school population never recovered its peak levels. The new growth in the city has not been among families with school-aged children. A comparison of the high school enrollment to overall Bayview city population demonstrates this difference.

YEAR	POPULATION SIZE	POPULATION GROWTH	HIGH SCHOOL STUDENT ENROLLMENT	STUDENT GROWTH
1960	72,700		3,629	
1970	93,165	+ 28%	7,460	+106%
1980	94,167	+ 1%	6,031	−19%
1990	111,498	+18.4%	6,535	+8%

The change in Bayview from a city of families with young children to an increasingly adult and senior population is primarily a phenomenon of the past twenty years, Overall, the school-age population in the state of California has risen by 14 percent in the decade from 1980 to 19909, but in Bayview it has only grown by 6 percent overall.

10. The 1980 U.S. Census reported that 12 percent of Bayview's population, or 11,125 people, were foreign born, out of a total population of 94,167.

11. In 1980, three-quarters of the population spoke only English, and 26 percent spoke a language other than English as their primary language. According to the International Institute, there are now an estimated 25,000 to 30,000 immigrants and refugees in Bayview. Approximately one-fifth of these were Spanish origin (60 percent of which were Mexican, 12 percent Puerto Rican, and 28 percent other), 56 percent Asian. By 1990, almost 18 percent of the city was foreign born, but most consider this an underestimate. The International Institute warned:

These foreign born numbers should be considered a minimum figure for several reasons: census figures significantly undercount ethnic groups, and within ethnic groups, immigrants are the most undercounted; the increase in population bewteen 1980 and 1990 was increasingly based upon immigration, so the 1990 proportions of foreign born based on our conservative calculations are likely to be significantly lower; and, recent undocumented immigrants, because of their illegal status are likely to be excluded from governmental counts.

These rates of growth were based primarily on people moving into Bayview, most as newcomer immigrants, rather than birth rates.

12. Every year, the California Department of Education releases new figures through its R-30 Language Census, detailing the number of limited English proficient students in the state and their languages.

CHAPTER TWO

13. My exploration of "social maps" of Madison High began because I decided to base my selection of students for in-depth interviews on a social map of the school. I assumed there would be a consistent sociological and demographic map that would direct me to the major student groupings in the school. In addition to interviewing teachers for their descriptions of the social map at Madison, I enlisted Lisa Stern to give me access to her social studies classes so I could work with students to elicit an initial student view of the salient social groupings in the school. Social mapping is a technique often employed by social scientists, and I was interested in enlisting students to create their own. In exchange for providing some information to her classes about the process and methods of doing sociological research, they would do a project on "social mapping" at the school. It happened that Stern taught both "regular" social studies classes and "sheltered" classes for newcomers. We decided that I should do the project in both contexts. In addition to the construction of social maps, students were asked to write their own analyses of what they had found and to present these to the class for discussion.

I have chosen to use of the term "American" throughout this book to refer to U.S.-born students. This is not an accurate term, nor is it politically preferable. Peoples of the entire North American continent are Americans, as are immigrants from anyplace in the world who come to live in the United States. However, the popular use of "American" among the students and adults at Madison High is used in a narrower sense, to refer to people born in the United States who seem to them to be of a U.S. culture. Because it is such an important conceptual term in how they view the world, I chose to adopt their terminology for this book.

14. "Sheltered" instruction is an approach to teaching academic subject matter in English to students who are limited or non–English speakers by presenting material in a way that helps to overcome the language barrier. It is sometimes referred to also as "specially designed academic instruction in English" or "content based English as a Second Language." "Sheltered" classes are supposed to cover the same curriculum as regular classes. They are supposed to be composed solely of limited English proficient students. The term "sheltered English" was coined by linguist Stephen Krashen (1984) to mean instruction in subject matter made comprehensible through specially designed instructional approaches for LEP students. In the

sheltered English classroom, the focus is on subject matter and the student's attention is on the message (content), not the medium (language). Krashen argued that native English-speaking students should be excluded from the "sheltered" class so that instruction can be directed at the LEP students' level of comprehension.

Theoretically, sheltered English classes use special instructional strategies, including: (1) emphasis on extralingual cues (visuals, props) to help the student understand what is being communicated; (2) linguistic modifications (pauses, repetition, elaboration); (3) interactive lectures in which there is continuous teacher/student dialogue; and (4) focus on central concepts rather than on details. However, not all teachers assigned to teach sheltered classes at Madison (or at the majority of schools throughout California) have the training and materials that support such special instructional strategies. And sheltered classes have come at a high price to students, who thrive on being sheltered from hostile American peers, but who pay for the separation in academic and social ways.

CHAPTER THREE

16. This process of white consciousness is reflective of the larger societal trends described by Howard Winant:

> The shifts brought on by the civil rights movement and the reforms it engendered also had an impact on white racial identity, which was rendered much more problematic than in the days of segregation. Whites had to change their attitudes towards minorities, which meant they had to change their attitudes towards themselves. A desirable feature of this shift was the beginning of racial dualism in whites. On the negative side, whites were threatened by minority gains. They sense a loss of their majority status. They suddenly noted an identity deficit. Formerly their whiteness since it constituted the norm was invisible, transparent, but not in a more racially conscious atmopshere, they felt more visible and more threatened (166).

CHAPTER FOUR

17. English is a national language of the United States. It is used extensively throughout the country and is the language symbolic of national identity. An "official" language is somewhat different. An official langugae is that language that is declared formally and officially as the language of government and beyond. The United States does not have an official language. Although many people assume that English has always been the official language of the United States, in fact, the founders of this nation and framers of the Constitution chose to be silent on the issue. The nation was then and has continued to be multilingual.

Periods of intolerance toward languages other than English were specifically tied to more general attitudes toward a specific group. Thus, the deliberate campaign of separating enslaved Africans so that people of a single-language group would not be together was less about attitudes towards those African languages than it was about social control of an enslaved population. During the treaty period between the U.S. government and Native American tribes, a campaign to "civilize the savages" included incorporation of children into boarding schools where their tribal languages were forbidden. During the early part of the twentieth century, and during World War I, a promotion of English and a campaign against use of the German language in the United States was part of the overall war campaign. After the war with Mexico, and the incorporation of Southwestern states, intolerance and repression of Spanish was related to attempts to break allegiances of the peoples of the Southwest with Mexico. However, it was not until 1981 that the subject of designating English as an official language for the nation was brought up in Congress.

Because English is so well established in the United States, efforts to officialize it are primarily about language relations and language status. In 1986, California passed an English-only initiative. Since then, twenty-three states have passed laws, primarily through referendums and initiatives. At the time this book was going to press, there is legislation in the U.S. Congress to declare English as the official language of the United States. An excellent source on the official-language movement in this country is James Crawford's *Language Loyalties: a Source Book on the Official English Controversy*.

18. A national study directed by linguist Lily Wong Fillmore, entitled the "NABE No Cost Study," documented widespread patterns of language loss among first-generation immigrant youth. As they become English speakers, they abandon their home language. Most immigrant families do not consider this possibility, and note too late that the loss has occurred. Some immigrant communities do provide their own mechanisms for maintaining the home language and culture. In Bayview, a small number of students appear to attend classes in their communities that provide home language instruction (usually mixed with religious or cultural instruction). These "Saturday schools" are often run by temples or churches. However, the enrollment in most of these Saturday schools are not immigrant children themselves, but the next generation, who are raised as monolingual English speakers and whose parents desire them to recapture native language usage.

19. Linguist Stephen Krashen has described the conditions under which second-language learning can occur. In addition to comprehensible input—that is, some interactive involvement that gives the words meaning—he has described what he calls "a low affective filter." The affective filter determines whether a person is able to absorb and take advantage of the opportunities to acquire a second language. Stress, fear, anxiety get in the way of learning. Strong motivation, self-confidence, a sense of safety, low anxiety are necessary, he claims, for students of a new language to be able to absorb and begin to use that language. In situations such as those described at Madison High, where students are afraid to use English for fear of being laughed at or humiliated, the fear acts as a high affective filter and makes second language acquisition much more difficult.

20. The number of needed courses has been figured by analyzing the annual R-30 Language Census required by the state of California that designates the number of students who are LEP and in need of services. This was figured by the staff at the Newcomer School, who attempt to monitor availability of courses for LEP students.

21. Sociologist Ruben Rumbaut reports that the self-esteem of immigrant students is linked to how they are labeled by their schools. Specifically, he found evidence that self-esteem was diminished by being labeled "Limited English Proficient." "The Crucible Within: Ethnic Identity, Self-Esteem, and Segmented Assimilation Among Children of Immigrants," 1995.

22. Skutnabb, Kangas, 1977 and 1994.

23. The use of the term "disabling" is a reference to a framework developed by linguist Jim Cummins (1984). Cummins describes the educational contexts that are "empowering" to language-minority students, and those that are "disabling." A disabling context emphasizes subtractive cultural and language incorporation—that is, the emphasis is on gaining a new language and culture *and* on leaving behind or neglecting the child's home language and culture. A disabling context emphasizes a transmission approach to teaching, whereby the new information and culture are transmitted to the student in a one-way process, as compared to an interactional pedagogy. And in a disabling context, the assessment of achievement is aimed at legitimizing the institution and the existing cultural and language relations.

Another useful framework is provided by Phelan, Davidson, and Cao's "Student's Multiple Worlds: Navigating the Borders of Family, Peer and School Cultures" (1991). The authors identify five borders that immigrant students must navigate. One is "linguistic borders," which result when communication between students' worlds (home/school, peer/home) is obstructed not because of different languages per se, but because one group regards the other group's language as unacceptable or inferior. This border is created not only because immigrant students, limited in English proficiency, are taught their academic curriculum in English so that their native language and culture are invalidated, but also because of the psychosocial aspects of anxiety, depression, apprehension, or fear block their ability to participate in their school and campus environment, because of cultural components related to their cultures' being invisible or put down by others, and because of the structural limitations making needed instruction and supports unavailable. Certainly, these borders are present in full force at Madison.

24. Ruben Rumbaut found that Mexican immigrant youth were the most loyal of all national immigrant groups to their mother tongue. He found that three-fourths of immigrant students prefer English and will choose to use English over their mother tongue. Mexicans, however, were the exception, with almost half preferring Spanish ("Crucible Within," 16).

CHAPTER FIVE

25. This discussion rests on an understanding of the social order in our nation as highly structured by race, and of our public life as engaged in shaping racial relations. The state (meaning our political and public institutions) is a site of ongoing struggle over racial meaning and power. Schools are institutions of the state and are involved in this struggle. As Omi and Winant write (1986), "The state doesn't just intervene in racial conflicts. It is the pre-eminent site on which and over which such conflict occurs." Although Omi and Winant do not speak directly to the issues of racial formation vis-à-vis public education as a state institution, their formulation seems particularly useful in pursuing a study of the dynamics of demographic change within schools. The dialectical relationship they present frames issues of how dominant and minority racial groups shape and reshape their own (and each other's) racial identities. Omi and Winant's work is theoretical, historical, and political analysis. It does not, therefore, provide a close-up look at the dynamics within a public institution of community negotiation, renegotiation, and racial formation. It is this dynamic that the study of immigrants in the process of "racialization" at Madison High attempts to illuminate.

26. *Chola* is a word used by young Latinos in California to refer to a female of a certain style. Originally, it applied to girls in gangs or with gang affiliations, but has come to be used more loosely. There is a certain dress associated with cholas: loose khaki pants or jeans, black sandals or sneakers, flannel shirts. The general image is very feminine, a lot of makeup and hair spray, pierced ears, a little belly showing, and a strut and stance in the world that is strong and not afraid. As one girl described it: *Cholas* look the world straight in the eye and never flinch."

27. Sociologist Ruben Rumbaut's "The Crucible Within" describes immigrants in inner-city schools who were found to be significantly more likely to develop a racial or pan-ethnic identity than immigrants in other contexts. They are also significantly less likely to hold on to their identification with national origin for very long. Rumbaut describes the stages of "assimilation" among adult immigrants. In the first few months of arrival, they experience a kind of euphoria. In the second year, they " hit the wall" and experience the highest rates of depression and anxiety. He defines this as the point of "psychological arrival" as immigrants realize the enormity of what they have gotten into. It is a kind of exile shock. The third year, there is some rebound, but it is characterized by great accommodations to Americanization. For the high school students at Madison High, the patterns for the majority I studied were somewhat different. For almost all, the immediate euphoria and high hopes for social acceptance were dashed quite quickly. Few chose to immigrate, and many feel waves of homesickness and anger that they have been uprooted. Some of them hit the wall in that first year, and begin a relatively early process of accommodation, including accepting their racialization into a U.S. system. Others hold on to their national identities for much longer.

CHAPTER SIX

28. Anthropologist Catherine Raissiguer (1993), Lois Weis in her book, *Working Class Without Work*, and studies by Angela McRobbie (1978) and Linda Valli (1986), all describe working-class female students developing marginalized wage-labor identities because they were secondary to their home or "domestic" identities. Particularly reminiscent of the young women at Madison High, Raissigeur found among immigrants of Algerian descent in France similar patterns of attitudes toward romance and the consideration of education in terms of postponement of marriage. She writes:

> Girls of Algerian descent . . . seem to have less access to notions of idealized
> heterosexual pairings, because in their communities and families mar-
> riage is still separate at some level from "romance" and because romance
> outside of wedlock is seen as highly problematical. Moreover, marriage is
> often used and perceived as a form of punishment. In this context, and in
> spite of the romanticization of heterosexual pairing in France, marriage,
> love and romance cannot be seen simply as desirable. Because the girls of
> Algerian descent I interviewed were not for the most part in total conflict
> with their families, and their expectations, they often opted to postpone
> marriage—perhaps as a way to choose their partner—through education
> and employment, but did not reject marriage as a whole.

CHAPTER SEVEN

29. In California, students are considered "limited English proficient" and in need of special language services until they reach a designated and measured level of English proficiency on a standardized test, and demonstrate academic success in content classes taught in English. At this point they are "reclassified" as "fluent English proficient."

30. There is no precise count of undocumented immigrants in California or in the nation. The best estimates, however, show that nearly half of all immigrants to California between 1980 and 1993 were illegal immigrants. According to the Public Policy Institute of California, in a report authored by Hans Johnson, the number is placed at over 200,000 per year. Net illegal immigration rose to these levels throughout the late 1980s. During the 1980s, there were 1.8 million legal immigrants to the state and between 1.4 million and 2.5 million illegal immigrants. The middle estimate used by the Public Policy Institute is 1.6 million undocumented immigrants in the state. Public schools do not have a count of undocumented immigrant students, because they are expressly forbidden from asking for immigration status under a Supreme Court action in the *Doe v. Plyler* case ruling on the protection of equal opportunity.

31. It was unclear what the actual issues were regarding the Afghans, but many school staff were experiencing the influx of Afghans as particularly problematic. The problems reported by school staff were that the new wave of Afghans were "too aggressive." School staff viewed this as a contrast to a Judeo-Christian perspective about turning the other cheek in the face of violence, their cultural and religious orientation was being described as "strike, don't be struck." One teacher explained that "if they think someone might offend them or their family, they figure they better hit them or strike out first as a matter of honor." Many of the Afghans were fresh out of the war back home. A number of the teenage males fought in that war. Many had seen killing; some had killed. Many had fathers who were imprisoned and who had not come with the family. The students interviewed for this study viewed themselves as in the United States temporarily, until the situation back home became tenable again and they could return.

32. These patterns seemed similar to those explained by Judith Warren Little (1991) in discussing responses of teachers to multiple ambitious goals in teaching, "the prospect of perpetual failure may defeat and discourage capable teachers who find that the challenges always seem to outstrip institutional resources and personal rewards."

CHAPTER EIGHT

33. In the early 1990s, a battle over the multicultural content of textbooks erupted in California into a profound but deeply divided debate over what children should be taught and over whose voices were to be represented in shaping curriculums. The occasion was the selection of a new set of state-approved social studies textbooks. In California, the State Board of Education formally adopts textbooks in subject matter cycles of seven years. Schools are limited to the use of their textbook and materials funds for books that have been formally adopted. The process of adopting texts is undeniably a political one. From 1990 to 1992, the state was engaged in reviewing and adopting social studies textbooks.

In the fall of 1992, the California State Textbook Commission adopted a new social studies textbook series for the upper elementary school grades. The books, which portray a history of America built by diverse peoples but based on the values of Europe, were welcomed by a majority of the commission as the most balanced and unbiased texts available to date. Meanwhile, during months of public hearings and private commission meetings previous to the adoption, legions had protested the books on the grounds that they skewed and marginalized the histories of many of California's ethnic and cultural communities.

Few educational issues galvanized as much reaction in California as the process that led to the selection of these textbooks. It was not simply an argument over books. The textbook authors and proponents were termed "pluralists" and said they applaud multiculturalism, but not at the expense of a common culture. "Too much" focus on diversity was posed by this group as a barrier to unity. These arguments flowed directly from a national discourse about curriculum framed largely by academicians such as Diane Ravitch, E . D. Hirsch, Arthur Schlesinger, and others.

The terms of the academic debate over cultural literacy were framed formally by E. D. Hirsch with the publication of his book, *Cultural Literacy* (1987). The argument he put forth is such a powerful articulation of the dominant paradigm about diversity that shaped Bayview, it is worth discussing in some depth in this note. In the midst of a plethora of school reform reports reiterating the economic needs of the nation and the necessity that schools provide the workers needed for a strong national labor market, Hirsch's voice added a new spin, combining a view of schools as instituitons responsible to serving the economic needs of the society, with an emphasis on schools as sites of cultural production. Hirsch views our society as in the midst of a cultural crisis, as well as an economic crisis, signified by the weakening of a public culture. In his view, schools have reneged on their public responsibility to educate students in the dominant traditions of Western culture. He is concerned not only with skills but with knowledge, and in this sense, Hirsch greatly expanded the dominant contemporary concepts of the role of schools. Students should graduate from our schools not only with basic skills but with basic cultural literacy.

National culture must be taught and it must be learned. Hirsch divides students into the culturally literate and the culturally deficient. It is the amount of literate knowledge a child has that accounts for their school performance. His solution is that those weak in literate culture must catch up. Culture is a canon of knowledge or information that simply has to be transmitted as a means of promoting social order and unity. The only problem is to define that culture. Hirsch is concerned about inclusion and equity, but his solution is to find ways that deprived children can have access to the same cultural wealth from which they have been excluded in the past. Traditional literate culture is equated with a European, Western-based canon.

Cultural literacy sparked an intense dialogue about whether a common culture and a traditional canon were appropriate, whether they could be agreed on at all, who had the right to determine what would be taught, and the nature of American culture as a whole. The depths of societal insecurity and anger tapped by this debate were evident in the explosion of name-calling, the plethora of forums and articles generated, and widespread debate on college campuses throughout the nation about Western Civilization requirements and ethnic studies. Some entered the debate to try to define the canon. Lining up to argue against Hirsch's notion of cultural literacy were those with a different view of culture, a different understanding of teaching and learning, a different analysis of the crisis facing our nation, and a different political agenda. Citing a more dyanmic, productive, lived view of culture, and citing the same demographics and problems in school achievement that Hirsch had referenced, these voices called for a school curriculum based in cultural pluralism and cultural transformation. The focus raised by Hirsch continues to rage in debates about cultural unity and curriculum. It was echoed with particular furor in the fight over the adoption of social studies textbooks in California.

The large, loose coalition of civil rights and community groups who opposed the California social studies textbooks called the pluralist version of a unified America evolved through assimilation and integration a "myth." They cited the inequalities and segregation prevalent in society today as resounding proof, and demanded that the texts be adequate to teach their children the story of how these came to be. Those who opposed the texts viewed themselves as inclusionists; their mission was to see their diverse experiences and perspectives included in the core curriculum of the schools.

California's board of education had the job of formally approving the books, and only one K-8 series, by Houghton Mifflin, was finally adopted by a split vote. After the adoption, the fight moved to local school boards as they deliberated whether to buy the books, knowing alternatives and the resources to buy them would be scarce. The Bayview School Board, after lengthy and polarized hearings involving active community voices, rejected the state texts. It was not a decision of consensus, and the rattlings of dissatisfaction with this decision continue to be felt.

34. Sorting students into different "tracks" to provide them with varying levels of instruction is one of the most widespread practices of U.S. public schools. It results in tracking students by race, ethnicity, and class into very different educational and economic futures. One group is given access to a superior education, while others are consigned to a lower-quality curriculum. One tracks student towards college and the other prepares them for low-paying service sector jobs. The rationale for such grouping is that it is based on "ability" or "achievement." Once a student is labeled as a slow, average, or high achiever, however, several things result. Research has shown that teachers' expectations change, and along with them is a watering down of the curriculum and the rigor for students in the lower tracks. Such labelling begins in the first few years of school and is compounded by the time students reach high school.

The practice of tracking is based on incorrect assumptions about teaching and learning. Most people believe that students of varying abilities learn best in separate tracks. This, however, is not true. Students of middle or low tracks perform poorly in homogenous groups, while high achievers do no better in homogenous groups than in mixed-ability groups. Additionally, vocational training does not increase a student's chances of getting a good job. Therefore, with the use of untracked hetereogeneous classes, nobody loses and the majority of children gain. Many people believe that students with lower abilities need to be protected from the unfair competition of high-track students. In fact, however, research documents that the labelling of students as low track is a source of great humiliation and shame, and results in lowered aspirations, a poor self-concept, and negative attitudes toward school. The experience of the skills and sheltered students at Madison High underscores this. The third erroneous assumption is that the techniques used to assess and place students into tracks are fair and accurate. Yet, research has demonstrated that tracking systems are based on inaccurate, unreliable, often subjective, or biased methods (Green and Giffore 1978; Moore and Davenport 1988; Oakes 1985 and 1986a).

Minority, limited English proficient, or low-income students are consistently and dramatically overrepresented in low academic tracks throughout the levels of schooling. White and more affluent students are conversely overrepresented in advanced tracks (Oakes 1985; Salvin 1987a; First and Carrera 1988; Dentzer and Wheelock 1990; Green and Giffore 1978). For a more complete review of the research literature, the reader is urged to read *The Good Common School* (National Coalition of Advocates for Students, Boston, MA).

35. The following table shows the comparison by racial/ethnic group of two outcome measures from California high schools: a three-year drop-out rate measuring the loss of stu-

dents from tenth grade to graduation, and the percentage of graduates from high school who have completed the course requirements for admission to a four-year college.

TABLE 1
Student Outcomes from California High Schools
(California Basic Educational Data System, 1992) by race/ethnicity

	3-YEAR DROP-OUT RATE	% GRADUATES COMPLETING A-F
White	10.8	34.2
Black	26.4	27.2
Hispanic	24.6	21.0
Filipino	10.2	43.8
Pacific Islander	16.0	24.9
Asian	9.2	54.5
Native American	19.2	19.3

For the county in which Madison High is located, a college board report gives a similar racialized picture of senior class preparation for higher education.

TABLE 2
High School Student Preparation for College 1992
Scoring at least   Scoring at least A-F course

	900 ON SATS	3 ON AP TESTS	A-F-COURSE COMPLETION
White	22.6	5.5	33.2
African American	7.6	.6	29.1
Hispanic	8.6	4.0	20.5
Asian	28.1	11.8	51.5
American Indian	19.2	4.8	25.9

CHAPTER TEN

36. Although all programs addressing the language needs of limited English proficient students may be called "bilingual education," in fact there are important programmatic distinctions. Transitional bilingual education provides some instruction in a child's home language to help them learn academic content and also provides ESL instruction. The use of a child's home language, however, is only until such a point that the child can understand English in a mainstream English-taught classroom. The goal is transition as soon as possible, and is usually completed within three or four years. Maintenance or "developmental" bilingual education programs strive to achieve bilingualism, both preserving and enhancing the child's home-language development *and* developing fluency in English. Thus, the home-language instruction is continued even after the child can function in English in an English-taught classroom.

37. In 1969, Whittier College, established by the federal government Title VII funding as the first Multifunctional Resource Center to support Title VII projects, held a very activist-oriented bilingual conference. It is remembered by many bilingual activists in the state as the starting ground of their movement. These people organized a lobbying effort to get the passage of California's first bilingual education bill.

38. The response was AB 1329, introduced in 1975 by Assemblymember Chacon and passing through the assembly to the senate during that year. Once the 1975 session adjourned, Assembly Speaker McCarthy appointed a special committee on bilingual education. The committee held six hearings and published a comprehensive report entitled "Towards Meaningful and Equal Educational Opportunity." The charge to the committee was to determine the status of the present bilingual programs, formulate a legislative response to *Lau*, and improve the present state program. The report laid out a series of options. The less prescriptive (and most desirable to those who resisted primary-langauge instruction) was a minimum plan in which districts could design their own programs, but the cost would be borne by the state. The second option (a compromise version which closely resembled AB 1329) was a phased-in mandate for transitional bilingual education funded by the state. Maintenance bilingual education would be a local option. The third option (strongly supported by bilingual educators) was for a mandated maintenance bilingual program in which the primary-language literacy would be a goal as well as English literacy.

AB 1329 (known by then as the Chacon-Moscone Bilingual Bicultural Education Act) came out looking like the reasonable compromise. The bill included provisions for a mandated trigger that bilingual programs be provided whenever there were ten or more students speaking the same language at the same grade level, and ensuring that one-third of the students in each bilingual class had to be English only. The legislation required that teachers be trained, but allowed substantial numbers of waivers. It also established a language census, an initial language assessment for all language minority students, and formal exit criteria governing when LEP students would be done with bilingual programs. The release was timed for the end of the 1976 session when the bill was in the Senate Education Committee. In August, the bill was passed after a massive lobbying effort. It included a provision that after July 1979, districts would be required to comply with state law. Once this occurred, the pressure of resistance to bilingual education began to mount for amendments to the law. It was explicitly resistant to the idea of using children's home languages in the schools and to the implication that more Spanish speaking and Latino teachers would need to be hired. The compromise provisions were new options that districts and schools could provide "planned variations" of the bilingual models outlined in the original legislation, allowances for exceptions to the requirement that one-third of the students in a bilingual class had to be English speakers, provisions of parental approval for placement in bilingual classes, and a June 30, 1987, sunset of the law.

39. In the 1994 legislative calendar, the debate over teacher qualifications has also resurfaced. To address the shortage of teachers with preparation in serving LEP students and the increasing need for all teachers to have basic understanding of principles of culture, language, and second-language acquisition, a bill requiring all teachers in California to receive training in a new credential authorization was killed by an intensive lobbying effort by the teachers union, which fed on the feelings of some in Sacramento who had never been happy about the bilingual legislation. During a legislative hearing, Senator Leroy Greene again voiced the now familiar sentiment that bilingual education is simply an employment program for Hispanic teachers.

CHAPTER ELEVEN

40. Olsen, Laurie, et al. *The Unfinished Journey: Restructuring Schools in a Diverse Society*. San Francisco: California Tomorrow, 1994; Gandara, Patricia. "The Impact of the Education Reform Movement on LEP Students," In *Language and Learning: Educating Linguistically Diverse Students*, ed. Beverly McLeod. Binghamton, NY: SUNY Press, 1994.

Almaguer, Tomas. *Racial Fault Lines: The Historical Origins of White Supremacy in California.* Berkeley, CA: University of California Press, 1994.

American Jewish Committee. *The Newest Americans: Report of the American Jewish Committee's Task Force on the Acculturation of Immigrants to American Life.* New York: Institute of Human Relations, 1987.

Apple, Michael W. *Ideology and Curriculum.* Boston: Routledge, 1979.

———. *Education and Power.* Boston: Routledge, 1982.

Apple, Michael and Linda K. Christian-Smith. "The Politics of the Textbook." In *The Politics of the Textbook*, edited by Michael Apple. New York: Routledge, 1991.

Aronowitz, Stanley and Henry Giroux. "Textual Authority, Culture, and the Politics of Literacy." In *The Politics of the Textbook*, edited by Michael Apple. New York: Routledge, 1991.

Attorney General of California. "Attorney General's Commission on Racial, Ethnic, Religious, and Minority Violence." Sacramento, CA. 1990.

Bach, Robert. *Changing Relations: Newcomers and Established Residents in U.S. Communities.* A Report to the Ford Foundation by the National Board of the Changing Relations Project. New York: Ford Foundation, 1993.

Banks, Sandy and William Trombley. "New Textbooks: In with Diverse," *Los Angeles Times,* 12 October 1990.

Bennett, Tony, Colin Mercer, and Janet Woollacott. *Popular Culture and Social Relations.* Philadelphia: Open University Press, 1986.

Berrol, Selma Cantor. *Immigrants at School: New York City, 1898–1914.* New York: Arno Press, 1967.

Booth, W. C. "Cultural Literacy and Liberal Learning: An Open Letter to E. D. Hirsch." *Change*, July/August 1988.

Bourdieu, Pierre. "Cultural Reproduction and Social Reproduction." In *Power and Ideology in Education*, edited by Jerome Karabel and A. H. Halsey. New York: Oxford University Press, 1977.

Bourdieu, Pierre and Jean-Claude Passeron. *Reproduction in Education, Society, and Culture*, trans. by Richard Nice. London: Sage Publishers, 1977.

Bowles, Samuel. "Unequal Education and the Reproduction of the Social Division of Labor." In *Power and Ideology in Education*, edited by Jerome Karabel and A. H. Halsey. New York: Oxford University Press, 1977.

Bowles, Samuel and Herbert Gintis. *Schooling in Capitalist America*. New York: Basic Books, 1976.

Breen, T. H., "The Giddy Multitude." In *Different Shores: Perspectives on Race and Ethnicity in America*, edited by Ronald Takaki. New York: Oxford University Press, 1987.

California Department of Education. "California Basic Education Data System, School Site Reports for 1993." Sacramento, CA, 1993.

Comaroff, John and Jean Comaroff. *Of Revelation and Revolution: Christianity, Colonialism, and Consciousness in South Africa*. Vol. 1. Chicago, IL: University of Chicago Press, 1991.

Church, Robert and Michael Sedlak. "Educational Reform in the Progressive Era." In *Education in the United States: An Interpretive History*. New York: Free Press, 1976.

Crawford, James. *Bilingual Education: History, Politics, Theory and Practice.* Trenton, NJ: Crane Publishers, 1989.

———, ed. *Language Loyalties: A Source Book on the Official English Controversy.* Chicago, IL: University of Chicago Press, 1992.

Cremin, Lawrence. *American Education: the Metropolitan Experience 1876–1980.* New York: Harper and Row, 1988.

———. *The Transformation of the Schools: Progressivism in American Education: 1876–1957.* New York: Vintage Books, 1961.

———. "The Revolution in American Secondary Education 1893-1918." In *Teachers College Record* 56:6 (March 1955).

Cummins, Jim. "From Multicultural to Anti-Racist Education." In *Minority Education: From Shame to Struggle*, edited by Tove Skutnabb-Kangas and Jim Cummins. Albany, NY: SUNY Press, 1991.

———."Empowering Minority Students: A Framework for Intervention." *Harvard Education Review* 56 (1984): 18–36.

———. Cummins, Jim. *Empowering Minority Students.* Sacramento, CA: California Association for Bilingual Education, 1989.

DePalma, Anthony. "The Culture Question." *New York Times Supplement,* 4 November 1990.

Eckert, Penny. *Jocks and Burnouts: Social Categories and Identity in the High School.* New York: Teacher's College Press, 1989.

Elder, Jr. Glen. "Time, Human Agency, and Social Change: Perspectives on the Life Course." *Social Psychology Quarterly* 57:1 (1994): 4–15.

Erickson, Frederick. "Transformation and School Success: The Politics and Culture of Educational Achievement." *Anthropology and Education Quarterly* 18:4 (1987): 335–55.

Fass, Paula. *Outside In: Minorities and the Transformation of American Education.* New York: Oxford University Press, 1989.

Fillmore, Lily Wong. "When Learning a Second Language Means Losing the First," *Early Childhood Research Quarterly.* vol. 6, pp. 332–46, 1991.

First, Joan and John Wilshire Carrera. "New Voices: Immigrant Students in U.S. Public Schools." An NCAS Research and Policy Report. Boston, MA: National Coalition of Advocates for Students, 1988.

Fine, Michele. *Framing Dropouts: Notes on the Politics of an Urban Public High School.* Albany, NY: SUNY Press, 1991.

——— ."Silencing in Public Schools." *Language Arts* 64:2 (1987).

———."Perspectives on Inequity: Voices From Urban Schools." *Applied Social Psychology,* Annual 14, edited by L. Brickmann. Beverly Hills, CA: Sage Publications, 1983.

Fix, Michael and Jeffrey Passel. *Immigration and Immigrants: Setting the Record Straight.* Washington D.C.: The Urban Institute, 1994.

Franklin, John Hope. "Jim Crow Goes to School: the Genesis of Legal Segregation in Southern Schools." *The Southern Atlantic Quarterly* 58:2 (spring 1959).

Gandara, Patricia. "The Impact of the Education Reform Movement on LEP Students." In *Language and Learning: Educating Linguistically Diverse Students,* edited by Beverly McLeod. Binghamton, NY: SUNY Press, 1994.

Gibson, Margaret. *Accommodation Without Assimilation: Sikh Immigrants in an American High School.* Ithaca, NY: Cornell University Press, 1989.

Gibson, Margaret and John Ogbu, eds. *Minority Status and Schooling: A Comparative Study of Immigrant and Involuntary Minorities.* New York: Garland Publishing, 1991.

Goode, Judith G., Jo Anne Schneider, and Suzanne Blanc. "Transcending Boundaries and Closing Ranks: How Schools Shape Interrelations." In *Structuring Diversity: Ethnographic Perspectives on the New Immigration*, edited by Louise Lamphere. Chicago, IL: University of Chicago Press, 1992.

Greer, Colin. *The Great School Legend: A Revisionist Interpretation of American Public Education.* New York: Basic Books, 1972.

Harklau, Linda. "Jumping Tracks: How Language Minority Students Negotiate Evaluations of Ability." *Anthroplogy and Education Quarterly* 25:3 (1994): 347–63.

Hatcher, Richard and Barry Troyna. "Racialization and Children." In *Race, Identity, and Representation in Education*, edited by Cameron McCarthy and Warren Crichlow. New York: Routledge, 1993.

Hirsch, E. D. *Cultural Literacy: What Every American Needs to Know.* Boston: Houghton Mifflin, 1987.

Hodgkinson, Harold L. "Here They Come, Ready or Not." Special Report for *Education Week.* Washington D.C., 1986.

Holland, Dorothy C. And Margaret A. Eisenhardt. *Educated in Romance: Women, Achievement, and College Culture.* Chicago, IL: University of Chicago Press, 1990.

Katz, Michael. *Reconstructing American Education.* Cambridge, MA: Harvard University Press, 1987.

———. *The Irony of Early School Reform: Educational Innovation in Mid-Nineteenth Century Massachusetts.* Cambridge, MA: Harvard University Press, 1968.

Katznelson, Ira and Margaret Weir. *Schooling for All: Race, Class, and the Decline of the Democratic Ideal.* New York: Basic Books, 1985.

Kirp, David. "The Battle of the Books." *Image Magazine, San Francisco Examiner,* 24 February 1991.

Kliebard, Herbert M. *The Struggle for the American Curriculum, 1893–1958.* New York: Routledge, 1987.

Krashen, Stephen. "Bilingual Education and Second Language Acquisition Theory." In California State Department of Education ed. *Schooling and Language Minority Students: A Theoretical Framework.* Los Angeles: Evaluation, Dissemination and Assessment Center at California State University, 1981.

Lazerson, Marvin. *Origins of the Urban School: Public Education in Massachusetts, 1870–1915.* Cambridge: Harvard University Press, 1971.

Little, Judith Warren. "Conditions of Professional Development in Secondary Schools." *The Contexts of Teaching in Secondary Schools*, edited by Milbrey McLaughlin, Joan Talbert, and Nina Bascia. New York: Teachers College Press, pg 187–223.

Litwack, Leon. "Education: Separate but Unequal." *North of Slavery: The Negro and the Free States, 1790-1860*. Chicago, IL: University of Chicago Press, 1961.

Lopez, David. *Language Maintenance and Shift in the United States Today: The Basic Patterns and their Social Implications*. Los Alamitos, CA: National Center for Bilingual Research, 1982.

Lucas, Tamara. "Into and Beyond Secondary Schools: Critical Transitions for Immigrant Youths." Commissioned Paper for the Immigrant Education Program. Washington, D.C.: Center for Applied Linguistics, 1995. Unpublished.

Lucas, Tamara, Rosemary Heinze, and Ruben Donato. "Promoting the Success of Latino Language Minority Students: An Exploratory Study of Six High Schools." *Harvard Education Review* 60:3 (August 1990).

Mar, Eric. "1990 Census Poses Challenges for California's Future," *California Perspectives* 2 (fall 1991).

Matute-Bianchi, Maria Eugenia. "Situational Ethnicity and Patterns of School Performance Among Immigrant and Nonimmigrant Mexican Descent Students." In *Minority Status and Schooling: a Comparative Study of Immigrant and Involuntary Minorities*, edited by Margaret Gibson and John Ogbu. New York: Garland, 1991.

McCall-Perez, Zaida. "The Latina Adolescent Experience, Participatory Research: Listening to Voices in a Newcomer Center." Unpublished diss. University of San Francisco, 1991. *Dissertation Abstracts* #9409604.

McDonnell, Lorraine and Paul T. Hill. *Newcomers in American Schools: Meeting the Educational Needs of Immigrant Youth*. Santa Monica, CA: Rand Corporation, 1993.

McRobbie, Angela. "Working Class Girls and the Culture of Femininity." *Women Take Issue: Aspects of Women's Subordination*. London: Center for Contemporary Cultural Studies, 1978.

Miller, Herbert Adolphus. *The School and the Immigrant*. New York: Arno Press, 1970.

Minicucci, Catherine. "Bilingual Education Legislation in California." Commissioned paper for California Tomorrow. San Francisco, CA, 1994. Unpublished.

Minicucci, Catherine and Laurie Olsen. "An Exploratory Study of Secondary LEP Programs." *Meeting the Challenge of Diversity: An Evaluation of Programs for Pupils with Limited Proficiency in English*. Vol. 5, Berkeley, CA: BW Associates, 1991.

Molesky, Jean. "Understanding the American Linguistic Mosaic: A Historical Overiew of Language Maintenance and Language Shift." In *Language Diversity: Problem or Resource?*, edited by Sandra Lee McKay and Sau-Ling Cynthia Wong. New York: Newbury House Publishers, 1988.

Muller, Thomas and Thomas Espenshade. *The Fourth Wave*. Washington D.C.: Urban Institute Press, 1985.

Nieto, Sonia. *Affirming Diversity: The Sociopolitical Context of Multicultural Education*. New York: Longman Press, 1992.

Oakes, Jeanne. *Keeping Track: How Schools Structure Inequality*. New Haven: Yale University Press, 1985.

Ogbu, John. "Minority Education in Comparative Perspective." *Journal of Negro Education* 59: 1 (1990).

———. "Understanding Diversity: Summary Comments." *Education and Urban Society* 22:4 (August 1990).

———. *Minority Education and Caste: The American System in Cross Cultural Perspective*. New York: Academic Press, 1978.

Olsen, Laurie. *Embracing Diversity: Teacher's Voices from California Classrooms*. San Francisco: California Tomorrow, 1991.

———. *Bridges: Promising Programs for Immigrant Education*. San Francisco: California Tomorrow, 1990.

Olsen, Laurie and Marcia Chen. *Crossing the Schoolhouse Border: Immigrant Children and California Schools*. San Francisco: California Tomorrow, 1988.

Olsen, Laurie, et.al. *The Unfinished Journey: Restructuring Schools in a Diverse Society*. San Francisco: California Tomorrow, 1994.

Omi, Michael and Howard Winant. *Racial Formation in the United States: From the 1960s to the 1980s*. New York: Routledge and Kegan Paul, 1990.

Peterson, Paul E. *The Politics of School Reform 1870–1940*. University of Chicago, IL: Chicago Press, 1985.

Peshkin, Alan. *The Color of Strangers, the Color of Friends: The Play of Ethnicity in School and Community*. Chicago, IL: University of Chicago Press, 1991.

Portes, Alejandro and Ruben G. Rumbaut. *Immigrant America: A Portrait*. Berkeley, CA: University of California Press, 1990.

Portes, Alejandro and Min Zhou. "The New Second Generation: Segmented Assimilation and its Variants." *The Annals of the American Academy of Political and Social Science* 530 (1993): 74–96.

Raissigeuer, Catherine. *Becoming Women: Becoming Workers*. New York: SUNY Press, 1994.

————."Negotiating Work, Identity, and Desire: The Adolescent Dilemmas of Working-Class Girls of French and Algerian Descent in a Vocational High School." *Race, Identity, and Representation in Education*, edited by Cameron McCarthy and Warren Crichlow. New York: Routledge, 1993, 140–156.

Ravitch, Diane. "Diversity and Democracy: Multicultural Education in America." *American Educator* (Spring 1990).

————."The Troubled Road to California's New History Textbooks" *Los Angeles Times*, 2 September 1990.

————. *The Troubled Crusade: American Education 1945–1980*. New York: Basic Books, 1983.

Ravitch, Diane and Chester Finn. *What do our Seventeen-Year-Olds Know?* New York: Harper and Row, 1987.

Ravitch, Diane and Chester Finn Jr., eds. *Against Mediocrity: the Humanities in American High Schools*. New York: Holmes and Meier, 1984.

Reese, William. *Power and the Promise of School Reform: Grassroots Movements During the Progressive Era*. New York: Routledge and Kegan Paul, 1985.

Roediger, David. *Towards the Abolition of Whiteness: Essays on Race, Politics and Working Class History*. London: Haymarket Series/Verso, 1994.

Roman, Leslie G. "White is Color! White Defensiveness, Postmodernism, and Anti-Racist Pedagogy." *Race, Identity, and Representation in Education*. Edited by Cameron McCarthy and Warren Crichlow. New York: Routledge, 1993, 71–88.

Rumbaut, Ruben G. "The Crucible Within: Ethnic Identity, Self-Esteem, and Segmented Assimilation Among Children of Immigrants." To be published in *International Migration Review*, special issue on "The Second Generation" edited by Alejandro Portes. 1997.

————. "Immigrant Students in California Public Schools: a Summary of Current Knowledge." CDS Report No. 11. Baltimore Center for Research on Effective Schooling for Disadvantaged Students, Johns Hopkins University, 1990.

Rumbaut, Ruben G. And Silvia Pedraza, eds. *Origins and Destinies: Immigration, Race, and Ethnicity in America*. Belmont, CA: Wadsworth Publishing Co., 1995.

Schlesinger, Arthur. "When Ethnic Studies are Un-American." *Social Studies Review* 5 (summer 1990).

Schrag, Peter. "Common Ground." *The Sacramento Bee*, July 1990.

Schensul, J. And T. G. Carroll (eds.). "Anthropological Perspectives on the Issue of Cultural Diversity." Special Issue of *Education and Urban Society* 22:4 (1990).

Skutnabb-Kangas, Tove. "Multilingualism and the Education of Minority Children" in Tove Skutnabb-Kangas and Jim Cummins eds. *Minority Education: From Shame to Struggle.* Philadelphia: Multlingual Matters Ltd. pp. 9–44.

Stanley Schultz, *The Culture Factory: Boston Public Schools, 1789–1860.* Cambridge: Oxford University Press, 1973.

Sirkin, Gerald. "The Multiculturalists Strike Again." *Wall Street Journal,* 18 January 1991.

Skuttnabb-Kangas, Tove. *Bilingualism or Not: The Education of Minorities.* Clevedon, England: Multilingual Matters, 1981.

———. "Multi-lingualism and the Education of Minority Children." *Minority Education: From Shame to Struggle.* Edited by T. Skutnabb-Kangas and J. Cummins. Clevedon, England: Multilingual Matters, 1988, 19–44.

———. "Guest Worker or Immigrant: Different Ways of Reproducing an Underclass." *Journal of Multilingual and Multicultural Development* 2 (1981): 89–113.

Sleeter, Christine. "How White Teachers Construct Race." *Race, Identity, and Representation in Education.* Edited by Cameron McCarthy and Warren Crichlow. New York: Routledge, 1993, 157–171.

Spener, David. "Transitional Bilingual Education and the Socialization of Immigrants." *Harvard Education Review* 58:2, l988.

Spring, Joel. *The American School 1642–1990.* New York: Longman, 1990.

Suarez-Orozco, Marcelo M. "Immigrant Adaptation to Schooling: a Hispanic Case." *Minority Status and Schooling: a Comparative Study of Immigrant and Involuntary Minorities.* Edited by Margaret Gibson and John Ogbu. New York: Garland, 1991.

Suarez-Orozco, M. Marcelo and Carola Suarez-Orozco. "The Cultural Patterning of Achievement Motivation: A Comparative Study of Mexican, Mexican Immigrant and Non-Latino White American Youths in Schools." *California's Immigrant Children: Theory, Research, and Implications for Educational Policy.* Edited by Ruben Rumbaut and Wayne A. Cornelius. San Diego: Center for U.S. Mexican Studies, University of California, 1995.

Takaki, Ronald T. *Iron Cages: Race and Culture in Nineteenth-Century America.* New York: Alfred A. Knopf, 1979.

———. Reflections on Racial Patterns in America." *From Different Shores: Perspectives on Race and Ethnicity in America.* Edited by Ronald T. Takaki. New York; Oxford University Press, 1987, 26–37.

———. A *Different Mirror: A History of Multicultural America.* Boston, MA: Little Brown and Co, 1993.

Tifft, Susan. "Education Of, By and For—Whom?." *Time*, 24 September 1990.

Trombley, William. "History Curriculum Stirs Passionate Dissent." *Los Angeles Times*, 9 October 1990.

Trueba, Henry T. *Raising Silent Voices: Educating the Linguistic Minorities for the Twenty-First Century*. Boston, MA: Heinle and Heinle Publishers, 1989.

Tyack, David. T*he One Best System: a History of American Urban Education*. Cambridge: Harvard University Press, 1974.

Viadero, Debra. "Battle over Multicultural Education Rises in Intensity." *Education Week*, 28 November 1990.

Watson, Aleta. "New History Textbooks Blasted as Racist." *San Jose Mercury News*, 13 September 1990.

Waugh, Dexter, "East Bay Parents, Students Call New Textbooks Racist." *San Francisco Examiner*, 19 March 1991.

———. *Francisco Examiner*, 8 September 1990.

———. "History Textbook Feud Splits Sides on Racial Lines." *San Francisco Examiner*, 30 August 1990.

———. *San Francisco Examiner*, 20 May 1990.

Weis, Lois. *Class, Race, and Gender in American Education*. Albany, NY: SUNY Press, 1988.

———. "Disempowering White Working Class Females: The Role of the High School." *Empowerment Through Multicultural Education*. Edited by Christine Sleeter. Albany, NY: SUNY Press, 1991, 95–121.

Willis, Paul. *Learning to Labour*. Westmead, Farnborough, Hunts, English. Saxon House, 1977.